T0272750

OVER THE INFLUENCE

KARA ALAIMO

OVER THE INFLUENCE

WHY SOCIAL MEDIA IS TOXIC FOR WOMEN AND GIRLS— AND HOW WE CAN TAKE IT BACK

alcove
press

Published in the United States by Alcove Press, an imprint of The Quick Brown Fox & Company LLC.

Alcove Press and its logo are trademarks of The Quick Brown Fox & Company LLC.

Library of Congress Catalog-in-Publication data available upon request.

ISBN (hardcover): 978-1-63910-668-4
ISBN (ebook): 978-1-63910-669-1

Cover design by Sarah Brody

Printed in the United States.

www.alcovepress.com

Alcove Press
34 West 27th St., 10th Floor
New York, NY 10001

First Edition: March 2024

10 9 8 7 6 5 4 3 2 1

For my daughters, and for yours

CONTENTS

AUTHOR'S NOTE

With the exceptions of Noor, Kate, Ryan, and Christina, when individuals in this book are referred to with a first name only on first reference, their names have been changed at their request to protect their privacy. No other details of their lives have been changed.

INTRODUCTION

Two big developments have changed the way humans live over the last four million years, according to Justin Garcia, PhD, head of the Kinsey Institute, which studies sex and human behavior. The first was the agricultural revolution, around 12,000 years ago, when humans stopped being migratory. The second was the arrival of the Internet over the past few decades.

The Internet—and especially social media—has had a seismic impact on everyone, not always for the better. But it's been particularly awful for women and girls. And we're only just beginning to reckon with what it's doing to us. In this book, I'll show you how social media is affecting every aspect of our lives—from how we feel about our bodies to how we parent our children and how successful we are in our careers.

My name is Kara Alaimo, and I'm a communication professor at Fairleigh Dickinson University. I'm also a social media user and a mom. I've been writing about the social impact of social media and issues women face for *CNN Opinion* since 2016, reacting to mounting evidence of the devastating toll social networks are taking on women and girls—and the fact that tech companies have known about these things all along.

For this book, I've talked to people who identify as women and nonbinary about how social media has affected their lives. They represent a wide range of ages, races, ethnicities, classes, sexual and gender identities, physical abilities, and political affiliations. Some live and work on social media. Others have deleted their profiles forever. Their stories have left me with a single conclusion: social media is toxic for women.

But I believe we can and must fix these problems—and the change needs to start with the way each of us uses social media. In this book, I'll explain how women can reclaim the Internet to empower ourselves by radically changing who we follow, what we post, what we like, and what we do when we see sexism and misogyny online. I'll also lay out what we need to demand from tech companies and lawmakers.

*   *   *

Here's what we're up against.

The average girl now joins social media before she turns 13. But long before then, her parents may have been "sharenting" intimate information about her online that people can later use against her—to bully her in high school or discredit her when she grows up to become a public figure.

The primary way teen girls use social media is to compare their bodies and lives to others. When they find that they don't measure up to the filtered, glamorized images posted by influencers and friends, many girls feel jealous and unhappy. Girls who use social media more are likelier to have concerns about their body images and symptoms of depression.[1] And young girls quickly learn that one of the most effective ways to create content people will (literally) like is to make themselves look "hot." So they sexualize themselves at shockingly young ages.

As I conducted interviews with experts for this book, I was struck by how many of them ended our conversations by asking me the same question: could I tell them how they should handle their own daughters' use of social media? So many parents who I meet at playgrounds and birthday parties talk and worry about the same thing. In Chapter 1, I offer up that advice, informed by research and interviews with leading experts.

In Chapter 2, I discuss how social media affects our body image. All those pictures we post on social media keep everyone's attention on our appearances. What's more, influencer culture sets near-impossible standards for what our lives and bodies should look like. It's fueling a wave of body dissatisfaction and plastic surgery. It's also keeping women busy focusing on how we look instead of a whole lot of other things we might prefer to be spending our time on—like, say, dismantling the patriarchy by helping elect women to political office.

In Chapter 3, I look at the way the world judges women. Thanks to social media, billions of people can now pronounce judgment on not just our bodies, but also our behavior—and they're taking the opportunity to do so. On social networks, women are coming under siege for everything from the hosiery they wear to their tone of voice when an airline screws them over at 2 AM. As I probably don't have to tell you, men simply aren't judged by the same standards. And now, people have discovered they can make bank by secretly recording women's worst moments in public and selling the rights to companies who can help these clips go viral, so the whole world can come together to shame us.

In Chapter 4, I talk about another topic of endless discussion among my friends: how to use online dating sites to find the right partner. It's now standard for single women to turn to dating apps, which ostensibly offer freedom of choice and possibility. In reality, most women are unhappy with their dating experiences. The majority of American women now say dating is harder than it was 10 years ago, according to a 2020 Pew survey. (The majority of men disagree.)[2]

Many heterosexual women get serious about settling down in their mid-thirties, while they can still have children. But since men don't live as long and tend to pair off with younger women, the number of single, straight men available to women at this life stage is shrinking. On top of that, being able to hide behind a computer screen tends to bring out men's basest behavior.

Women of color have it the worst. While today no one would dream of openly disqualifying people of color when they apply for jobs or try to book Airbnbs, dating sites are the last mainstream place where people are invited to practice racism so overtly.

That explains why some of the women who I interviewed for this book told me they've stopped using dating apps. The other reason? They say many of the men they're being matched with aren't real. Catfishing—pretending to be someone else, forming emotional relationships online, then hitting up victims for money—is now a major global business. And women are considered easy targets because we're perceived as emotionally vulnerable, especially when dating. But I also tell the story of a friend who applied the same degree of strategy and savvy she used in her elite global business consulting work to online dating—and is now happily married. I share her tips for protecting yourself and finding the person you're looking for online.

In Chapter 5, I discuss the new forms of sexual violence and femicide that have been enabled by the Internet. Online dating sites now make it easier for rapists to find victims. There are almost no statistics on how many violent crimes are tied to dating apps, which conveniently helps platforms evade responsibility for endangering women's lives. However, according to a report released by the United Kingdom's National Crime Agency, more men are becoming sex offenders because *it's now so easy to find victims*.[3] And in a nonscientific survey conducted by Columbia Journalism Investigations, out of 1,200 women who dated online, a jaw-dropping 31 percent said they'd been sexually assaulted by someone they met on a dating app.[4]

What's more, thanks to social media, it's now possible to sexually exploit women and girls remotely—and it's happening with alarming frequency. Sextortion—blackmailing a woman to engage in sex acts, often by getting her to share a racy image, then threatening to release it publicly if she doesn't do more—is just one example. One 13-year-old girl was sextorted by a 30-year-old man in Israel while her mother was in the same room.

I also discuss the nonconsensual sharing of nude images. While this is often called revenge porn, Kamala Harris points out in her autobiography that it's not the right term. Revenge often isn't accurate *because the women haven't done anything wrong*—and the images frequently weren't ever intended to be porn.[5] For women—who, unlike men, are frequently shamed rather than celebrated for our sexuality—this is often life-destroying. Former California Congresswoman Katie Hill resigned from Congress when her nude images were released online, while so many men who have been accused of sexual abuse—including the then-president, Donald Trump—have remained in office.

I also look at how, on social media, when like-minded sociopaths like "men's rights activists" get together, their beliefs become even more extreme. Now, the men who have been radicalized in online communities for misogynists are going out and committing real-world violence. For example, since 2014, there have been numerous acts of mass violence against women committed by "involuntary celibate" men who believe they've been wrongly deprived of sex with beautiful women.[6] And now, so-called "incel" ideology has permeated youth culture on TikTok, where jokes about violently abusing women are commonplace—and considered hilarious.

In Chapter 6, I take on the world of influencers. If you watch or read the news, you'll see regular stories about the rare people who make millions of dollars from their social media content. But the truth is that most of the people who try to work as online content creators—the people popularly called "influencers"—are women who never earn a living wage for their labor. One scholar now calls them "digital housewives."[7] Meanwhile, when women in other professions try to use social media to bolster their careers, they often end up with fewer followers, reposts, and speaking opportunities than their male counterparts.[8]

In the next two chapters, I look at how misinformation is directly targeted to us because of our gender. In Chapter 7, I explain how, when women become mothers, they routinely turn to the Internet for information and support. What they often find instead is misinformation that encourages them to make dangerous, potentially deadly decisions. While experts have been sounding alarms about the impact of fake news on elections, they've mostly ignored what I call misinformation for mommies. On social media, people with no medical training declare themselves to be experts and urge women to go into childbirth—a process that poses significant risk of deadly complications—without the benefits of modern medicine. Women are made to feel guilty for using safe pain medication during labor, while no one advocates withholding pain management from men who undergo excruciating medical procedures.

And "sanctimommy" culture makes mothers feel like failures if the realities of their lives don't match up to Instagram images of other people's children smiling beatifically in starched white dresses while eating their homemade, organic snacks. Beneath these veneers, Instamoms are every bit as vulnerable as the women they may inadvertently shame, of course, as they look online for validation in a culture that makes it near impossible for women to balance their careers, children, and sanity—and contend with the reality that, if they want to make money from sponsors, their posts must be cheerful.

In Chapter 8, I discuss how anti-vaxxers convince women that safe, life-saving vaccines are dangerous. One way they've built their movement online is by reaching out to women when they're most vulnerable—after their child has died or received a devastating medical diagnosis—and convincing them vaccines were responsible, turning them into fierce anti-vax advocates. This has been going on for years, and it laid the groundwork for people to be skeptical of coronavirus vaccines. Anti-vaxxers successfully convinced many women not to get vaccinated against Covid by using social media to spread a deceptive claim uniquely designed to frighten us: the contention that the vaccine causes infertility. Then, when they or their family members got sick or schools were shuttered due to community spread, women were largely the ones left to handle the fallout.

In Chapter 9, I discuss the new ways women are trolled online and what we can do about it. A 2020 study conducted by The Economist Intelligence Unit found that 38 percent of a sample of women in 51 countries have been victims of online violence, from violent threats to stalking to doxing—posting private information, like someone's address, online.[9] Women of color are hardest hit. Amnesty International found that Black women are 84 percent more likely than white women to be on the receiving end of online abuse.[10] So when people like Elon Musk claim to be promoting "free speech" when they host abusive content on their platforms, what they're really doing is silencing the women and girls who flee social media when they're targeted.

One reason online abuse against women isn't taken more seriously is because tech companies and law enforcement agencies are, of course, largely run by men. Women routinely say that when they file reports of abuse after men threaten to attack them online, tech companies either don't respond or claim their terms of service weren't violated. When women report online death threats to police, officers often don't investigate. By contrast, people who make death threats against police officers online are often promptly identified and prosecuted.

In Chapter 10, I look at the shocking sexism and misogyny that women who work in Silicon Valley and as social media managers for brands are up against. The cultures inside tech companies have been described as "brotopia." But they're far from utopia for the women who come up against rape jokes and sexual passes from their bosses as a normal part of trying to do their jobs. Meanwhile, most of the people who run the social media accounts of companies and other organizations are women.[11] The average salary for a social media manager is roughly a third of the average salary in the male-dominated tech sector,[12] even though many of the skills social media managers draw upon are remarkably similar to those in tech jobs. I also discuss how, by reading our emails, tracking our physical locations via our phones, and following our every online move, modern tech companies have created what Al Gore calls a "stalker economy."

Finally, in Chapter 11, I explore the predominant way feminism and female empowerment have been portrayed online in recent years: through viral videos made by companies telling women we can solve all our own problems if we just feel beautiful, act confident, and buy the right body wash—instead of looking to others (like, say, the corporations who put out these videos while continuing to objectify and underpay women) to change the way they treat us. All this has triggered an epic backlash that has reduced the rights of millions of women and girls. We can see this in everything from the election of Donald Trump in 2016 to the 2022 Supreme Court decision that took away women's right to decide whether and when we become mothers and terminate pregnancies that threaten our lives.

*   *   *

While writing this book, I came to a shocking realization: life now seems to be imitating social media. We all know social media has become a cesspool of sexism and misogyny, but we can't escape it by turning off our phones or deleting our accounts, because what's happening on social media is changing our offline world. It's making it more socially acceptable and commonplace to abuse women and deprive us of our rights. An example of this is how incels who have been radicalized online have gone on to commit so many mass shootings.

And violence targeting women in politics is on the rise all over the world, according to the Armed Conflict Location & Event Data Project.[13] It's hard not to trace this back to the shocking abuse women politicians are facing online, which I describe in Chapter 9. It can also help explain why, in 2021, women were less likely to say they'd consider running for office than they were in 2001.[14]

Some people say we should stop using social networks because they're toxic places. But I don't believe we should turn social media into what Saudi Arabia was like when I visited a decade ago, where women are run out of public places in which we could empower ourselves. It's also increasingly clear to me that this "solution" wouldn't work anyway, because as men become more radicalized online, they're becoming more emboldened to abuse and even kill women offline. We can't stand down and let this keep happening. We have to fix what's wrong with social media.

*   *   *

This book is motivated by my fears about how using social media—and living in the world wrought by social media—will affect my own young daughters. It's a rallying cry for us to use our collective power to upend this entire system. I'll explain exactly how we can do it—by recognizing and calling out the subtle (and not-so-subtle) sexism and misogyny we find online, rejecting the misinformation that is directly targeted to us because of our gender, using our platforms to boost one another and call attention to the injustices we collectively face, and demanding that tech companies and lawmakers crack down on the astounding new forms of violence and abuse we're up against online.

Let's do this.

GIRL MEETS INSTAGRAM

The typical girl's relationship with social media now begins long before she enters the birth canal. That's when many elated expecting parents start sharing sonogram photos and other details of their daughter-in-development. So-called "sharenting" is when parents post pictures of their kids on social media, which can include shots of them in diapers and, as they grow up, anecdotes about their embarrassing questions and misdeeds. Children have practically no privacy rights to prevent this from happening or, crucially, to later demand that tech companies remove it from the Internet.[1]

That's what bothers Mikaela, 15, whose parents are both comedians with public Instagram accounts followed by tens of thousands of people. Mikaela's parents love posting photos and videos of her on their accounts—like pictures of her in a Halloween costume, or videos of her dancing or awkwardly trying to figure out how to hit a tennis racquet. She hates it so much that she doesn't allow her dad to take photos or videos of her at all anymore, she told me, because she worries they'll end up online. But since she's asked them to stop, her parents now post photos they still have of her when she was younger—which she doesn't appreciate either.

Mikaela's main worry is that kids in her school will see the posts. "It's embarrassing, and it's scary that they might make fun of me," she told me. Most of the bullying in her high school doesn't happen in the hallway, she says. It happens on social media.

"A lot of times [bullying] takes place in group chats on Snapchat where people send photos of one specific person," she explained. "Boys love to do this. They make these group chats and will add random people and be like 'you're so weird.'"

Girls experience online bullying at almost double the rate of boys, according to a 2023 report from the Centers for Disease Control and Prevention (CDC). Twenty percent of girls have to contend with it.[2]

Mikaela told me she wouldn't mind if her parents posted about her on private accounts for family and friends. "It makes sense for a family member to see their niece growing up," she says. "It doesn't make sense for Randy who lives in Texas to see video of me growing up. I don't know if there's gonna be a creep seeing photos of me."

Leah Plunkett, a lecturer at Harvard Law School and author of *Sharenthood: Why We Should Think Before We Talk About Our Kids Online*, says sharenting can be especially detrimental to young girls like Mikaela. "They're coming of age in a society where girls and women are judged on their physical appearance and ability to please an audience," she says. "If girls are raised to please the audience of a parent's camera and become aware that those pictures and videos are going to a larger audience, the message is, 'you should learn to comport yourself even in your private life in a way that will please us as your parental audience and other viewers.'"

As they grow up, they may keep seeking affirmation by trying to make other people happy instead of focusing on their own needs and desires. And Plunkett points out that putting pictures of kids in the bathtub or otherwise unclothed online sets an especially dangerous precedent for young girls, because it suggests that it's appropriate for them to post photos in which they're undressed in the future, too.

What's more, those pictures and potty-training anecdotes might later show up in the media when their daughters grow up and try to position themselves, let's say, as serious candidates for political office. We can expect these kinds of scenarios to become increasingly common as the offspring of parents who began using social networks over the past couple decades come of age and become public figures. And as we'll see in Chapter 3, when they grow up, their daughters will likely be judged for this content by especially unforgiving standards, simply because of their gender.

* * *

Social apps also teach girls to judge themselves unforgivingly. Vivian was 15 years old when Instagram launched in 2010. She was an early adopter. "Initially when I joined, I took pictures of flowers and nature and it was more of a creative tool," she told me. "But as it became more popular, fitness pages started to turn up."

Vivian loved yoga, so she posted a picture of herself doing a handstand, which was shared by a "fitspo"—short for "fitspiration," or fitness inspiration—account. Soon she was following fitspo accounts, along with models and influencers. She decided she wanted to look like them.

But the people girls follow online often set unattainable standards. Humans don't tend to naturally have the "Instagram body." Achieving it usually involves surgery.[3] Unfortunately that doesn't stop teens from comparing and despairing that they don't look like influencers.

"I used to run track, I used to enjoy exercise for the sake of exercise, for its mood enhancing effects, for the competition, and just for the joy of moving," Vivian says. "But it became about the aesthetic when these images started flooding into my world. I wanted to look like these people who appeared to be killing it at life. I was trying to be and look like something that didn't really exist before Instagram."

What about all those Kate Moss ads and glossy women's maga-zines that taught generations of young women to count their calories before they all started counting their social media followers? Unsur-prisingly, research shows that seeing idealized women's bodies in ads makes girls feel lower body satisfaction afterwards.[4] But past generations of girls didn't necessarily spend hours each day staring at them.

On social media, "it's the amount of accounts, women, bodies that are put in front of us," Vivian says. "It's so easily accessible and in your hands at all times. There's this mass amount of comparison at your fingertips, where you can feel good about yourself and then see a picture and you don't, because you don't look like these things that have been airbrushed."

On many Instagram accounts, "the women are naturally lean and slender," Vivian, who is white, says. "That's not my body type, and it's really difficult for anyone to change your body's set point."

For the record, she's right: biology, rather than our own behav-ior, plays an enormous role in determining what we weigh. Identical twins who are raised apart from one another tend to have practically the same weights, while kids who are adopted end up with body mass indexes similar to those of their biological parents.[5]

This means that, if you want to change your body, "you have to go to extremes," Vivian says. "So that's what I did."

Vivian says high school was already a difficult time. Her par-ents fought. Her classes were hard. She was bullied at school. And "when you're that age, you're not thinking clearly," she says. So in high school she restricted her calories, eating as little as possible, to try to look like the influencers she followed on Instagram. She also did lots of cardio workouts, since that's what she saw recommended on Instagram. And she acted on other information she found on the app: "Twelve thousand-calorie diets, how to cut carbs, how to not eat sugar, how to say no to food at the holidays," she recalls, "all approaching nutrition from 'you are fat and need to not be.'"

* * *

The average child joins social media at an even younger age than Vivian: 12.6, according to Common Sense Media.[6] That's just before they're legally allowed to have accounts in their own names without parental consent at age 13.[7] And it's over a decade before the part of the brain that controls decision making fully matures, around age 25.[8]

What's more, in the early teen years, a girl's confidence plunges—a drop far beyond anything the average boy experiences.[9] And she becomes fixated on her body.

Body image is central to the identities of teen girls, says Jean Twenge, PhD, author of *iGen: Why Today's Super-Connected Kids Are Growing Up Less Rebellious, More Tolerant, Less Happy—and Completely Unprepared for Adulthood—And What That Means for the Rest of Us.* "That occurs for boys and men as well but is not as acute."[10]

This is the vulnerable state young girls are in when they first sign up for Instagram.

What's more, it's an especially critical time for their development. "When girls are going through puberty between the ages of 11 and 13, their brain is rewiring," social psychologist Jonathan Haidt, PhD, tells me. "It's the most sensitive time other than in utero for a girl's brain development. So parents should be very concerned about what girls are exposed to during this very important window."

What Vivian was being exposed to, of course, was lots of filtered, idealized images. To make herself look like the other women she was seeing online, she used an app to smooth her skin, whiten her teeth, and reshape her figure. Using social media felt performative, Vivian recalls.

"The difference between having social media and not is there was no rest from it, there was no break. I didn't get to go home and relax after school and not worry what people thought. It was like, 'oh my gosh, I have to go post a picture that people will think is relevant.' Every moment of your life, you're thinking about whether or not it's postable."

Vivian enjoyed the validation she got from getting likes on her posts, which made her dependent on other people for her happiness and well-being. It was nerve-wracking. "It was that anxiety factor of wanting to constantly check if people are commenting or noticing you or giving you approval," she said. "I've never experienced such a heightened sense of 'oh my god, no one responded, I have to take this down,' or 'what have I done wrong to not get a reaction?' That definitely determined whether I felt good or bad about myself."

Soon, she was paying for services to get likes on her posts. "You're paying someone in Bangladesh like $200 a month," she remembered. "I didn't want people to be like, 'oh, that post didn't do very well.'"

When she got validation from real people, she felt it was tied to her body. "I didn't think, 'they think I'm smart, they think I'm funny,'" she recalls. "I was so conscious of wanting to feel liked, and looking good was a quick and easy way to do that. Instagram provided a platform to advertise that you look good."

But, looking back, while Vivian was cultivating online followers, she was missing out on true female friendships. "In high school I didn't learn where or how to find real friends, and that was hard," she says. "In college, I lived in a dorm with other girls, but then once I got older, I didn't know where to find friends." Social media, she says, provided "a false sense of connection. It was a placeholder for actual real relationships." It left her feeling lonely.

She's not the only one. These days, it's more typical for people to feel lonely than to feel connected, according to psychologist Marisa

Franco, PhD. Dr. Franco says we're living in a time of "friendship famine." Americans have fewer friends than ever before. It started decades ago, with the arrival of television, when people started watching sitcoms instead of getting together with friends. But, since 2012, when social media took off, loneliness has surged. And being lonely is toxic. Studies show that having friends is more important for our health than even diet and exercise.[11]

Of course, social media is also a place where friendships can be forged. Natasha Varela, a licensed clinical professional counselor in Illinois who specializes in working with youth and their families, is Latina. She says it can be empowering for Latina girls and girls of color who live in a predominantly non-Hispanic, white society to find online communities with other people who "look and talk like me."

It's easy to see how social media can be an especially important tool for teens who are minorities in their physical communities. Take game developer Zoë Quinn, who uses they/them pronouns. Internet trolls obtained naked photos of them and sent the photos to their friends and family. Trolls also doxed them, deluged them with rape threats, encouraged them to commit suicide, reported them en masse to the IRS, forced them to live in hiding, and caused them to be put on post-traumatic stress disorder (PTSD) medication. It was part of a series of attacks on women in gaming—particularly women who aren't white—that became known as Gamergate.[12] Still, Quinn writes in *Crash Override: How Gamergate (Nearly) Destroyed My Life, and How We Can Win the Fight Against Online Hate* that "everything I have, everything good in my life, I owe to the internet's ability to empower people like me, people who wouldn't have a voice without it."[13]

In particular, Quinn says that, as an LGBTQIA+ teen, the anonymity of the Internet helped them overcome their "massive social anxiety" and the awkwardness of asking potential dates whether they were queer. People who they met online helped them fight loneliness and the desire to kill themself. And Quinn learned and established their career as a game developer online.[14]

Varela tells me she also sees teens exploring a wide range of identities and communities on TikTok. Some of it—like communities for youth activists, or interests that can turn into careers—can be healthy. The options feel practically limitless.

But, while some teens use social media to find healthy communities, others like Vivian end up cultivating online followers at the expense of deeper friendships. One thing that can leave teens feeling isolated is the sense of envy they may develop from keeping up with their friends' seemingly perfect lives on social media. If you've ever used a social app, I'm not going to blow your mind right now when I tell you that one of the main things we do on social networks is compare ourselves to others.[15] On Instagram, what racks up likes isn't generally depictions of what a lot of girls' lives are really like: dragging themselves out of bed to the sound of too-early alarms, doing tedious homework after school, fighting with their parents, lacking the freedom to do what they really want.

"On social media, almost every girl sees that her life is worse than average and she is below average. That is a terrible thing to do to a kid at any age, but it's especially damaging during puberty," Dr. Haidt tells me.

Social media also allows teens to become aware of every party to which they *weren't* invited—or to which they weren't allowed to go.

"With this ability to share your location with friends on Snapchat, I've had clients talk about seeing that all of their friends are together at a friend's house and they know that but can't talk about it because it's kind of creepy to snoop on your friends, so they're just holding this hurt and these feelings of rejection and exclusion," Varela told me.

This can be especially devastating for girls. "Social connectedness is much more important for girls than boys, typically," Igor Galynker, MD, PhD, director of Mt. Sinai's Suicide Research and Prevention Laboratory, tells me. "It starts in middle school and continues for a lifetime. And because it is much more important for girls, girls spend a lot more time on social media. So they're more affected by cyberbullying and the hostility they find online, as well as feelings of being left out."

Vivian felt badly about herself when she compared her life to photos posted by other girls her age. Her mom had strict rules and didn't let her go out to socialize much. "Seeing friends go places on social media, I wanted to look like I was keeping up even though I didn't really do that much. So I channeled that into fitness. I wanted an identity I could show on Instagram that made me cool—and hot, of course," she recalls.

When girls feel jealous of what they see, they often respond by trying to emulate or outdo their friends in their own posts, triggering a vicious cycle that only sets an impossible standard for everyone.[16] It's easy to see how an adolescent girl like Vivian, already low in confidence, would walk away from Instagram feeling like she doesn't measure up to the shiny, happy (but, also: filtered, fake) pictures she finds online. The feeling can stay with her long after she logs off.

To make things worse, the algorithms designed by social networks amplify their insecurities. In 2022, researchers at the Center for Countering Digital Hate created a TikTok account pretending to be a 13-year-old girl and liked videos about mental health and body image. In under three minutes, TikTok was recommending suicide content. Within eight minutes, it was recommending eating disorder content. And the account was absolutely deluged with mental health and body image content. These kinds of posts—like videos advertising tummy-tuck surgery and weight loss drinks *to a 13-year-old girl*—appeared every 39 seconds. When an account was set up with a username suggesting the girl was vulnerable, she was shown even more harmful content.[17]

Senator Richard Blumenthal's staff also created an Instagram account purporting to be a 13-year-old girl and followed accounts about eating disorders and dieting. Instagram was soon recommending accounts with names like "I have to be thin" and "eternally starved."[18] Is it any wonder Vivian developed an eating disorder?

Vivian still remembers what happened when she went to extremes to try to look like the women she followed on Instagram: "Your brain fixates on food because your body is starving, and it feeds into the calorie counting, the anxiety," she told me. "I had gut issues. I was cold and exhausted all the time."

Vivian's fitness obsession continued when she moved across the country for college. Things came to a head when she was hospitalized for malnutrition. Along with the rest of her muscles, her heart had weakened. It nearly stopped. Nurses had to wake her in the middle of the night to feed her protein shakes.

After ten days in the hospital, Vivian went to an outpatient treatment center for six months, missing her spring semester of junior year. Her mom moved in with her and her roommates, driving her to treatment each day.

But even after intensive treatment, she continues to struggle with eating issues as a woman in her 20s, Vivian says.

Sometimes the results of what girls see online are even more tragic. In 2022, a British coroner ruled that social media contributed to 14-year-old Molly Russell's suicide. In the six months before she took her life, Molly liked, shared, or saved 2,100 posts about suicide, depression, or self-harm on Instagram.[19]

* * *

In her late twenties, Vivian now works in the healthcare industry. She also works as a part-time physical trainer. On Instagram, where she posts photos and fitness content, "I get so many negative comments, like 'why do you do that exercise, that's so stupid,'" she tells me. "I don't think anyone would say that to a dude. They think they can push you around a little bit because they think you're sensitive. So they're mean, and they're hurtful, and people take things out on you online that they would never say to your face."

As a trainer, she's also come to recognize the same terrible effects Instagram had on her in her clients who tell her they want to look like influencers. As *The New York Times* explains it, "the so-called Instagram body, seen on rappers, reality stars and actresses, includes an extreme hourglass shape, [and] a flat tummy, with voluptuous hips and buttocks."[20]

But Vivian tells me that "the Kim Kardashian aesthetic is impossible. You're not going to have a thin waist and a butt at the same time, that just doesn't happen. But clients will show me pictures of people they want to look like, and it's like, 'this woman works out for a living and is 20 years younger than you.' It's not attainable, but we think it is because it's all over our feeds."

This helps explain why visually oriented platforms like Instagram are the most detrimental to our mental health. One study of 14–24-year-olds in the United Kingdom found that Instagram and Snapchat, which place the greatest emphasis on images, were the platforms that were worst for their well-being.[21] And girls are the ones who use these platforms the most.[22]

Documents leaked by Facebook staffer turned whistleblower Frances Haugen show that Meta, Facebook and Instagram's parent company, is well aware of these problems. "Thirty-two percent of teen girls said that when they felt bad about their bodies, Instagram made them feel worse," according to internal research leaked by Haugen. "Comparisons on Instagram can change how young women view and describe themselves."

Facebook later pointed out that the data was based on a small sample size, since 150 girls out of a few thousand who they interviewed reported this. And self-reports like this can be unreliable, since teens may be repeating the conventional wisdom that social media is bad or not accurately diagnosing themselves.[23] Still, according to the company's internal research, "aspects of Instagram exacerbate each other to create a perfect storm." That's partly because "social comparison is worse on Instagram." Staffers noted that TikTok is more about performances, while even on Snapchat people tend to focus on faces rather than bodies and lifestyles. In the company's surveys, teens said Instagram made them less confident that their friendships were strong. All of this can promote eating disorders, unhealthy body images, and depression, according to the company.[24]

The effects are amplified by the way social media comes to consume girls' lives. Half of teen girls say they're almost always online (compared to 39 percent of teen boys).[25] When I spoke to Haugen, the whistleblower, she pointed out that "it used to be that you got to go home from junior high if you had a really bad day and someone made fun of how lame your jeans were and it would evaporate. Now, it doesn't. Social media lets you obsess until the moment you fall asleep or people can harass you till you go to bed and then the first thing you see is more mean comments when you wake up."

But many young people like Vivian have parents who don't let them go where they want offline. So they're stuck at home—where they turn to social media and have potentially far more dangerous experiences. These platforms have also changed the way many girls lead their lives offline. Now, instead of doing things and getting photos for social media, girls like Vivian do things *so* they can share them on social networks.[26] The work of curating their lives for Instagram or TikTok can become a full-time job in itself, on top of the other (important) things they need to do at this stage of life.[27]

Developmental psychologist Erik Erikson says the key project of adolescence is identity formation.[28] But if a girl is constantly worried about following, reacting to, and staging her life for others, she's less focused on her inner self. It can also be tough for other healthy activities to compete with the dopamine rushes girls get from racking up likes on social media.

Yet "the more the need for the 'others' is fed, the less able one is to engage the work of self-construction," Shoshana Zuboff, PhD, writes in *The Age of Surveillance Capitalism: The Fight for a Human Future at the New Frontier of Power*. This is a profound loss. A woman who doesn't achieve an appropriate balance between her inner and outer lives is more likely to have trouble coping with solitude and lack a strong sense of self.[29]

It's therefore not surprising that, as teen use of social media exploded, alarm bells began ringing everywhere that they weren't faring well. Between 2011 and 2021, the percentage of high school girls who felt persistently sad or hopeless skyrocketed from 36 to 57 percent, according to the CDC.[30] Between 2009 and 2015, the number of 10-to-14-year-old girls admitted to the emergency room after intentionally hurting themselves *nearly tripled*.[31] And between 2007 and 2015, the suicide rate for 15-to-19-year-old girls *doubled*, according to the CDC.[32]

Researchers disagree about whether this is caused by—or even correlated with—the use of social media. Candice Odgers, PhD, a professor of psychological science at the University of California, Irvine who studies the effects of online experiences on adolescent health and development, told me there isn't a causal link between the use of social media and suicide and depression. Girls today are stressed because we live in a sick society, she says. They've had to deal with the Great Recession. Covid. School shootings. Climate change. Because of demographic changes, there are more girls of color, who contend with racism and other challenges. Many of the movements that are making social progress, like #MeToo, Black Lives Matter, and increased acceptance of diverse gender and sexual identities, are also causing lots of social strife.

But Dr. Haidt says the problem with studies that don't find negative outcomes associated with social media use is that they tend to study both boys and girls and include screen-based activities like texting. He says this masks the ways visually oriented platforms like Instagram are affecting girls in particular.

One thing both Dr. Odgers and Dr. Haidt do agree on, though, is that research conducted in the United Kingdom finds that, among girls between the ages of 11 and 13 (when they typically go through puberty), greater social media use predicts lower life satisfaction a year later.[33]

Social media also comes with real potential safety risks for girls who try to become influencers and post content for public consumption in the hopes of getting enough views to be compensated by social networks or attract brand sponsorships.

By college, men Vivian didn't know were reaching out to her on social media asking to go have drinks so they could help her become a model or offer her other kinds of connections. She was intrigued, so she would exchange messages with them, she recalls.

It was tempting to engage with these men because Vivian wanted to be a fitness influencer herself, just like the women she was following on Instagram.

Ultimately, she decided not to meet up. Looking back, she realizes she was possibly in far more danger than she ever realized. "You just never know what someone is going to do," she told me. "I know so many girls who would go and meet up with these guys and it's scary." She pointed out that sex trafficking is a huge problem in the area where she lived.

Vivian did try reaching out to healthy food and activewear brands to ask them to sponsor her but ultimately never made any money from influencing. "It was all just a big waste of time," she says. "All this stuff is not actually feasible because of how saturated it is."

But that doesn't stop other girls from trying to make money from their posts. Of course, if a teen girl were starring in a film or television show, she'd be protected by laws designed to safeguard her welfare.[34] But when a tween strips on TikTok Live and is rewarded with Venmo payments by her male admirers, there aren't safeguards in place for her protection.[35]

"There's an emerging informal economy where girls seem to be recruited to monetize their private behavior explicitly for money in ways that would be uncomfortable and in many cases illegal if it were being done in a brick and mortar way through the formal economy," Plunkett, the *Sharenthood* author, told me. "We don't have exact numbers, but I'm very comfortable saying our working understanding should be that the adult market for this content tends to be males who are looking for girls and female teens."

Even if girls don't post racy content, they still risk attracting the attention of unsavory men. Florida teenager Ava Majury started posting videos of herself dancing on TikTok at age 13. They caught the eye of 18-year-old Eric Rohan Justin, who initially paid Ava $300 for selfies. When he asked to buy "booty pics" and pictures of her feet, she blocked him, and her dad texted Justin to say Ava was a minor and he should stop contacting her. In 2021, Justin showed up at her family's home with a shotgun and blew open the front door. Ava's father shot and killed him. The next month, Ava's parents discovered that a man who contacted Ava offering to pay for her phone number was a registered sex offender. And after Ava said another boy in her class was watching and following her, she stopped attending school in person. But she stayed on social media.[36]

* * *

The other kinds of risks girls disproportionately face when they post on social media can haunt them long into the future. In today's cancel culture, kids can ruin their chances at college admission or future jobs with a single post—before they're mature enough to fully appreciate the possible consequences. Girls are, of course, especially vulnerable.

"A boy can be a star athlete and good at school and also make a mistake and people say he did something stupid," Laura Otton, a New York–based psychotherapist, told me. "There doesn't tend to be this domino effect of a mistake negating all his other good characteristics. Whereas, even in childhood, girls are judged based on their mistakes. If a girl makes a mistake and posts something inappropriate, it is judged as a reflection of her worth, her morality, and who she is."

But kids still post things that could come back to bite them in the future all the time. "The prefrontal lobe is the last part of the brain that fully develops, later in young adulthood," Varela says. "It's the part of the brain that can pause and understand long-term consequences of actions. So when they take a risk, they think, 'the consequences aren't really going to happen to me.'"

Charlotte, 16, is from New York City. Her mom, Melinda, constantly reminds Charlotte to be careful what she posts on social media. Melinda follows Charlotte on Instagram to make sure she follows the rules. No bikini photos allowed. But guess what? Kids don't always listen to their parents.

So, two years ago, Charlotte posted photos of herself in bikinis on a website called VSCO that her mom didn't know about. She remembers it was spring break and she was on vacation in the Caribbean when she discovered those bikini shots she'd posted of herself were being used by someone else on Instagram profiles that seemed to be designed for trafficking girls. So she went to her mom for help.

Melinda filed a report with Instagram, but says she never got anything more than an automated response saying it had been received. Melinda has lots of connections through the rarefied Upper East Side world in which she lives. One of her mom friends was close with one of the most senior people at Facebook. That mom sent the top Facebook executive a letter from Melinda asking that the profiles be removed. She never got a response. Melinda also spoke to an assistant district attorney, who told her there was nothing he could do.

Charlotte told me the scariest part of all this wasn't thinking about what it could do to her reputation. It was the possibility sex traffickers would try to come after her in real life. "I was scared they could find me and take me," she says.

Charlotte now goes to boarding school.

* * *

Why do girls post bikini shots or sexualized photos? It doesn't take long for girls on social media to figure out that one of the easiest ways to create content people will like is to make themselves look "hot" in pictures.[37]

So, many girls start sexualizing themselves for social media at shockingly young ages. They're often using "finstas"—Instagram accounts without their real names, so their parents can't track them.[38] But the American Psychological Association warns that the sexualization of girls is linked to depression, eating disorders, low self-esteem, anxiety, and shame.[39]

"This is objectifying girls, turning them into bodies who are there for other people's pleasure, to look at and to like," Otton warns. "It's anxiety provoking, this acute pressure to fit into a mold and give more and more in order to be accepted and get recognition and love."

And if another measure of a girl's popularity is the number of friends she has, she may accept friend and follow requests from men she doesn't know without registering the possible danger of predators who are attracted to these kinds of images of young girls. Charlotte told me she's extra cautious online after the bad experience she had with her bikini photos. So she only accepts follow requests from strangers if they have a friend in common. But she thinks a majority of her friends "would accept requests even from someone they don't know," she told me. "It means more followers, more likes, more attention, and it's validating when you see an older guy request to follow you that doesn't look like a creepy old man."

Then there are sexts. Vivian told me that, in high school, some boys would ask her to sext. She shared photos of herself in underwear with a few of them. They never went public, she said. "That could have been so bad," she thinks now. At the time, she worried about getting a reputation as a slut. The possibility that the photos she shared could end up online and haunt her as an adult never entered her mind.

"I don't blame myself because I was so young, but I just wish I could have known I had the option to tell these guys to fuck off,"

Vivian told me. "But it was this lack of knowledge and curiosity of what it's like to have a guy interested in you."

A 2020 meta-analysis of 50 studies found that over 47 percent of young people engage in reciprocal sexting, sharing nude or practically nude images of themselves.[40] While this may be shocking to their parents, many teens don't see it as a big deal.

"Nudes are pretty normal," Charlotte told me. "I'd say most of my friends and I have nudes in our lives." A lot of girls take them and keep them on My Eyes Only on Snapchat, so they have them at the ready when boys ask for them, she explained. And, in her experience, only boys do the asking. "A girl would never ask for a penis picture, because that's the weirdest thing ever," she says.

Charlotte told me it's rarer for boys who aren't in a relationship with a girl to ask for nudes at her boarding school because it's such an incestuous community. "If a guy asked me here, I would immediately tell my friends," she explained. "And even though it's normalized, it's also looked down upon." But "if you don't know the person or live in the same state, you're more likely to send it because there's no repercussions," she explained.

Why do girls send them? "Obviously if you send someone something like that they're going to respond in a positive manner, so some girls do it for attention, some do it for validation," Charlotte said.

Justine Ang Fonte, an intersectional health educator, told me teens often ask for sexts as a "way to gain power by owning this piece of reputational property and using it as a way to maintain power, disempower someone else, or manipulate and create control in a relationship." And Fonte said that girls share them for the exact reasons Charlotte explained. "For young people, but especially hetero girls, a lot of times the reason is 'I want him to like me,' even if it's something they're not comfortable with," Fonte told me. "They think, 'if I don't have the hottest body and this guy is giving me attention, all I have to do is press send' and it can fill their need for validation. Teen girls can be that vulnerable and they want that sense of belonging that badly."

"It's not that girls are not worried about being slut-shamed," Fonte says. "It's just not at the forefront of their decision making. That instant gratification is more attractive to them in that moment."

This also makes them vulnerable to adult predators online, Fonte says. "Most young people who are going through puberty are insecure because their bodies are changing so fast, so predators just have to say the right things to get what they want. Then they can say 'now I have these photos, Venmo me this money and if you don't, I'm going to share this photo with your whole class.'"

Think I'm not talking about the girls in your life right now? Almost one in three girls between the ages of 13 and 17 has had a sexual interaction with an adult on social media.[41] Carrie Goldberg, a victims' rights attorney who often advocates for women and girls who have been abused online, told me when girls get into a situation like this after sexting, it's especially catastrophic if they're afraid to tell their parents about it because they're worried about being slut-shamed, or berated for sexting in the first place, or having their phones taken away. That's because victims are often "sextorted" for more and more explicit content, so the longer they go without getting help, the more material the perpetrator accrues and the worse the situation becomes.

What's more, when kids are involved, sexting is a serious crime. Under both federal and state law it's a felony to produce, share, or possess sexually explicit images of minors, so kids can be—and have been—charged under severe child pornography laws, even for images they've taken of themselves.[42]

Laws are especially punitive toward (often female) victims. "If a minor takes a nude selfie, in theory she's produced child pornography," Goldberg writes in *Nobody's Victim: Fighting Psychos, Stalkers, Pervs, and Trolls.* "If she has it on her phone, she's in possession of child porn. If she sends the image to anyone else, she is guilty of distribution. If she sends it to one of her peers, that's another crime, distribution to a minor. By comparison, say she sent the image to her boyfriend, they break up, and he retaliates by forwarding the image to all his friends. In that case, he might face only one possible felony charge for distributing child porn, compared to the victim's four."[43]

In Chapter 5, we'll talk more about sextortion and so-called revenge porn. The reason the release of these images is so devastating for girls socially, of course, is because they must walk razor-thin lines between being called hot and being branded as sluts. Remember how Vivian said what she worried about when she sexted was her reputation? The modern term for a girl who is trying too hard to get sexual attention on social media is "thirsty"—and it isn't a compliment.[44]

* * *

Social media is also where girls and boys now learn about sex– specifically, from porn. "Most adolescent boys and girls are exposed to porn," Fonte told me. She says their typical first exposure can happen between the ages of 8 and 11.

"They're not necessarily proactively searching for it," she says. "It could be a pop up on a screen they accidentally click on, it appears because of a virus, or a friend holds up a screen. Or they google 'how do I kiss someone' and it leads them to all sorts of things."

And when they watch porn, they're taking notes. In a 2021 study, 18-to-24-year-olds said pornography was the most helpful source of information they received about how to have sex.[45]

It's not necessary to take sides in the debate between anti-porn and "sex-positive" feminists to acknowledge a simple fact:

mainstream porn often depicts violence against women. A 2010 study of porn videos found that 88 percent depicted aggression. Women were the ones receiving the aggression over 90 percent of the time.[46] Online porn is also racist: Black women are more likely than white women to be shown as the victims of aggression, while Black men are more likely than white men to be shown as the perpetrators.[47]

"This reinforces power structures," Fonte says. "Seeing how often women are dominated by men in hetero scenes and behaviors, the suggestion is you're supposed to like this or this is normal or common."

So it's not surprising that girls who watch porn at younger ages are more likely to be sexually submissive[48]—which puts them at greater risk of being on the receiving end of dangerous, potentially deadly behavior. A 2019 study found that 12.5 percent of adolescent women and 23.9 percent of adult women in the United States say they've become scared during sex as a result of something done to them, such as choking.[49]

I used the term choking here because it's what has been used in research. But attorney David Lauren told me what we're really talking about is strangulation. "Choking is when you eat something and it goes down the wrong way," he says. "Strangulation is a conscious act by one person against another."

Fonte told me that "when we interrogate what's going on there, college men say, 'this is what I think women like because this is what I see in porn.' The assumption that all women are into aggressive, violent behaviors when engaging in sexual acts can have fatal consequences. The normalization of this is what is really scary."

In 2015, a meta-analysis of twenty-two studies from seven countries found "little doubt that, on the average, individuals who consume pornography more frequently are more likely to hold attitudes conducive to sexual aggression and engage in actual acts of sexual aggression."[50] For example, a 2011 study found male college students in the United States who have consumed porn were less likely to intervene if they witnessed a sexual assault and more likely to commit sexual assault themselves—if they were confident they could get away with it without being caught.[51] Other researchers found that one of the key characteristics of boys who disagreed or only somewhat agreed with the statement "I want there to be equal numbers of men and women who are leaders in work, politics, and life" was that they had been exposed to online porn.[52]

Watching porn can also be harmful to girls' body images because they come to think the bodies they see in porn are realistic or common, Fonte says. "These people are performers and have been curated to play in the scene," she said. "It's not a typical body. So much of our society values female bodies based on what they look like, so especially young girls think their body is only worth being desired or has power and capital if it looks a certain way, and if it doesn't they don't feel like they have the same right or privilege to be able to assert themselves or have the confidence to demand what they want to do or feel comfortable with."

What's more, Fonte says, porn gives girls a skewed idea of what pleasure looks like. "A lot of female performers on the screen seem to be enjoying themselves, and it seems like it's very easy and common to orgasm, when it's actually very much a minority experience," she told me. "So, in real life, it must seem like something is wrong with them if they don't. There are these feelings of insecurity and shame from partners suggesting something is wrong with them, because they're exposed to the same visuals."

But when schools try to teach porn education to push back against these ideas, parents freak out. Just ask Fonte, who garnered national media attention after she gave sex ed workshops at Columbia Grammar and Preparatory School which outraged parents. *The*

New York Times interviewed multiple sex educators who found nothing wrong with what she had taught and reported that it was in line with national and international standards for sex education. But she still stepped down from her position as director of health and wellness at Dalton, the elite Manhattan prep school.[53]

* * *

What We Can Do

How can we make social media a safer place for our daughters? For starters, we've got to sharent responsibly. Here are a few ways to do it: when you post, refer to your children by their initials or pet names. Limit who can view such content. Your family and close friends will be delighted to see pictures of baby Olivia sleeping peacefully in her nursery. But there's no reason why the random guy you met at a professional conference who later friended you on Facebook needs access.

In *How to Be a Woman Online: Surviving Abuse and Harassment, and How to Fight Back,* Nina Jankowicz offers advice for sharing real-time location photos that also makes for smart sharenting strategy. "Using the 'close friends' feature on Instagram stories or creating a Facebook list containing people you know in real life and trust is a good way to scratch your sharing itch but keep yourself relatively safe," she writes.[54]

When you get connection requests from people, talk to them offline to confirm they are the ones who actually created the accounts. Set up a different account with a pseudonym to use when you seek out or share sensitive information, like support groups for parents of kids with illnesses or disabilities—or at least post anonymously as a group member. And before you post anything, ask yourself whether your daughter will be mad about it if it's published on the cover of *The New York Times* when she runs for president.

Dr. Galynker recommends selecting schools for our daughters that use minimal technology and screen time. We also have to delay the age at which our kids start using social media. Remember there's a documented association between using social media and bad mental health outcomes in the youngest girls—ages 11–13. They don't belong on social networks in the first place. But if all their friends are already online, it will be near impossible to win that battle. So we need to talk to parents of our kids' friends and classmates while they're very young and collectively agree to hold off on letting our kids join social networks until high school (Dr. Haidt recommends waiting until at least age 16).

We've got to be on top of this and start uniting as parents early on this front, because we can count on social networks to only come after our children at younger ages. Even at the height of the fury at Instagram over Frances Haugen's leaks, chief executive Adam Mosseri wouldn't commit to not rolling out a version of Instagram for kids ages 10–12 in the future.[55] We can't just worry and moan about this—we've got to act preemptively to protect our daughters.

This also means it's on us to give them other safe things to do. Contrary to popular perception, today's teens say they'd much rather hang out with their friends in person than interact with them on social media, danah boyd writes in *It's Complicated: The Social Lives of Networked Teens*. The reason they spend so much time on social networks is because their overscheduled lives, lack of transportation, and parents' rules prevent them from getting together offline.[56]

We also have to instill values in our children early on that they can later draw upon when they're faced with challenges on social media. Varela encourages families to discuss this together. "Talk about, 'who do we aspire to be as human beings?'" she says. "Maybe it's being kind and respectful and accepting other people no matter where they come from and what they look like. You can build that early in childhood by planting seeds and watering them, and hopefully they grow so when they're more independent and autonomous to make choices, that's there." Then, she says, kids can grow up to post content on social media that aligns with their values—like kindness, body positivity, and acceptance.

And we all need to get savvier about understanding how platforms work and how they affect our daughters so we can teach them how to use social networks safely. boyd points out that we often call teens who grew up with social media "digital natives" and assume they're tech savvy by virtue of their ages. But in reality, our young daughters are often what sociologist Eszter Hargittai, PhD, has called digital *naives*, totally unaware of some of the dangers they face online.[57]

One place to start is the Common Sense Media website, which provides guides for parents on helping kids navigate different social platforms (Resources, page 234).

Varela also says one of the most important things parents can do is communicate with our daughters and be there to help them talk about and navigate the challenges they face online. "Teen moods change, the resistance can be there, but continue to open the door and offer the opportunity to communicate and check in," she says. "You're the adult. You have to be the one to make the move, to offer support and attention. Even when your teen rejects you and pushes you away, you don't stop. You keep choosing to show up and try."

Most important, Goldberg told me, is that "parents need to tell their kids they forgive them for anything bad that happens online but they need to know about it and no secrets. We see children scared out of their minds that their parent is going to take their phone away"—and that can prevent them from telling their moms or other caregivers that they're in very dangerous situations.

We also have to talk to our daughters about "context collapse": in person, they'd act differently around their friends than they would with their parents, teachers, and college admissions counselors. But, online, the content they post could be viewed by anyone. Even snaps that they might think quickly disappear could actually be saved or hacked, then used against them years into the future. We also have to talk to them about the ways girls and women are unfairly judged in our society (more from me on this in Chapters 2 and 3) and how things can be taken out of context, so they can think about possible repercussions before they post.

What's more, we have to remind our girls—*repeatedly*—that their bodies or the number of likes and online friends they rack up are not the source of their worth. And we need to discuss why the filtered, photoshopped photos they see online aren't good representations of anyone's lives.

We also need to talk to our daughters about body image and self-compassion (treating themselves as they would a friend) *before* they start using social media. In a 2022 study, Canadian researchers found that when women were asked to conduct a writing exercise designed to build self-compassion before comparing themselves to images of the "ideal" woman on Instagram, they had less dissatisfaction with their appearances. But those who didn't complete the exercise before seeing the Instagram images had more concerns about their bodies.[58]

In addition, we need to talk about how to handle the many dangers they'll find online, from the pressure to sext boys in their school to professional sextortionists and scam artists (much more from me on this in Chapters 4 and 5). We need to tell them to only connect online with people they know offline. We also have to teach them to be on the lookout for friends who might be struggling or in trouble—and discuss when to give them positive affirmation and when to get them more help.

And we should talk to our daughters about who they follow, and why it's more important to keep up with people like Greta Thunberg and Amanda Gorman than the Kardashians. "When I was growing up, Hollywood picked one version of what a female should look like," Dr. Odgers told me. "She was thin and she was blond. But now, there are diverse types of women represented in influencer networks around different interests and cultures and kids are finding the people they gravitate towards." We should help them find these kinds of healthy groups—and avoid the potentially very dangerous ones, like the fitspiration community.

We should also encourage our daughters to use social networks to connect with people around shared interests and issues and nurture deeper friendships through things like messaging close friends, rather than seeking validation from endless acquaintances.

And we should steer our girls away from the more visually oriented platforms like Instagram. As we've seen, social media can be a place for teens like Zoë Quinn to connect with one another and find a healthy community or even a lifeline. Or it can be a place where girls like Vivian learn to starve themselves. It's about how they use it. When they're our daughters, we have to help them get it right.

We also have to talk to our daughters about healthy relationships. "I tell my kids it's OK not to know every single moment where our friends or boyfriend or girlfriend are," Varela says. "There are lots of different reasons why people get together and don't include everyone every time and that's OK. It helps to depersonalize it because the youth brain is so self-focused. They think, 'something must be wrong with me.'"

We also need to teach our daughters about consent. Remember how Vivian said she didn't know she had the option to tell guys who asked for sexts to get lost? Our daughters need to know that they not only have the right to refuse to sext, but they must, because they *don't want to go to prison* or have their intimate images be the first thing potential employers find when they google them later on. And they should also say no to anything else that makes them uncomfortable.

Similarly, Fonte says we need to speak with our girls before they're exposed to porn. Think your daughter isn't going to see it because of her gender? "It's a big myth that this is something only teenage boys are watching," Fonte tells me. "All genders are exposed to and looking at porn. Caregivers like teachers and parents should be talking about it well before they see it, so when they are inevitably exposed to this they realize they are looking at an entertainment industry and not an education industry."

And while I'm writing about girls in this book, it should go without saying that boys are part of the solution as well. Parents need to instill these same values in their sons and teach them about consent and refusal too, so they grow up to treat people with respect on (and off) line.

These conversations about social media can be especially hard because many of us don't have memories of our own parents having this talk with us to look back on. But Varela also advises being open to therapy. "Sometimes it's harder for kids to go to their parents and communicate," she says. "Recruit a therapist and think about this person as a coach and advisor for you and someone who can check in and help youth navigate and explore how social media is impacting them."

We also need to ensure that our daughters balance their screen time with things like sleep, homework, and extracurricular activities. When I spoke to Frances Haugen, she told me one of her biggest concerns is kids missing out on sleep because they're on social media. According to the American Academy of Pediatrics, not getting enough sleep increases a child's risk of everything from accidents to obesity and depression, and is associated with behavior and learning problems.[59]

We also have to be good role models, putting our phones away at the dinner table and when our kids are trying to talk to us—and not oversharing details of our own lives online, either.

"I'm really firm on this," Varela says. "We have to pay attention. We have to put our phones down and close our laptops and look our teens in the eye and talk to them and connect with them, because if they're in their screen and we're in our screen, you're gonna lose them. Check your behavior and what you're modeling."

Varela says we should also watch for signs that something is wrong with our daughters—such as significant changes to their mood, personality, or appearance or if they're isolating more than usual or not doing their normal activities. Some of this is typical adolescent behavior, she says, but if it's very significant and a lot of signs are present at once, it's time to be concerned—and seek outside help.

We should also demand that our kids' schools implement more rigorous curricula to help them handle what they see on social media in healthy ways. From the time they learn to read and write, Finnish schoolchildren are taught how online content affects their emotions and how to identify altered images and fake news.[60] It's downright negligent that American schools don't universally have curricula of the same quality. Dr. Odgers says a big problem is that girls from higher-income families tend to get this kind of guidance from parents and teachers, while girls from lower-income families don't.

Comprehensive sex education is also important, Fonte says, because it makes children less vulnerable to online predation. "We have to teach them to know their worth, assert themselves, and look out for others in their peer group who are in unsafe situations," she says. Porn literacy is needed as part of this education. To be clear, porn literacy does not involve watching porn. It involves critically analyzing how the industry is misconstruing reality, Fonte says, and discussing healthier ways for romantic partners to interact with one another.

But Ron Bartley, a retired educator and college president, points out that we can't reasonably expect teachers to solve all of society's ills. "Educators are being attacked and criticized for addressing topics in the classroom that are not purely academic," he told me. Many feel under siege. That's why every state should mandate specific curricula about how to use social media in healthy ways, to be taught by experts. This would ensure that students in both rich and poor areas receive this education and that educators don't come under fire for teaching it.

As for social networks, they have a social responsibility to alter their tools and algorithms to fix these problems. Documents leaked by Haugen show that staffers have proposed offering filters that are "fun" instead of ones that help people beautify themselves.[61] That's exactly what they should be pushing. Their algorithms should amplify *unfiltered* photos and content that promotes body positivity instead of thinspiration.

Dr. Odgers told me teen girls turn to social media when they struggle with their mental health. So social networks should also have resource boxes that pop up when they search for terms related to mental health and body image, linking to organizations that can help them.

But ultimately the horror of what Haugen revealed wasn't just what social networks are doing to some girls. It was that we can't trust them. After all, Haugen testified that Meta executives have been aware of these problems all along but choose to prioritize profits instead of addressing the ways their products are harming users—*even when they are vulnerable young girls.*

So it's on us to protect our daughters. Ultimately, the most important thing we can teach our girls is that, instead of focusing on how they look on social media, they need to think critically about how they look *at* platforms like Instagram.

THE FACE IN THE FILTER

We've seen how over-exposure to toxic content on social media fed Vivian's eating disorder. But, sadly, she wasn't crazy to think people were judging her body when she posted pictures on Instagram. In fact, social media has dramatically dialed up the volume and venom of the judgments women face.

When you think about it, social networks are designed to elicit people's judgments of us. When we post something on a social network, users are invited to signal their approval or disapproval with likes, shares, reposts, comments, and emoticons. And, unless you've made your profile private, it has connected us with literally billions of other people on the Internet who are accepting that invitation.

It's easy to see that pictures elicit way more reactions than text. According to Adobe, posts with images get 650 percent more engagement.[1] So that's what we often share. Posting photos instead of text keeps the focus on our appearances. And it allows the whole world to weigh in on them.

Take pregnancy. Before, a celebrity snapped by paparazzi leaving her home might have had to contend with snarky tabloid headlines. But now, thanks to social media, the public can participate in "bump watches" to guess whether she's having a baby or merely ate an extra french fry for lunch.

"Deciding when to tell friends or family or your employer that you're expecting is a really big deal," Renée Cramer, PhD, provost of Dickinson College and author of *Pregnant With the Stars: Watching and Wanting the Celebrity Baby Bump*, told me. "Your comfort depends on whether you or your friends have experienced pregnancy loss and where you are in your education and your career. It's a personal decision."

But the comments people post on social media when they "out" women in the public eye for being pregnant make *The National Inquirer* look tame. "You get these vicious comments on Instagram and [X, the platform formerly known as Twitter] that you'd never have gotten in a tabloid," Dr. Cramer says. "And now she can read those comments."

Before, an overweight teen might have had to contend with snickers from her classmates. But now, when she posts a picture of herself in her prom dress, people across seas and continents can all tell her she's fat and ugly.

"We used to say those things behind her back," Dr. Cramer says. "Now it's said right to her face, literally under her body on social media. We're all just public property."

If a picture is worth a thousand words, what a picture usually can't represent about a woman is worth a hundred thousand: our thoughts and values and struggles and personal histories and hopes and dreams, our views on issues, the contributions we have made and have to make to the world. And, even if they can be conveyed visually, they usually can't be appropriately responded to with an emoji. But apps like Instagram put our pictures front and center. On Tinder, people make split-second decisions to swipe left or right, based on a single selfie. (I'll have much more to say about dating apps in Chapter 4.)

The availability of images of most women on social media means we're now judged for our appearances more than ever before. For example, the vast majority of employers use social media to screen people who apply for jobs.[2] Researchers at the University of the West of Scotland found that when prospective employers evaluate social media profiles of applicants, they judge women primarily based on their appearances. (Men tend to be judged on the content they post.)[3]

We're also judging ourselves more now that we have all these pictures to scrutinize. Before social media, we might have had our picture taken when we went to a wedding or birthday party, but we didn't see photos of ourselves all that often, plastic surgeon Dr. Dennis Schimpf points out. So "you were kind of unaware of what you look like because you weren't seeing yourself in all these different sorts of environments and angles," he told me. But now, thanks to all the photos we (and our friends) post on social media, "it's non-stop. You see women who struggle with their weight or different things and they're constantly being reminded of that."

So it shouldn't register as a surprise that a wide body of research confirms that using social media is associated with feeling badly about our bodies—and it seems that this association only grows over time.[4] For example, a 2018 study found that women who use Instagram more compare themselves with celebrities more and objectify themselves more.[5] And a 2015 study found that the more involved people are on Facebook, the more they surveil their bodies and the greater their body shame.[6]

Dr. Schimpf says this self-surveillance on social media also helps explain why so many more women are having plastic surgery. Between 2000 and 2020, there was a 131 percent increase in cosmetic procedures, according to the American Society of Plastic Surgeons. In 2020, 92 percent of those procedures were done on women.[7] Then, during the Covid-19 pandemic, when we all spent even more time on social media and were constantly confronted with our faces on Zoom, plastic surgery really took off. Between 2020 and 2021, there was a 63 percent increase in body procedures and a 54 percent increase in facelifts, according to the Aesthetic Society, a group of plastic surgeons.[8]

Social media has also given us loads more pictures of other people to examine. But so many of the photos of others we're seeing online are filtered. "They're making it almost impossible for you to be comfortable with your body because you're constantly looking at things that are probably not achievable and maybe not even real, trying to be something you can't even match," Dr. Schimpf says.

Of course, women have long tried to imitate the appearances of famous models and actresses. Dr. Cramer writes that looking at these kinds of images "enables our self-discipline by providing examples we are meant to follow, bodies we are meant to emulate and adore, [and] attitudes and poses we are meant to strike and hold."[9] But while we might give ourselves a free pass for not achieving the waiflike look of a 1980s supermodel, why shouldn't we look like our friends?

We're also more likely to think we should look like the influencers we follow online because we think of them as more similar to ourselves than movie stars and models. That's because the remarkable thing about today's influencers is they're often not people who have done anything remarkable. Many are simply, in the (in)famous words of Barbara Walters, "famous for being famous."[10]

As Nicholas Kulish writes in *The New York Times*, "there is no longer so much difference between slick, professional media content and the way ordinary people document their lives—less and less distance between the photos you want of your night out and the photos you would see" produced by advertisers and influencers.[11] This puts tons of pressure on us to beautify ourselves—even if we don't have the time, money, and professional help to do so that are enjoyed by the influencers we follow. And Dr. Cramer points out that when we don't measure up, our culture teaches us to blame ourselves, rather than society for setting these impossible standards.

What's more, some of the trends influencers set are far from pretty. One study of the content shared by Black female celebrities in

South Africa found that they bleach their skin and do their hair in ways that are "unnatural to many African women."[12] They've bought into the messages we're all bombarded with that white bodies are beautiful—and they pass the idea that African women need to erase their identities on to the people they influence. Plenty of white people, obviously, send the same message. Women of color around the world feel these pressures acutely.

Some social media challenges send the same kinds of sick messages. A trend that emerged in China a few years ago had people snapping and sharing pictures of themselves holding pieces of A4 paper vertically to show that the paper covered their entire waists—which requires being shockingly slim. But, as Chinese feminist Zheng Churan posted, "bodies don't need eyes staring at them." She posted a photo of herself holding the paper horizontally, which was considered cheating.[13] These are the standards women around the world are internalizing on social media.

To help us augment our appearances, sites like Instagram offer an array of filters that allow us to artificially enhance our perceived attractiveness. This doesn't only promote unrealistic standards. Some filters, like those which lighten our skin and make us look slimmer, also promote racism and body image dissatisfaction.[14] And if they're not enough, outside apps can help us make other adjustments to our photos, like whitening our teeth or airbrushing our skin. They're used by an astonishing number of people. Ninety percent of young women and nonbinary people in the United Kingdom report using a filter or editing their photos to appear slimmer, reshape their nose or jaw, whiten their teeth, or bronze or brighten their skin, according to a 2021 study conducted at City University London.[15]

This increased discomfort with the way we look is reverberating through our society. Architects are now redesigning everything from primary bathrooms in homes to changing rooms in gyms to create more privacy because Americans have gotten less comfortable being seen naked—even by their own spouses.[16]

Keeping women focused on our appearances is a proven strategy for holding us back. In her book *The Beauty Myth: How Images of Beauty Are Used Against Women,* (written before she sadly fell for conspiracy theories), Naomi Wolf reminds us that the idea that women, but not men, must be beautiful isn't really about our appearances at all. It's an invention of modern Western culture—and it's designed to control us.

There's nothing natural or inevitable about the idea that a woman's worth is based on her body. Before the 1830s, women who weren't aristocrats or prostitutes were valued for their fertility and contributions to their families' earnings—not their BMI. "Physical attraction, obviously, played its part; but 'beauty' as we understand it was not, for ordinary women, a serious issue in the marriage marketplace," Wolf writes. But during the Industrial Revolution, men began to work outside the home and women were relegated to the domestic sphere. Victorian society therefore invented the beauty myth, according to Wolf, "as a means to expend female energy and intelligence in harmless ways."[17]

Wolf says after the feminist movement of the 1970s, when women won more reproductive and legal rights and began to make major advances in their educations and careers, society doubled down on the beauty myth to try to keep women insecure about their bodies. After all, companies have a major interest in keeping us consuming products to support the multi-billion-dollar diet, beauty, and apparel industries. What's more, stereotypes of powerful women as masculine and unattractive are used "to punish women for their public acts by going after their private sense of self." Wolf argues that in the 1970s, the strategy became "the paradigm for new limits placed on aspiring women everywhere."[18] A quick scroll through some of the things said about women leaders on social media is enough to remind us this hasn't changed.

All the time and money we spend on our appearances adds up to an enormous tax that men simply don't pay. Hillary Clinton calculated that she spent 600 hours—or about 25 days—getting her hair and makeup done while campaigning during the 2016 presidential election.[19] That's all time she wasn't holding rallies that could have helped her win the electoral vote. While I don't want to turn around and judge men based on the same unfair standards to which women are held, I do think a cursory look at Clinton's male rivals, Bernie Sanders and Donald Trump, confirms that having passable hair is not a requirement for male aspirants to the presidency. That gives them an enormous and unfair advantage.

The rest of us face the same double standards. The average woman in the United States spends nearly two hours more per week than the average man on her appearance, according to one national survey.[20]

Bodies, Brawls, and Bimbos

But social media doesn't just keep all of us judging women based on their looks. Some of the other content women are incentivized to post about our bodies on social media threatens our physical and mental well-being and even our lives. And it sets us back—individually and collectively.

Scroll through a social media feed for five minutes and it quickly becomes clear that if you want to get attention or even earn money from the content you post, a surefire strategy is to post audaciously. Pakistani social influencer Qandeel Baloch, who was described as her country's version of Kim Kardashian, lived by this approach. As her biographer Sanam Maher wrote, Qandeel "was aware that in order to sustain her audience's interest, she had to continue to give it something worth watching." Or, as Qandeel herself said, "to become popular, you have to do a lot. It's necessary to do some bad things. You have to show yourself, take off your clothes."[21] So she shocked her deeply conservative country by wearing revealing clothing and posting provocative videos, like one promising to perform a strip dance if Pakistan won a cricket match against India (the team lost) and another saying people would keep loving one another even if the government prevented them from celebrating Valentine's Day—a holiday condemned by many religious and political leaders in Pakistan.[22]

Of course, social networks encourage provocative content. "Getting a user outraged, anxious, or afraid is a powerful way to increase engagement," early Facebook investor Roger McNamee writes in *Zucked: Waking Up to the Facebook Catastrophe*. "Anxious and fearful users check the site more frequently. Outraged users share more content to let other people know what they should also be outraged about. Best of all from Facebook's perspective, outraged or fearful users in an emotionally hijacked state become more reactive to further emotionally charged content."[23]

Obviously the more time we spend on social media, the more money social networks make by showing us ads. So social networks program their algorithms to show users this kind of inflammatory content.

But Qandeel was sometimes shocked by the torrent of abuse her content provoked. "Please shoot her wherever you find her," one person commented on one of her posts. "You ugly b****, people like you should go die. . . . f****** c***," read another.[24] (Stars are mine.)

It's easy to question the wisdom of Qandeel's decision to transgress standards that are strictly enforced in her culture—by force, if necessary. But it becomes harder to judge her when you fully appreciate the circumstances of her life. According to her biographer, Qandeel was forced into marriage with a man who she said stubbed out cigarettes on her skin, threatened to throw acid on her face, and wanted to kill her. When she reported this to her parents, they told her she had no choice but to live with him. Qandeel eventually ran away to a women's shelter with her young son. By becoming Internet famous, she was able to not only support herself but also send money home to her family. It was a survival strategy.[25]

None of this, however, was justification enough for Qandeel's brother, who was so incensed by the shame he felt she brought on her family that, by his own admission, he strangled her to death in 2016. She was 26.

*   *   *

Like Qandeel, other women who use social media to try to get the kind of attention they can monetize are up against the reality that what audiences love to like are the kinds of retrograde representations of women that reduce us to our bodies. Kim Kardashian once shared a secret recording of Taylor Swift talking on the phone with Kardashian's then-husband, who now calls himself Ye, to try to prove that Swift had consented to a reference to herself in one of his songs. Then, when teen actor Chloë Grace Moretz posted on X (then called Twitter) suggesting that people look at what was going on "in the REAL world" instead of focusing on the feud, Kardashian's sister Khloé sexually shamed Moretz by posting a picture of a woman with her rear end exposed after her swimsuit shifted on the beach. Moretz denied the photo was of her.[26]

"As critical as I am of Kim Kardashian, she's a genius because she or someone in her camp knows how to keep the spotlight on her," Veronica Arreola, a Latina women's rights activist, tells me. "But the actions that happen in this kind of conversation reify the worst stereotypes of women, that we can't all get along. She's playing on these tropes that put feminism back in a lot of ways."

Women also have incentives to post content showing themselves harming their bodies and encouraging other women to do the same. People love a TikTok with the latest beauty craze—like sunscreen contouring (only applying sunscreen on the parts of your face to which you want to draw attention), slugging (slathering your face with Vaseline to try to hydrate it), or microneedling (sticking needles into your skin to try to generate collagen). What happens when people get skin cancer from all that contouring, or breakouts from the slugging, or infections and scarring from the microneedling?[27] They can turn their wrath on the women who promoted the trends, triggering the kind of outrage off which social networks (literally) feed.

What We Can Do

So, to sum up where we are, apps like Facebook and Instagram have made our world more visual, prompting us and others to focus on our appearances. This isn't just unfair and hasn't just made us unhappy. It's also a remarkably effective way of holding women back from achieving equality with men. And it has encouraged women to post the very kinds of content that incite public furor and flagellation and play into sexist stereotypes of us.

How do we fix all of this?

Instead of liking pictures of our friends when they wear tight dresses and mountains of makeup, let's instead all start liking their posts about their work and issues they care about. Instead of commenting and telling women they look beautiful, let's tell our women friends they're brilliant.

Instead of using filters, let's post what we really look like—which will give others permission to do the same (and like their posts when they do). If we all redirected our behavior like this, social media platforms would look very, very different.

We should also post content about our lives that helps reshape views of women. Veronica Arreola, the Latina women's rights activist, started the hashtag #365FeministSelfie to encourage women to share more of our lives. It was partly pushback against the narrative that women are vain navel-gazers when we post selfies, she told me. It was also a way of encouraging women to insert themselves in public conversations.

"I often don't see myself in the media, so me taking a selfie and sharing it is putting myself in the media, in the narrative," she said. The effort was also sparked by her recognition when going through family photos after her mom died that women are often the ones taking the photos rather than the ones *in* pictures.

By asking women to post pictures of themselves with their kids, or on their way to job interviews, or transitioning to a new gender, Arreola wants to encourage women to show that we're powerful and remind people that the personal is political.

"We need to be talking about feminism on an everyday basis," she says. "It's not just for elections, it's not just for crises, it's not just when the Supreme Court does something. Every day we live, we are doing something political."

Let's also use social media in ways that work for us. Instead of scrolling through #fitspiration posts that make us feel badly about our bodies, let's join Facebook groups or meetups for walking or running or other healthy activities in our communities. Instead of measuring ourselves against how classmates we haven't seen since high school look in filtered photos of their fanciest clothes and most fabulous moments, let's use social platforms to keep up with our true friends, since fostering close relationships is what makes people happy.[28]

We also have to demand that social platforms step up to confront these problems. They should publicly identify when photos have been manipulated. Using social media is widely documented to hurt women's body images. Being reminded that the photos we're seeing often aren't real could help change that.

As we've seen, there's a lot not to like about the ways women are represented on social media. But there's a whole lot we can do and demand to change this ugly system.

SOCIAL MEDIA AND WOMEN'S "PERPETUAL STATE OF WRONGNESS"

In 2017, human rights lawyer Amal Clooney delivered an impassioned address at the United Nations pleading for an investigation into a genocide being perpetrated by the Islamic State. She exhorted the international community to act quickly to stop the terrorist group from raping, torturing, and murdering the Yazidi people. "If we do not change course, history will judge us, and there will be no excuse for our failure to act," she warned.[1]

If I'd written about her speech for CNN, I might have suggested a title like "Amal Clooney Implores World to Stop Genocide." But here's *TIME* magazine's post on X (then called Twitter) about her testimony: "Amal Clooney shows off her baby bump at the United Nations." For *TIME*, what mattered wasn't what she was trying to say. It was her body.

In 2021, First Lady Jill Biden, EdD, traveled to California to commemorate the birthday of labor organizer César Chávez in her unpaid role as America's first lady.[2] As a result, according to *Glamour* magazine's website, X (then called Twitter) "broke."[3] The reason? Dr. Biden wore a pair of black hosiery that many people described as fishnet stockings. She was called everything from a prostitute to a witch—though plenty of others jumped to her defense by praising her sartorial selection.[4]

We are all Amal Clooney and Jill Biden. It's not just women in the public eye who face what writer Jill Filipovic describes as a "jeweler's loupe scrutiny" over their bodies and every deed.[5] The biblical first woman, Eve, is pinned with responsibility for the fall of mankind all because she ate an apple, and modern-day women are judged no more charitably.

We saw in the last chapter how social media makes it possible for more people than we would ever encounter in the physical world to pronounce judgment on our bodies. But that's just the start of the ways people use social media to socially sanction women. In this chapter, we'll see how it also gives perfect strangers incentives to shame women for money—and, of course, for our sexuality.

How It Started

We all know the part of this that predates social media. To be a woman is to live in what writer Rebecca Solnit has called "a perpetual state of wrongness."[6]

What happens if you disagree with others? You're a "mean girl." (Never mind that girls aren't more aggressive than boys.[7]) What happens if you raise your voice in public? You're shrill and unstable. (Men who do so are leaders.)[8] What happens if you go for a job that has traditionally been held by men? You're unqualified, unkind, unlikeable, and untrustworthy.[9] (A man who does so is being, well, a man.)

What happens if you sleep with multiple men? You're a slut. (A man who has sex with many women is a *success*. But really, there are simply no male equivalents for words like *slut* or *mistress*—because they're not needed. People don't judge them the same way.)

And if people don't like the length of your skirt or neckline, you might be called out for that, too. "Anything can be slut-shamed— literally anything," Charlotte, 16, who you met in Chapter 1, told me. "I'll post a photo of myself and my friends and people will take it the wrong way. I don't post anything wrong, my mom follows me. Something so simple can be taken out of proportion. But when a guy posts some shirtless photo, no one gives a fuck."

What happens if you're transgender? You'll be asked by perfect strangers about the state of your genitals, even though no one goes around asking cisgender men whether they're circumcised, says Julia Serano, author of *Whipping Girl: A Transsexual Woman on Sexism and the Scapegoating of Femininity.*[10]

What happens if you're lesbian? "The old stereotype is we're these sad, fat women who can't get men so we take each other instead and it's a lesser life," my friend Eve tells me.

What happens if you don't get married and have children? You're pathetic and unfulfilled. Emily, 37, who is single, is a physician in a Florida hospital, where her coworkers constantly ask about her dating life. "Well-meaning colleagues will mention they have a friend who froze her eggs and tell me where she did it," she told me. "The assumption is I'm going to want to have children and I'm too old to have them. But nobody ever goes up to the men and asks, 'are you planning to have children? When are you planning to have children?'"

When she goes to a restaurant by herself, Emily says, "there's typically a lot of questions. I'll be asked, 'is anyone joining you?' and I'll say no. 'Oh, so no one's coming,' the waiter will reply. And I'm like, 'nope, no one's coming!' But I never hear men complaining they get second questions or looks if they go out alone. I think the assumption is they're traveling for business."

Recently, Emily went on a trip on her own to recover from a bad breakup. "When I told the person at the hotel that I didn't need a second key, they asked, 'what are you going to do on your own?' And I said, 'I don't know, the same thing couples do! I'm going to go shopping, I'm going to go to museums!' And they looked at me like I was the saddest person on the planet."

What happens if you do get married and have children? You're either tedious and unproductive for not working while you raise your kids, or not fully committed to your kids or your job if you do work. And if you're a poor Black stay-at-home mom, you're also a drain on society—even though minimum wage jobs don't pay enough to afford quality childcare.

What happens if you go out in public sans enfants? People will ask where your kids are. (When dad goes out *with* the kids, he'll be admired for "babysitting.") But what happens if you tote your kids along with you in public places? You may annoy others if they behave like children.

Of course, the United States stacks the deck against mothers. It's the only one of 41 countries that doesn't ensure moms get paid time off work after having children, according to the Organization for Economic Cooperation and Development.[11] So lots of moms have to go back to work quickly after having a baby—but it can be exceedingly difficult and expensive to find childcare options, because the United States spends 28 times less than the average rich country on childcare.[12] And when we send our kids to daycare, we have to teach them survival skills in case someone tries to murder them and all their friends, since guns are the number one killer of American children.[13] Most working women also take on the majority of the childcare and domestic work in our homes.[14] But what happens when, up against all this, you drop the ball and forget to pack your kid's lunch or help him with his homework?[15] "Dads get the at-least-he's-trying pat on the back when people see them mess up," journalist Gemma Hartley writes in *FED UP: Emotional Labor, Women, and the Way Forward*. "Moms get the eye rolls and judgment."[16]

What happens if you ask your male partner to do half the work of arranging playdates and childcare? You're high maintenance. (This is "a term almost explicitly reserved for women who ask for emotional labor from their partners," Hartley writes, and "there are few insults greater."[17])

My husband and I recently attended a birthday party where the fact that I "don't cook" became a major topic of conversation. No one was interested in the fact that I'd traveled to all seven continents and served in a presidential administration where I met everyone from Saudi princes to Togolese mangrove farmers. What was fascinating to people was that I don't do all the domestic labor in my home—while also, like my husband, working full time.

What happens when your mother-in-law comes to visit and the house is a mess? "She's blaming you," sociologist Claire Kamp Dush, PhD, reminds us.[18]

What happens if you don't appear happy? Men you don't know may tell you to smile. What happens if you do things to make yourself happy? You're selfish for not putting others first (*especially* if those others are your children).

My good friend Noor, a stay-at-home mom, was the sole caretaker for her first child when he was born. She didn't have family living nearby who could help. It was hard not to have any space to take care of herself, she recalls—and it made her unhappy. So after her second son was born, she was determined not to have a repeat experience.

"For me, taking care of myself means going to the gym and being away from the kids for a little bit," she explained. "I need to take care of myself so I can take care of my kids."

So Noor started going to the gym and putting her baby in the gym's infant care room when he was three and a half months old, while she did one-hour workouts a few times per week. She was right there in the building if her son needed anything. In fact, if he needed a diaper change, the staff would interrupt her workout so she could take care of it.

"They did the same things in the infant room that we did at home," Noor told me. "They played and let him sleep. But people around me—friends, extended family, people I met at the gym—kept telling me my baby was too young for me to leave him. People would tell me to wait until he was a year old."

What happens if you tell your doctor you're in pain? You might be diagnosed with a psychological problem. (Men are more likely to be given *painkillers*.)[19]

Rana Awdish, a physician and author of *In Shock: My Journey from Death to Recovery and the Redemptive Power of Hope*, told me she was once in the hospital and recognized that she had sepsis—a life-threatening condition. "I asked for a hospitalist to come in and he looked at me and said, 'I'm sure you're having a lot of anxiety right now, but I'm not worried about sepsis.' I'm a critical care physician and I was very aware of my own symptoms, so I worked back channels to get into the Intensive Care Unit," she said. "But I could have died if I had let him attribute my symptoms to anxiety. It was so infuriating and wrong."

What happens if you spend time making yourself look attractive? You're narcissistic and vain. What happens if you *don't* keep up your appearance? You'll be more likely to get lower grades in school[20] and be fired from your job[21]—and less likely to make it to the top of your field[22] or land a romantic partner.[23] (I'm sure I don't need to point out that unattractive men pay less severe penalties.)

And what happens if you end up in the public eye? Your every word and move will be scrutinized so strangers can render a verdict on whether you're fake. Men simply aren't "authenticity policed" in the same way.[24] Like Jill Biden and Amal Clooney, you'll also be apprised for your body, rather than your brains. And even if you please some people, you'll almost certainly displease others (remember that Dr. Biden was both praised and pilloried for her pantyhose).

So it pretty much doesn't matter *what* you do. If you're a woman in our culture, everyone thinks they have the right to judge you—often unkindly.

How It's Going

Now, all these judgments of women are publicly proclaimed on social media. As we saw in the last chapter, online, people will post what they think about you, in no uncertain terms, for you and the world to see.

One reason people will post things online that they'd never have the audacity to say to your face is because the Internet allows them to cower behind their computer screens—a phenomenon known as the online disinhibition effect. Psychology professor John Suler, PhD, says this is partly because trolls can remain anonymous online, so they don't have to "own their behavior."

Even when they use their real names, "people often perceive that what they say or do online won't stick to them," law professor Danielle Keats Citron writes.[25] What's more, Suler says, some people view the online world as a fantasy realm or game. It can be easy to lose sight of the fact that the people they're interacting with are human beings with feelings.[26]

And because other people's reactions aren't visible, users may make their posts extra extreme to ensure they have their desired effect. One teenage boy, for example, was asked by author Peggy Orenstein about a group account he posted in that contained more than 100 sexist and racist "jokes" about his high school classmates. "You wanted to make your friends laugh, but when you're not face-to-face, you can't tell if you'll get a reaction or not so you go a little further," the 15-year-old said. "You go one step beyond."[27]

So a lot of the content people post on social media shamelessly conveys their sexist and misogynistic views of women. Quick definition of terms: sexism, according to Cornell philosopher Kate Manne, PhD, involves the idea that men are superior to women.[28] An instructive example would be Nigerian president Muhammadu Buhari's post on X (then called Twitter) that his wife's proper place is in his kitchen.[29]

By contrast, Dr. Manne defines misogyny as punishing women for doing things that cause displeasure to men—like, for example, challenging them in an election.[30] One example would be Donald Trump's repost of a doctored video of himself hitting a golf ball and knocking down his former rival, Hillary Clinton. Witnessing acts of violence in media is correlated with committing acts of physical aggression. So, as I argued for CNN in 2017, this single post made the world less safe for women.[31]

Memorializing Mommy's Meltdown

Now social media also gives people monetary incentives to post content about women so we can be vilified by the masses. If you secretly record video of mommy melting down on the playground, you can try to sell it to one of a cottage industry of companies that will buy the rights to clips primed to go viral, then try to make money from selling ads or collecting royalties when people view them or put them on TV. Women are, of course, especially strong targets because of our perpetual state of wrongness.

In 2017, a stranger recorded a mother arguing with a gate agent at the airport at 2:00 AM after she experienced a 12-hour flight delay which stood to make her family miss their Disney cruise. True, this was a first-world problem. It's also true that a stranger captured what was quite possibly one of this mama's worst moments and it was posted to the Internet presumably without her consent, where it will now be used as a (possibly totally inaccurate) measure of her overall character for time immemorial. I think most people would be ready to lose their minds after that level of sleep deprivation and stress—especially with kids in tow.

What could the stranger's motivation have been for sharing this clip? Money, Sue Scheff, author of *Shame Nation: The Global Epidemic of Online Hate*, told me. Junkin' Media offered to buy the rights to the video.[32]

Documenting other people's alleged transgressions and sharing them with the world is known as public shaming. Monica Lewinsky considers herself "patient zero" for the practice. As we all know, Lewinsky's "friend" secretly recorded hours of private phone conversations with her which were released publicly in 1998, revealing that Lewinsky had a sexual relationship with then-president Bill Clinton. Back then, people turned to the comments sections of websites and to email to judge and excoriate Lewinsky. But now, social media has provided a space that allows for the mass "stealing of people's private words, actions, conversations or photos, and then making them public—public without consent, public without context and public without compassion," Lewinsky said in a TED Talk.[33] Social media users then render judgements on the person's entire character based upon a single piece of (often very unrepresentative) evidence.

The practice is now commonplace. In 2017, a national poll found that 60 percent of mothers say they've been "mom shamed" (on or off social media).[34] Things are especially appalling for women in the public eye. Moms like Meghan Markle and Emily Ratajkowski have been attacked for the ways they held their babies in pictures shared on social media.[35] (For the record, as I've mentioned, the number one killer of kids in America is guns,[36] not mishandling by mothers. But instead of looking at the lawmakers who refuse to effectively regulate firearms, many on the Internet prefer to unleash their wrath on women.)

Sometimes, angry hordes turn on women for things they post themselves. When comedian Amy Schumer shared a picture of herself performing standup comedy—in other words, *doing her job*—on Instagram, she was criticized for going back to work soon after giving birth. "Like, I can still smell your placenta," one person posted. And model Chrissy Teigen was pilloried on social media for going out to dinner and giving her baby a bottle (rather than staying home to care for and breastfeed her baby).[37]

In 2021, TikToker @jessilynmariee_ got so fed up with comments from users saying she should be taking care of her infant son, Ace, when she posted short videos of herself without him that she posted a TikTok with the words "if ace isn't on my hip or in the background he's asleep, in play pen playing, or with sean [his father] playing/bonding," "so next time anyone tries to come for my parenting KNOW YOUR FACTS FIRST." Or how about this: don't go after her parenting at all.

Of course, both men and women are shamed on social media. But something feels different about the ways that women are publicly pilloried. The public flagellation of Lewinsky was, as she rightly pointed out, an example of slut-shaming. It's clearly a practice reserved for women. (Bill Clinton's popularity only improved after he was impeached over the scandal.)[38] Also consider the mom in the airport. Why did the clip go viral? Because it plays into many of the double standards we've been discussing.

But men have also long recognized that such attacks are unthinkably cruel. America's founders were so horrified by the idea of publicly shaming people for their transgressions that they abolished the practice in every state except Delaware by 1837. Benjamin Rush, a signer of the Declaration of Independence, described the practice as "universally acknowledged to be a worse punishment than death."[39]

Sadly, in our social media era, many victims have agreed with him. Suicide has become a shockingly common response to social shaming. Lewinsky acknowledged in her TED Talk that, after she was publicly shamed, "life was almost unbearable"—so much so that her mom made her leave the door open when she showered.[40]

Now, Lewinsky observes, "millions of people, often anonymously, can stab you with their words, and that's a lot of pain. And there are no perimeters around how many people can publicly observe you and put you in a public stockade."[41] The only part about this that feels quaint is her contention that mere millions have the potential to condemn women online. There are now nearly 5 billion people on social media.[42]

Sexual Shaming

Another time-honored reason for shaming women, we all know, is for our sexuality. Like Qandeel Baloch, who we met in the last chapter, other women have major monetary incentives to post racy content on social media. Angela Jones, a sociology professor at Farmingdale State College who studies the experiences of marginalized people who do online sex work, tells me that some people say online sex work is empowering for them. It gives them autonomy to set their own hours. If someone harasses them, unlike in real life, they can ban them (though trolls have a way of setting up new profiles). They have more physical protection, because they're working from home rather than in a strip club or dungeon. And the work is especially attractive to people who face challenges in conventional jobs. Many of the people who post sexual content on OnlyFans and do other online sex work are "poor Black and brown folks who because of racism and classism struggle in traditional labor markets," Jones says.

Jones says disabled women often turn to online sex work because "they tell me, 'the body I was born into cannot work a traditional 9-to-5 job.' So many workspaces are ableist ones and employers roll their eyes and grimace at the idea of providing people with accommodations."

But Jones, whose pronouns are they/them, says so-called "camming"—short for screen capturing, when someone takes unauthorized screenshots or recordings of sex workers and puts them on other parts of the Internet—is a widespread practice. And it destroys women's lives.

"The stigma against sex workers and our society's whore phobia is so pervasive that when this content is shared across the Internet without consent, it can have very adverse consequences," they tell me. "A lot of people straddle sexual economies and non-sexual ones. They work part-time on OnlyFans and part-time in an office, and if their employer finds out about their work on OnlyFans, it can jeopardize their job. I've talked with sex workers who say it impacts their access to housing. Women who are parents worry about what happens if teachers at school find out, what happens if state agencies find out. Sex workers have had their children taken away from them."

"And it's not just the deprivation of material resources," Jones tells me. "There's also the social aspect. People may not be open or out about their sex work to family or friends. There are lots of social sanctions, losing friends, the awkwardness of Grandma knowing."

Jones describes the online harassment these women receive as "disgustingly transphobic and violent, racialized and cis-sexist." A lot of women who do this kind of work tell Jones they accept it as part of the job. "They say, 'trolls be trolls, they're gonna troll. They're just empty rape and death threats,'" Jones says. "Being online creates this barrier, but that doesn't mean psychological harms don't permeate that barrier. I'm not convinced that what's happening here is harmless. I think there's a lot of psychological violence."

What We Can Do

First, we have to reckon with an uncomfortable truth: All of us—myself included—are sometimes guilty of implicit bias in the ways we judge, talk, and post about women. So we've got to take conscious actions to overcome it. For starters, we should compare the ways we talk about women and men. When tempted to criticize a woman on social media, we should consider whether we would say the same thing to her face—and whether we would judge a man the same way.

In particular, we've got to avoid "authenticity policing" women (picking apart and judging a woman's every word and action to render a verdict on whether she's "fake"),[43] since this is almost never done to men. And we shouldn't comment on a woman's body or appearance unless she herself clearly encourages it—for example, by posting a picture of herself in a new suit she bought for her first day on a new job. In these kinds of cases, you're clear to cheer her on—but it's even better to shift the conversation to what she'll contribute rather than how she looks.

Next, we need to hold other people to these standards. We've got to change the norms of socially acceptable behavior on social media to make people uncomfortable posting sexist and misogynistic content. When we see people we know practicing sexism and misogyny (even, and in fact especially, when it's subtle), instead of calling them out, we need to do what feminist activist Loretta Ross has termed calling them in.[44] Calling people out just fuels the outrage machine the Internet has become. But we can call our friends and family in for respectful offline conversations about what's wrong with their content.

"I always say that this movement is about showing solidarity and standing up for people," Muslim feminist activist and Women's March co-chair Linda Sarsour tells me. When you see someone you know posting something that is wrong, "say, 'I think that's wrong, and I want to have that conversation with you.' Anti-hate work starts with the people we know and love the most."

As for the trolls who are *trying* to get us to fight with them? *Don't clap back.* Remember that social networks amplify content that generates engagement, so if you respond to sexism, it will only give the post a higher profile. "Yes, it feels great to tell a misogynist 'you're a prick,'" Imran Ahmed, chief executive of the Center for Countering Digital Hate, told me. "But you know what feels better? Winning the strategic battle against them. Mathematics say the right thing to do is ignore it or take a mental health break, report it, and then move on."

But Ahmed says we also have to demand that social networks stop allowing this kind of abuse. "We've got to actively oppose the moral decisions taken by companies to allow dissemination of this kind of hatred, because a lot of people are getting rich off hate," he tells me.

So use the reporting tools social networks offer to flag content that violates their community standards—and call out the platforms publicly if they don't take action.

We also have to change what we reward with our attention. Let's all never, ever react to the public shaming of a woman, because we know we have all had a bad day at some point. And, above all, because men just don't face the same treatment.

On top of this, we need to actively create, seek out, follow, and share content that fights the sexism and misogyny we're up against on and offline. If we rewarded these kinds of posts with more of our attention, people would create more of them. And if they got a lot of engagement, algorithms would show users more of them. In Chapter 11, I'll suggest ways to do this.

For now, instead of using social media to judge women, let's turn our judgment on a society that tries to convince women and girls that we are perpetually somehow wrong, simply because of our gender.

4

PLENTY OF CATFISH

My good friend Akosua is the kind of person you might refer to as "good people." We worked together at the United Nations before she took her current job in New York at a humanitarian organization. A Ghanaian American, she went to an Ivy League college, then earned her graduate degree in international relations.

Akosua always leaves extra big tips for the waitstaff or hotel cleaning crew when we go out to dinner or travel together. She's beautiful on the outside, too: she works out and takes impeccable care of her skin and hair. You can tell she's interested in fashion from the way she dresses. Akosua is also super laid back. She takes life as it comes and is quick to smile or laugh.

Recently, for her 42nd birthday, Akosua gave herself two big gifts: she froze her eggs and shuttered her online dating profiles. She'd been dating online for five years by then, and she'd had enough.

Akosua is looking for a long-term commitment but says the men she met online didn't seem to be. "The most common men I met were ones who didn't want long term partnerships but had the trappings that they do," she told me. "Then their actions don't align with what they say. I feel like that's what I kept coming into contact with."

Akosua thinks online dating has created a mating market that favors men. "Traditionally, when it came to dating, men almost had to commit and then maybe you'd step out of that committed relationship," she says. "Now, you don't have to. There isn't this pressure to get married, which is liberating, but men have a longer range if they want to have children. They can decide to do so in their forties or fifties and pretty easily have them. Whereas for women, there's this finite amount of time."

Now, she says, "as dating apps become more popular and men are finding they have lots of opportunities, if someone upsets you for the smallest reason, you can go to a dating app and find someone else."

That's if you ever go out on a date in the first place. "A lot of men wanted to talk to me forever and never meet," Akosua says. It's a complaint I hear *endlessly* from my single friends. But why??

Akosua's theory is that one reason men pursue arrangements like "textationships"[1]—where you text and text without ever meeting—is because they use it as a form of emotional support. It gives them someone to talk to when they've had a bad day at work. But "it's a lot of emotional labor for women," she says.

When she did meet up with men in person, Akosua had to contend with her share of bad behavior. One man she met up with at a Brooklyn bar made her downright scared.

"He was talking about women he had dated who were in grad school, and he said they do it to have kids and stay home, and he knew I was in grad school," she told me. "I remember thinking 'I need to get out of here as soon as possible, I don't even feel physically safe.'" She thought about leaving when he went to the bathroom, but was worried he'd see her. When he returned, he asked her to go home with him. All she could think about was how to get away from him.

Looking back, Akosua realizes she was also put in danger by a man she never ended up meeting. He told her he'd been born in Mexico but came to the United States as a child and went to an elite college. She was in grad school at the same university at the time. Now he was in the navy. They would text for hours each day. He said he couldn't do video because he was on a ship.

"I noticed there were random errors in his grammar and spelling and I was like, *that's bizarre.* But I had to check myself: am I just being elitist? I'm like, OK, he wasn't an English major," she remembers.

"So the conversation keeps going, he's pulling me in more and more, he'd be concerned when I'd go places and I was like, OK, that's nice. But I wasn't going to keep talking to men and not meet them because that was a pattern in the past. So then he tells me he got special permission from his senior officer to leave early and come meet me. He tells me he's getting his ticket. The next thing I know, he asks if I can loan him $300 because he has a bank account at home, and he can pay me back."

That's when she realized she was being catfished.

"I was a little heartbroken because he'd done all this pulling me in for a week of conversation," Akosua remembers. "Then I think he created another profile saying he was this guy's friend and he was heartbroken. Then he created another saying he was the superior officer and had given permission and this guy just needed the money. After that, I was like, 'if you contact me again, I will call the police.'"

Afterward, she did a reverse Google image search and realized the photo the guy had used on his profile was one commonly used as part of online romance scams.

Akosua knows she dodged a bullet. He might have disappeared with her money. Or "I would have met him in person and who knows what he could have done to me," she says.

What's more, Akosua later read that, if she'd fallen for this scam, she could have ended up targeted by other cybercriminals. "If you fall for small things, they consider you an easy mark and put you on a list that's globally available for people, and then they escalate," she says. "It's a huge business and it's heartbreaking because you don't really hear about the emotional abuse and the toll it takes on people, since no one puts a gun to your head."

But, despite the anguish it caused her, Akosua is still magnanimous. "You have to also consider that a lot of the people who do this in other countries don't have another way to make money to feed their families," she tells me.

Another thing Akosua says online dating sites mask is all the discrimination that happens on them. "On some level I didn't see it because people who didn't swipe on me just didn't swipe on me, but then I read the data that Black women are the women least swiped," she says.

These days, Akosua is happy to have her online dating days behind her. But she still has to live in the world that online dating has created. "When I was younger, men used to approach me in real life more regularly," she remembers. "But now, with dating apps, they don't."

* * *

Like Akosua, my closest single friends are gorgeous women, inside and out, who travel the world, often speak multiple languages, hold graduate degrees, rock their jobs in fields like diplomacy and international aid (while also making the world a better place), are fun and vivacious—and spend year after year having one experience more disturbing and depressing than the last after meeting men on dating sites.

And, like Akosua, the majority of American women say dating is harder than it was ten years ago, according to a 2020 Pew survey. The majority of men disagree.[2]

One of the men who disagrees with this proposition is Stanford sociologist Michael Rosenfeld, PhD, who studies mating and the social impact of the Internet. Online dating is hard because dating is hard, he told me. It isn't easy to find someone who is physically attractive, charming, witty, kind, and smart with a great job but no debt or skeletons, because so many people are jerks. But at least dating apps connect us with more potential partners, so our options aren't just the people we meet through church, the corner bar, or mom.

He's right, of course. And this broadening of the pool is especially important for people in so-called "thin markets," who meet fewer potential partners offline. For example, lesbian, gay, and bisexual adults are more than twice as likely as straight adults to have met their partners online, according to the Pew survey.[3]

A dating app is also where I met my husband. He's a kind, fun, witty ER doctor who proposed to me in Antarctica. He whips up gourmet meals when he gets home from work and does all the voices when he reads our kids bedtime stories. But the problem with stories like mine is that people have this misperception (carefully cultivated by dating apps, by the way) that they're the rule when really they're more like the exception.

What I mostly remember from my online dating days is thinking it was hell. I was working in demanding jobs while also in grad school full-time, so I didn't have a ton of spare time. It was a sinking feeling to meet someone in person for the first time and know within seconds that I wasn't interested, but still have to sit through a drink and whole long conversation. If we'd met in person rather than connecting through an app, I would never have gone on some of those dates in the first place. Some of my girlfriends were better than I was about making the most of those kinds of situations, looking at them as a chance to have a conversation and maybe learn something from someone new. But I'm an introvert. I would have rather spent those nights in a yoga class or having dinner with a close friend. Also, I met my husband online a decade ago, before I think dating sites devolved to what they are today.

Like Akosua, the vast majority of women who want to date and are having trouble doing so—65 percent—say it's hard to find someone who wants the same kind of relationship as they do, according to the Pew survey.[4] So there's an enormous discrepancy between what women want and what they're getting.

The problem starts with demographics. Right around the time Akosua got serious about settling down, primarily because she wanted to have children, the pool of available men her age was narrowing. That's because men don't live as long as women and tend to pair off with younger women, Dr. Rosenfeld explains. Starting in a woman's mid-40s and continuing for the rest of her life, there aren't as many unpartnered heterosexual men as there are straight single women, he says.

What's more, because women now earn the majority of college degrees—which are the ticket to career success in our economy—many of the men in that pool don't have jobs that can comfortably support a family, Dr. Rosenfeld says. That narrows the pool of attractive partners for women like Akosua even more. (The pool of Black college-educated men is especially small. But some Black women prefer to date Black men in order to try to avoid the discrimination they contend with from many men of other races, as we'll see.)

Add to that the fact that men don't contend with the pressure women face to have children before they're no longer fertile. Then there's the evolutionary biology claim that men are biologically programmed to be more promiscuous while women value commitment more. There's a mountain of scientific evidence that this isn't true, Angela Saini writes in *Inferior: How Science Got Women Wrong—and the New Research That's Rewriting the Story*.[5] But our society *thinks* manly men sleep around, so that's how men who want to be seen as manly behave. Just look at who Hollywood has long celebrated: boy-men who are mostly interested in casual sex (see television shows like *Entourage* or hit movies like *Failure to Launch*), rather than courteous guys who commit to relationships.

When women ask for more than this from their partners, they're often pegged as needy or demanding. Contrast that with a man who demands things from other people, who would just be considered a man.

"Women are supposed to be open and say what they want and demand sexual reciprocity, but on the other hand, God forbid you express an attachment need too soon or appear to be cutting off someone else's options or make them feel trapped," Zoe Strimpel, PhD, a British historian of gender and intimacy, told me. "As soon as it becomes, 'I really like you, when can we see each other again,' then you're tapping into this age-old idea of women as black holes of excessive emotion, hysteria, drama, and entrapment."

Men also don't face the same scale of potential risks to their lives when they meet strangers online. (We'll see in the next chapter how dating apps are facilitating sexual assaults and even murder.) So the men Akosua might date have the upper hand in many ways. Being in the power position isn't exactly likely to promote boy scout behavior. And now, we've moved the mating game to online apps.

As we saw in the last chapter, people will treat others more appallingly than they would in person when they can then recoil behind their screens. This can help explain the behavior women face like ghosting (talking for days on end to a person, only to never hear from him again) or breadcrumbing, which Urban Dictionary describes like this: "When the 'crush' has no intentions of taking things further, but they like the attention. So they flirt here or there, send dm/texts just to keep the person interested, knowing damn well they're staying single."[6]

What's more, when people interact online, they don't see other people's facial reactions or body language that shows they're getting uncomfortable. "The worst of gendered behavior in dating—men overtalking women, sending dick pics, mansplaining, that kind of thing—is happening in the world around us but it's amplified on apps because there are not the visual cues that women want them to stop," Justin Garcia, the head of the Kinsey Institute, told me.

Nancy Jo Sales, author of *Nothing Personal: My Secret Life in the Dating App Inferno*, also argues that dating apps have "encouraged men to think of women as less than human—as hot pictures, as objects," which has normalized treating women with disrespect. As a result, she writes, "as women . . . achieved more and more professional and political power, the destabilizing trend with which they now had to contend was the outrageous sense of entitlement and disrespect from the men they were dating and with whom they were having sex."[7]

I suspect another reason some men treat the women with whom they match so deplorably is because they're strangers. If you're set up by a mutual friend, your reputation is on the line. If you act like a jerk, she'll almost certainly tell your friend. But when you meet a stranger online and treat them like crap, no one you care about is likely to ever find out—and you're probably also not going to run into the person again.

I can hear my male critics shouting at me from the future to point out that women on dating sites sometimes treat men like shit, too. I'm sure that's sometimes true. But when you take a situation in which women like Akosua are in a position of disadvantage and move it to a platform where many of the norms of appropriate behavior are stripped away, women are practically set up to be mistreated.

It's not that things were so much better before these apps landed in our lives. "Courtship has been a messy affair for millions of years," Dr. Garcia points out. "People die in courtship. They lose everything. They lose their hearts, they lose their resources, they lose their minds." Dating sites certainly haven't fixed these problems—but they've piled on new ones by taking away some of the constraints to treating women terribly that often exist when you meet in other ways.

*   *   *

Women of color like Akosua also have to contend with shameless racism on these apps. While today it would generally be socially unacceptable (not to mention illegal) to create filters to remove people of color when they apply for jobs or mortgages, men routinely and simply filter women like Akosua out of their search terms on dating apps—the last mainstream place where people are invited to practice racism so overtly.

On online dating sites, the vast majority of white men—over 59 percent—state racial preferences. (White women are even more guilty of doing so.)[8] Let's call this what it is: discrimination.

Sociologists Celeste Vaughan Curington, PhD, Jennifer H. Lundquist, PhD, and Ken-Hou Lin, PhD, interviewed online daters and analyzed over 1 million users' profiles and interactions obtained from a major online dating site. They found that "race is the most important predictor of how White daters select whom to date. More often than not, White daters ignore the overtures of racial and ethnic minority daters with (conventionally) more desirable education background, height, and body type, while being responsive to those without similar qualities" when they are white.[9]

It makes no sense that people would be attracted to others based on race. Race is a social construct, and personalities don't tend to differ much by race.[10] If a man met a woman of a different race in person, he'd have an opportunity to see that she is lovely and amazing and realize he was interested. But, on social media, many men filter women like Akosua out before they ever get that chance.

When I spoke to Dr. Curington, an assistant professor of sociology at Boston University, she pointed out that even men who don't consciously filter women of color out from their matches may unknowingly have this work done for them by dating apps. "Machine learning is based on people's discriminatory behavior," she says. So a man may be presented with fewer women of color on a dating app simply because men who are similar to him haven't seemed to like the profiles of women of color in the past. "That's the hidden algorithm."

Dr. Curington told me that, despite these filters, online dating has led to more interracial matches than in the past. But, she said, many of the experiences women of color have with the men they meet online are deeply traumatic for them.

"Many Black women describe being treated by white men and some men of color who they meet on these apps as fetishized, hypersexual, and appropriate only for sexual encounters," she says. "Asian women describe bumping up against these stereotypes of hypersexuality and aggressiveness or being expected to be extremely submissive and extraordinarily feminine. And Latina women are expected to be this feisty, fiery, aggressive woman who is perhaps a caretaker or a maid."

Women of color have these experiences regularly, Dr. Curington told me. And "it can be extremely traumatizing and emotionally exhausting. It's heavy."

Transgender women are also up against the impossible question of whether to disclose on dating apps that they're trans, Erique Zhang, a scholar who studies transgender identity and media representations of trans people and identifies as a nonbinary, transgender femme, told me. "There are a lot of cisgender people arguing online that it's deceitful for trans women not to disclose we're trans, reproducing all these older stereotypes of trans women 'tricking' straight men into dating them and not being 'real' women," Zhang told me.

But they told me that if trans women do disclose their status on dating sites, they open themselves up to possible hate crimes or "chasers" who want to date them for fetishistic reasons.

*   *   *

Like other forms of social media, dating apps also encourage men to focus on women's appearances. Men say that the number one thing they look at when deciding whether they're interested in a woman online is—I trust you don't need my help to finish this sentence—their pictures.[11] According to OKCupid cofounder Christian Rudder, the third of women who are most attractive on the site receive about two-thirds of the messages. And OKCupid has users create fuller profiles than other apps like Tinder, where people seem to swipe mostly based on looks.[12]

Part of the reason for this is that it's difficult to assess potential matches carefully when we're deluged with choices. Research finds that when people speed-date at events with large numbers of people, they evaluate them superficially, based on things like their weight and height, because it's tricky to fairly weigh so many characteristics of so many people.[13] The same thing seems to happen online.

Being flooded with options also paralyzes people. An enormous body of research finds that giving someone loads of choices—whether they're buying jam or looking for a romantic partner—can be so overwhelming that they decide not to choose any of them at all. And when people perceive they have lots of other options, they view their current romantic partners less positively, are less committed to them, and are more likely to eventually break up with them.[14]

"Greater choice breeds restless dissatisfaction," Victoria Coren wrote in *The Guardian* at the advent of online dating. "We end up frozen," she said, "certain that an even more congruent soul mate is waiting."[15]

The writer Dan Slater interviewed executives at online dating companies for his book *Love in the Time of Algorithms*. Greg Blatt, then chief executive of the Match Group—which owns Match.com and numerous other major sites—told Slater that, in the past, "relationships have been billed as 'hard' because, historically, commitment has been the goal. You could say online dating is simply changing people's ideas about whether commitment itself is a life value."

Slater wrote in *The Atlantic* in 2013 that "most" of the executives he spoke with "agreed with what research appears to suggest: the rise of online dating will mean an overall decrease in commitment."[16]

That time has now come. A 2018 study by Dr. Rosenfeld found that less than 12 percent of single, heterosexual American women had gone on a date in the past year.[17] In 2019, just 12 percent of American adults said they'd *ever* been in a committed relationship with someone they met online, according to Pew.[18] But not only are most people not finding true love online—in the world wrought by dating apps, they're less likely to find it at all. As dating apps have become more popular, it's become less likely for people to commit to relationships, period.

In 2004, 67 percent of Americans aged 18–34 had a steady romantic partner, according to the General Social Survey. By 2019, less than half did.[19] Women are also less likely to be living with partners today than they were before the rise of the Internet.[20] By 2018, the marriage rate had fallen to the lowest number since the federal government began collecting records on it in 1867.[21] And fewer women are having children: the birthrate has been falling for about 15 years. (In 2021 it rose slightly, a blip believed to be attributable to the pandemic.)[22]

It's actually a huge myth that all women want to be in relationships, marry, and/or have kids. In fact, just 38 percent of single women are looking for dates or a relationship, according to the Pew study[23]—though you have to wonder if that number would be higher if some of them hadn't had the same kinds of experiences as Akosua.

"A hundred years ago, a woman couldn't afford to support herself, so she needed to be married," Dr. Rosenfeld points out. "So whatever guy was willing to marry her, you know, that was what it was. And then, if they didn't really get along well, such was life."

It's empowering that we live in a society where many more women have options to leave bad marriages—or avoid them altogether—and where girls can dream of being world leaders instead of (or in addition to) wives. And, of course, I'm not worried about the women who choose to be single, because I know from the first 35 years of my own life that we're perfectly capable of being happy and fulfilled without being married. The women I'm talking about in this chapter are the ones like Akosua who are looking for relationships, turning online, and ending up not just disappointed but disrespected and even in danger. The majority of women who do want to date are dissatisfied with their dating lives, according to the Pew survey.[24]

As heterosexual women get older, it only becomes harder for them to find partners because there are fewer straight, single men available, Dr. Rosenfeld says. He points out that many women in their sixties and seventies don't want to date because they've been taking care of people all their lives and aren't looking for another person to nurse through their ailments.

But those who are looking for romantic partners often end up in the same place as Akosua. My former colleague Anna is Latina and has worked as one of the most senior women in the world of international diplomacy. Now in her 60s and divorced, she lives in Manhattan. After my husband and I met online, we pushed her to try online dating.

What astonished her, she said, was how many of the profiles seemed fraudulent. Despite how smart and savvy she is, initially even she was duped. It wasn't until she got on the phone with a man she'd been communicating with for some time that she instantly realized his accent was Jamaican, not German as he'd claimed.

Sometimes, she'd message a man and then go back to his profile to find it had been suspended. "I was absolutely shocked by the number of times this happened," she told me. "After a while you start picking them up, because they are sort of generic handsome guys and you know this is a stolen picture," she says.

Anna would occasionally message a man who seemed interesting and real, but he'd typically write back to say he had already matched with five or ten women, she told me. "They'd say, 'your profile looks really interesting, you look lovely, but my hands are full with what I already have.'"

Anna quickly realized it would be a full-time job to try to meet someone online. "I stopped a while back because I just couldn't stomach it," she told me.

But worries about online dating still keep her up at night because her daughter, who is in her early thirties, wants to settle down and has been dating online. Recently, Anna had to tell her daughter that a man she'd fallen hard for wasn't really off working on an oil rig. She was devastated.

These kinds of scams are growing. "Romance scams," or catfishing—where people pretend to be someone else, establish emotional relationships online, hit up their victims for money, then typically disappear—cost Americans $547 million in 2021, an almost 80 percent increase over the previous year, according to the Federal Trade Commission. That makes them the most common type of fraud reported by Americans.[25] And those figures are just the scams authorities know about. Most victims are believed not to ever report these crimes, out of shame or fear.[26]

Women are targeted by these scammers because "women are seen as easy targets emotionally," disinformation expert Nina Jankowicz told me—and online dating sites are places where women's emotional guards are often down.

In China, these kinds of scams are called pig butchering, because of the way victims are fattened up with the façade of a relationship before perpetrators go in for the kill. Think it's just doddering old ladies falling for these scammers posing as suitors? Think again. They're educated, worldly women like Akosua and Anna. According to an investigation by *The New York Times*, pig butcherers are now targeting tech savvy younger women, sometimes offering to help them invest their money and even creating professional-looking websites with charts and graphics where they think they're watching their crypto purchases grow.[27]

But really, the money they sent is long gone, and these men aren't the handsome, jet-setting investment banker-philanthropists they claim to be. Want to know who many of them actually are? Men from China who are lured to travel to Laos, Myanmar, and Cambodia with the promise of lucrative jobs. When they get there, they're held as slaves and forced by criminal syndicates to pig butcher Western women.

"If they resist, they face beatings, food deprivation or electric shocks," according to a 2022 ProPublica report. "Some jump from balconies to escape. Others accept their lot and become paid participants in cybercrime."[28]

Other times, Jankowicz warns the men you may meet online could be "real"—but they're targeting you because they want things very different from a long-term relationship. "If you are a powerful woman in a field—especially in hard-won, difficult-to-access fields—some men will attempt to use you to gain access to that field," she told me. "It could be access to career opportunities or also secrets in some situations."

And it's not just women's mental health and money on the line here. In 2022, a 15-year-old girl was catfished online by a 28-year-old man. He showed up at her Riverside, California home, murdered her mom and grandparents, and left with the girl (who was found alive by police).

"Anybody can say they're someone else and you could be in this situation," the girl's aunt warned in a tearful press conference.[29]

One thing that may be making women more susceptible to these scams is the effect of using social media in the first place. Think back to the previous chapters. Social media often causes women to feel badly about our bodies—and ourselves.

It starts young. "Girls who do not feel good about themselves need the affirmation of others, and that need, unfortunately, almost always empowers male desire," Joan Jacobs Brumberg writes in *The Body Project: An Intimate History of American Girls.* "In other words, girls who hate their bodies do not make good decisions about partners, or about the kind of sexual activity that is in their best interest. Because they want to be wanted so much, they are susceptible to manipulation, to flattery, even to abuse."[30]

This can also help explain why women put up with bad behavior from men they meet online. When women go on dating apps and meet men who aren't looking for commitment, they feel rejected, which hurts their self-esteem, which can make them less assertive.

Take my college friend Kate, who worked in a high-charging job for one of the world's most elite consulting firms. When she first started dating online, Kate, who is white, told me, "I met all the Peter Pans, who didn't ghost me exactly but it fizzled because they just wanted to have some fun. And I really lost a lot of self-confidence. I think we all think when men find the right person, they suddenly convert from being a player to someone who is committed, like in the movies. So when I met someone who didn't want to commit, I thought, 'there has to be something wrong with me. They must want something I don't have.' I never just thought maybe there's something wrong with them." This made her feel less comfortable asking for what she wanted from the men she met.

But Kate says when she posted on her online dating profile that she was looking for a relationship, the game changed. "I said if you are not, please don't bother messaging me," she told me. "I had to not be afraid to scare people away. There's this illusion that you have to get a man by being casual first and that he'll then on his own decide he wants something longer term, but you're wasting your time if a guy doesn't already know he wants a commitment."

After that, Kate met a succession of nice guys online. The seventh was named Ryan. Reader, she married him.

What also helped, Kate said, was carefully reading profiles and only engaging with men who seemed to have put some effort into creating them. Ryan had listed his Myers-Briggs personality type. She was also specific in her profile about what she's like, listing her quirks (lip synching to her favorite songs while walking down the street) and how she liked to spend her weekends.

If a guy didn't seem interested in talking and meeting, Kate moved on, assuming he was probably messaging lots of women. "Don't accept being on a back burner," she says. "Just push him to the side. The brilliant thing about online dating is you're not in a bar where a guy is really drunk and won't go away. You can just delete him from your phone. You can't take it personally because how much info does he have about you? Not that much."

What was liberating, Kate says, is when she realized "I have just as much agency as guys."

Still, she says, filtering all these men took *a lot* of effort. She gave herself breaks from online dating when putting in all that work without meeting someone promising felt like too much. "It's demoralizing when it's been a while since you've had a good date," she says. "That's why having your own filters is so important. Once I started weeding out men who had bad chat or didn't suggest meeting up in the first week or so, my actual dates got a lot better. I only went out with men who were also genuinely looking for a relationship. We weren't always a good fit, but the dates themselves gave me hope that there were still good men out there."

What We Can Do

There *are*, of course, plenty of good people on dating apps. Here's what you—and dating apps—can do to help you find them.

First, dating apps need to stop inviting prejudice. They can do this by removing features that allow users to state or filter by racial preferences and carefully programming their algorithms not to take race into account. Full stop.

As for users, use apps that at least place some importance on written profiles alongside photos. Do a reverse image search on Google to see if your match's photos have been used on other sites. Meet them on Skype or Zoom and spend some time having a real conversation before agreeing to meet up in person to make sure they seem to be who they say they are. (Pro tip: this is also a smart way to avoid spending your Saturday nights with people who aren't compatible with you.) Yes, rapists can still dress and act like choir boys, but this is a potential way of weeding out catfishers.

Don't let your guard down with someone you meet online until you have met their family, friends, and colleagues and you can verify their identity with certainty and have solid evidence they can be trusted. And I don't have to tell you not to send money to people you meet online, right?

Also, to try to find the right match, articulate what you're looking for. If a person can't handle it, they're not right for you—but you'll do a service to yourself and other women by setting the bar higher. Remember Kate's advice to filter profiles aggressively—and just walk away from people who don't seem serious.

Another reason why it's important to take the time to filter through profiles carefully is because, while dating apps may claim to do this for you by building proprietary algorithms that will match you with the right romantic partners based on your personal qualities, 75 years' worth of research on relationships suggests this can't really be done. That's because people's traits don't predict whether their relationships will be successful.[31] So it's really on users to weed through lots of profiles to find people who might be strong matches.

It also helps to have the right mindset going into online dating, Kate says: don't pin too much hope on any one date, but be optimistic that if you meet enough people, one of them will turn out to be right. Dr. Strimpel agrees. She says the sheer number of people on dating sites means that if a woman goes on enough dates, she can probably find a match.

So Dr. Strimpel's advice to women is to "hold your nose and play a numbers game." She acknowledges that "you go through lots of boring and demoralizing experiences, but those people I know who push through and have three coffees every Sunday with different people have always found people."

Repeat this next one after me, please: *don't take rejection as a referendum on yourself. Take it as a referendum on the other person and what they can't see.*

Of course, don't filter matches based on race, or you'll be depriving yourself of a lot of awesome people.

Don't blame yourself or let yourself become despondent or depressed if you find it hard to meet the right person online.

Recognize that these apps aren't the miraculous matchmaking machines they claim to be and go out and live your best life while you keep looking for the right person, just like Akosua.

Teach your daughters these things. Tell your girlfriends these things. And, whatever you do, make clear from the outset that you expect the people who swipe right on you to also treat you right.

SEX CRIMES AND MURDER IN THE TIME OF SOCIAL MEDIA

In January 2017, Aaliyah Palmer was in her first year of college at NC State University when she went to a party with a group of Fort Bragg soldiers who she and her friends met on Tinder Social—a service the platform no longer offers that used to match groups for dates. She ended up in the bathroom with one of the soldiers, where a sexual encounter started out as consensual, she told me. Then she asked him to stop, she explained. He didn't, she says. In North Carolina at the time, this wasn't considered rape, because she had provided consent before she says she revoked it. That law has now changed, thanks partly to Aaliyah's advocacy.[1]

Aaliyah says there was a large gap between the bottom of the bathroom door and the floor, and she could see one of the soldier's buddies on the other side of the door holding a phone upside down and filming the incident. One of the men later told police the video had been taken on Snapchat, she told me. The next morning, Aaliyah says she saw the soldiers bragging and joking about the incident on their Tinder group, before they unmatched with her and she could no longer access their conversations. But she says that when her lawyers contacted Snapchat and Tinder, neither company provided evidence to help her case.

"Especially with Tinder, they made a platform for the purpose of people who are strangers connecting," Aaliyah told me. "You can't create that kind of thing without analyzing what issues could arise. They should have been prepared for situations like this to happen, where something criminal happens and people need evidence. They make it very difficult to have evidence to get things prosecuted, especially when cases like rape are very 'he said, she said.'"

Aaliyah, who is biracial, was the first in her family to go to college. Between school and government scholarships, she was there on a full ride. She planned to become a veterinarian. But, after the incident, she struggled with anxiety and depression and dropped out.

"I was set for success and then this happened, and the anxiety it creates knowing they had taken videos on Snap, and I don't know who they know and I don't know who they sent it to. It could be someone sitting next to me in class. That just kicks your anxiety into overdrive," she told me. "I lost so many opportunities."

When I spoke to Aaliyah nearly six years after the incident, she was hoping to return to school at NC State. But she told me that, because she no longer has the scholarship she was awarded when she was originally admitted, she fears leaving with a huge load of debt she wouldn't have had if this episode hadn't derailed her.

There are almost no reliable statistics on how many violent crimes are tied to dating apps, which conveniently helps platforms evade responsibility for endangering women's lives. But, in 2019, Columbia Journalism Investigations conducted what it called a non-scientific survey of over 1,200 women who reported using a dating platform over the previous 15 years. A jaw-dropping 31 percent said they'd been sexually assaulted by someone they met on a dating app. More than half of the women who said they'd been sexually assaulted reported that they were raped.[2]

Part of the reason for this is that dating apps appear to be creating what the United Kingdom's National Crime Agency describes as "a new kind of sexual offender." In a 2016 report, the agency found that between 2009 and 2014, there was a six-fold increase in sexual offenses caused by online dating—and 85 percent of the victims were women. Now, according to the report, these crimes are being committed by men who are "less likely to have criminal convictions, but instead exploit the ease of access" to victims offered by dating sites."[3] And a 2022 study conducted in the United States found that sexual assaults tied to dating apps tend to be more violent than sexual assaults committed by acquaintances, with greater instances of injuries, assault, penetration, and strangulation, leading the researchers to "propose that sexual predators use dating apps as hunting grounds for vulnerable victims."[4]

Men with past convictions for sexual offenses have also freely used dating apps to connect with new potential victims, according to a 2019 report by ProPublica, Columbia Journalism Investigations, and Buzzfeed. Take Mark Papamechail. According to the report, in 2014, Janine Dunphy met Papamechail on the online dating site Plenty of Fish. A background check would have revealed that Papamechail had been convicted of rape multiple times and was a registered sex offender in Massachusetts. But Plenty of Fish didn't conduct background checks on its users. After a date, Papamechail invited Dunphy to his home. When she turned down his sexual advances, she says he threw her down, pinned her with his arms, and raped her.

Papamechail was found not guilty in a 2016 trial.[5] Dunphy said that although prosecutors tried to get copies of her communications with Papamechail from Plenty of Fish, the company refused to help, saying that because it is based in Canada, it's not subject to subpoenas issued in the United States. Afterward, she suffered from stress-induced blood clots and PTSD, and says she still thinks about her "date" with Papamechail every day.

Unbelievably, Papamechail returned to Plenty of Fish. There, in 2016, he was matched with Susan Deveau. In 2017, Deveau called the police in Peabody, Massachusetts, saying a man was attempting to rape her. Her last words on the phone call were "he's coming." She later told police Papamechail did the same thing Dunphy reported: threw her down, held her with his arms, and raped her.

Deveau's daughter told researchers for the report that her mother seemed undone by the ordeal. She drank excessively and eventually died of kidney failure.

I probably don't need to tell you where Papamechail seems to have turned up after that: back on Plenty of Fish. Dunphy says his username was Deadbolt56, and that she sent screenshots of his profile to the site but didn't receive a response.

Dunphy and Deveau are far from the only women to report being matched with serial sex offenders on online dating sites. And Dunphy is among a number of women who say that when they report users who assault them to dating sites the platforms don't take action, and they continue to see the men they report using the sites.

"There are definitely registered sex offenders on our free products," a spokesperson for the Match Group told Columbia Journalism Investigations in 2019.[6]

When you consider the nature of the crimes we're talking about, it's unconscionable that dating apps haven't done more to get sex offenders off their sites. Former Marine David J. Morris, who has written about PTSD, told Rebecca Solnit, "the science on the subject is pretty clear: according to the *New England Journal of Medicine*, rape is about four times more likely to result in diagnosable PTSD than combat. Think about that for a moment—being raped is four times more psychologically disturbing than going off to war and being shot at and blown up. And because there are currently no enduring cultural narratives that allow women to look upon their survival as somehow heroic or honorable, the potential for enduring damage is even greater."[7]

By 2022, the Match Group finally began offering users of Tinder, Match, and Stir (a site for single parents) the option to run background checks on people they meet on the sites.[8] It's an important offering, because background checks (and/or the fees associated with them) seem to deter sexual offenders. Columbia Journalism Investigations analyzed over 150 sexual assaults tied to dating apps in its 2019 report and found that most of them happened through dating apps owned by the Match Group. But there was not a single assault tied to Match.com—the only Match Group app that conducted background checks at the time.[9]

Still, background checks risk giving women a false sense of security. The vast majority of sexual assaults are never reported in the first place, so many sexual offenders won't be flagged by these kinds of tools. According to the Rape, Abuse & Incest National Network (RAINN), only 31 percent of sexual assaults are ever reported to the police, and 97.5 percent of perpetrators go free.[10] Plus, users could elude detection by using fake names. (As I'll explain, this is why dating apps should require users to take real-time selfies when they sign up and match them against official IDs.)

What's more, these background checks are a paid service. "Physical safety shouldn't be placed behind a paywall," Illinois Democratic Rep. Raja Krishnamoorthi said when the company announced the feature. "If Match Group wanted to show us they are serious about protecting people, they would make this feature available to all users at no cost."

Illinois Democratic Rep. Jan Schakowsky similarly pointed out, "while this may appear as if Match Group is taking safety more seriously, it's hard to tell whether this is an attempt to pad their bottom line or promote safety on the platform."[11]

Like Aaliyah, sexual assault victims told researchers for the ProPublica report that online dating sites wouldn't help them obtain evidence of their messages after they were attacked by men they met on their sites.

Meanwhile, some women pay for online dating with their lives. In 2022, Ethan Hunsaker was found guilty of stabbing his Tinder date, 25-year-old Ashlyn Black, to death.[12] Women including Grace Millane,[13] Samantha Stewart,[14] and Ingrid Lyne[15] met with similar fates after matching with men on dating apps.

Sexual Exposure and Sextortion

But dating apps are just the start of the ways that social media has enabled shocking new kinds of sex crimes against women.

Victims' rights attorney Carrie Goldberg met a man she calls "Badguy" on OKCupid in 2012. She was in her mid-thirties and living in New York City, where she was appointed by courts to make life decisions on behalf of elderly, mentally disabled, and poor clients who didn't have family to care for them—deciding where they'd live, who their caretakers would be, and how their money would be handled. She had also just been through a divorce.

"Badguy" claimed he'd just graduated from the prestigious Wharton School of Business, and he seemed smart and charming. He bought her jewelry and art. A few weeks later, for Valentine's Day, he gave her an iPad mini. He used it to film her when they were in bed, sometimes with permission, sometimes without, according to Goldberg.

But, a few weeks after their relationship began, "Badguy" became controlling—demanding to know where Goldberg was and what she was doing and falsely accusing her of cheating. She broke up with him.

He didn't react well. "Badguy" started emailing her racy photos he had taken. He sent a sexually graphic video of Goldberg that he'd taken without her consent and said he'd bcc'd her boss and judges with whom she worked. He told her he would post her intimate pictures online.[16] Goldberg told me she worried that if they ended up on the Internet, it would be impossible to get them removed.

These kind of scenarios in which someone shares intimate images without the consent of the person in them are often referred to as revenge porn. But Vice President Kamala Harris, who made fighting online abuse a priority when she served as attorney general of California, writes in her memoir *The Truths We Hold: An American Journey* that the word "revenge" isn't fair because, like Goldberg, many victims haven't done anything wrong. And they never meant for their images to be porn.[17]

In 2014, the iCloud accounts of celebrities including actress and activist Amanda Heard were hacked. The intimate photos they had of themselves were posted online for the world to see.[18] In an op-ed in *The New York Times*, Heard pointed out that another reason the term "revenge porn" isn't appropriate is because talking about revenge puts the focus "on intent rather than consent. What matters is not why the perpetrator disclosed the images; it is that the victim did not consent to the disclosure."[19]

Most American women are vulnerable to this kind of abuse. Almost 88 percent of American adults say they've sexted in the past[20]—and that doesn't even include all the women who've been photographed or recorded without their consent. A 2017 survey by the nonprofit Cyber Civil Rights Initiative found that nearly 16 percent of women have been threatened with or victimized by the distribution of sexually graphic pictures of themselves without their consent. Women are far, far more likely than men to be victims.[21]

People who are racial or ethnic minorities, LGBTQIA+, or disabled are even more vulnerable. One Australian study found that half of disabled people had been targets of nonconsensual porn and LGBT people were over 1.7 times more likely than straight, cisgender people to become victims.[22]

Cyber exploitation is, of course, one of the worst crimes imaginable. These days, Goldberg runs a law practice fighting for people who have been victimized by gender-based crimes. She says she's seen her clients suffer from anxiety and eating disorders and become depressed and suicidal.

"Harassers post women's nude images because they know it will make them unemployable, undateable, and at risk for sexual assault," law professor Danielle Keats Citron writes.[23]

In 2019, Katie Hill resigned from Congress after her nude photos ended up on the Internet. She blamed her estranged husband for leaking them; he denied it. Hill was urged by then-House Speaker Nancy Pelosi not to step down. She resigned anyway but acknowledged in her resignation speech on the House floor that "we have men who have been credibly accused of intentional acts of sexual violence and remain in boardrooms, on the Supreme Court, in this very body and, worst of all, in the Oval Office."

But, for Hill, the public exposure "felt insurmountable at that moment."

"I was completely overwhelmed by everything—how many people had seen my naked body, the comments, the articles, the millions of opinions, the texts, the calls, the threats," she wrote in her book *She Will Rise: Becoming a Warrior in the Battle for True Equality*. "I would start shaking, crying, throwing up."[24]

Many women who are victims of cyber exploitation don't report the abuse to law enforcement because they don't want to draw attention to their nude photos or have their names splashed across the Internet as part of criminal cases.[25] While most states have laws against nonconsensual pornography, Goldberg told me that even when women do report cybercrimes, law enforcement is sometimes reluctant to take on cases when the victims and perpetrators are in different states.

Of course, when this happens, society often blames women (and women blame themselves) for taking or allowing these photos to be taken in the first place. But, as Keats Citron argues, if our waiter posted our credit card information online, we wouldn't blame ourselves for going out to dinner. If our tax advisor publicly shared our Social Security number, no one would say it was our fault for having our taxes done.[26] We should have the same expectation of sexual privacy. What's more, often these photos are taken without the victim's knowledge. Hill said she had no idea many of the pictures of her that ended up online even existed.[27]

But now there's a cottage industry of websites that allow users to post nude images of other people and then charge the victims to take them down.[28] Other times these kinds of images are used to blackmail women to engage in sexual acts. One man hacked the webcam of Cassidy Wolf—former Miss Teen USA—and took nude photos of her while she was getting undressed in her bedroom. He told her that if she didn't want him to put them on social media, she'd have to send him naked pictures or video or do a live online show. This kind of blackmail is known as sextortion.[29]

Some sextortionists trick their victims into downloading a link that installs malware, allowing the perpetrator to access the content on their computers. Malware can also allow sextortionists to remotely turn on the webcams of their victims and record them. Other perpetrators gain access to the social media accounts of people they know by guessing answers to easy security questions, like the name of the street they grew up on or their high school mascot. Or they trick users into sharing their passwords. The man who sextorted women for six years from his office computer in the United States Embassy in London obtained their passwords by sending them emails pretending to be a member of Google's "Account Deletion Team."

Even if perpetrators aren't technologically savvy, they can buy their way into women's computers from others who are. One hacker website sold access to the computers of girls for $5 each (a premium compared to the $1 charged for access to those of boys).

Other times, sextortionists convince women and girls to send them graphic material—such as by pretending to be their boy-friend—then exploit them for more. One 30-year-old man in Israel convinced a 13-year-old girl to undress in front of her webcam while her mother was in the same room.[30]

And, in a case that made global headlines, Canadian teenager Amanda Todd agreed to briefly flash a man with whom she was chatting online. The man took a picture of her topless and then demanded that she perform a show for him. When she refused, he sent her photo to classmates on Facebook. When Amanda switched to a new school, the man set up a Facebook profile with her naked picture as the profile image in order to reach her classmates there. She switched schools again and again. In 2012, at age 15, she committed suicide.[31]

Other women and girls are sextorted for money. One set of perpetrators worked out of a facility that the Philippines' national police chief likened to a call center, friending people on social media, getting them to participate in cybersex, secretly filming it, then charging them up to $2,000 not to put the footage online. The enterprise was only shut down after a 17-year-old victim committed suicide.

The Brookings Institution describes sextortion as "a crime of often unspeakable brutality." Victims "spend every moment in fear of the next message demanding more compromising pictures or videos, living in perpetual anxiety of the risk of public exposure." According to a Brookings report, one teen said it "felt like I was being virtually raped." Another woman kept a knife under her pillow while she slept. "The mother of another victim explained that her daughter now becomes uncomfortable whenever she steps out onto the street, constantly wondering if any passersby have seen her naked." One girl was afraid to go outside or to school for fear of running into her perpetrator. Another left school and moved hundreds of miles to a new town "out of fear for her life."[32] At least 28 percent of sextortionists have at least one victim who attempts suicide, according to an FBI analysis.[33]

Some men sexually abuse women online because they derive a sick kind of pleasure from inflicting this kind of pain. William, who grew up in public housing in Britain, dropped out of school at age 15 and became an Internet troll. He would hack into victims' accounts, obtain naked photos of them, and send them to their family members, colleagues, and friends. Journalist Parmy Olson explains, "ruining people's lives gave William a thrill, and a sense of power unlike anything he had felt in the outside world." And "he got a buzz from knowing that at least for a moment, his victims felt their lives crumbling around them."

"I'd be lying if I said there was any great reason," William later said. "I don't feel guilty, it makes me laugh and it wastes a night. That's all I want . . . I want something that's going to leave me not depressed and give me something to focus on. And it's fun to make someone feel that awful."[34]

There's a term for using a person's social media account without her permission. It's called "fraping"—a portmanteau of Facebook and raping. Urban Dictionary defines fraping as editing a person's Facebook content "when they leave it open and vulnerable."[35] The definition is fitting, when you think about it. The allusion to rape points to the gendered nature of the abuse, since victims are usually women, and outrageously places the blame on victims for not better protecting themselves from violation.

In the future, we can expect that it'll only get easier to sexually shame women online. That's because it has now become easy to use artificial intelligence tools to create fake "revenge porn" by putting a real woman's face on a naked body.[36]

From the Manosphere to Murder

We've seen how social networks facilitate sexual crimes. But another element in all of this is how they radicalize men to commit violent crimes against women in the first place.

In 2021, a man went on a rampage, killing eight people in Atlanta spas, six of whom were women of Asian descent. He told police he did so to get rid of his "temptation."[37] In 2022, a man followed 35-year-old Christina Yuna Lee into her building in New York City's Chinatown and stabbed her to death in her apartment. The suspect was charged with murder and sexually motivated burglary.[38]

"Where are men getting the idea that Asian women are a sexual temptation based on how they look? That's exactly how Asian women are depicted in mainstream porn: hypersexualized, fetishized, exotified, and seen as subservient," Justine Ang Fonte, the sex educator we met in Chapter 1, tells me. "There are real consequences, with women actually dying because of this stereotype."

As we saw in Chapter 1, mainstream porn is also how strangulation has become part of sex for many women. So now, the violence men are witnessing in online porn is spilling over into physical violence offline—and even murder.

Another place men are radicalized to harm women is on the so-called manosphere—the web of "men's rights" advocates on social networks.

A major hub of the manosphere is a community called The Red Pill on Reddit. The name comes from the movie *The Matrix*, in which taking a red pill sends someone down a rabbit hole. As *The Daily Beast* explains, "in manosphere-speak, the rabbit hole is feminism, which the red pill reveals to be a War on Men."

Red Pill members often share the views that women are dumb and lack substance, trick men into marriage for their own financial gain, cheat on men, and falsely accuse men of rape when they regret sexual encounters. They believe women do these things in order to retaliate, get attention, or avoid feeling like sluts. "In addition to anti-feminist screeds, The Red Pill teaches 'sexual strategy,'" *The Daily Beast* reports. "This includes how to 'spin plates,' or balance sleeping with several women at once; how to respond to women's 'shit-tests,' a social device used to determine a suitor's 'fitness'; and how to practice 'negging,' a game tactic involving a backhanded compliment calculated to undermine confidence and make a woman more vulnerable to advances. Red Pillers practice 'dread game,' or intentionally instilling 'dread' in a partner that you have other options, and various other techniques."

Another group of misogynists on social media are the men's rights activists who believe our society is empowering women and holding men back. Members commonly say they need to "take the pussy off the pedestal."[39]

Then there are the communities of so-called "pickup artists," who share predatory tips about how to manipulate women into having sex with them while disparaging women and the idea of consent, Lydia Bates, a program manager at the Southern Poverty Law Center, told me.

A similar community on Facebook, Reddit, and other parts of the Internet is Men Going Their Own Way. Many of these men have had bad experiences in relationships with women and believe men must reassert their masculinity and reject feminism.[40]

Internet forums have also brought together a community of men who identify as "incel," or "involuntarily celibate." (They've appropriated a term initially coined by a Canadian woman who tried to create an online community for lonely singles.)[41] According to Dr. Kate Manne, the Cornell philosopher, "incels believe they are entitled to, and have been deprived of, sex with 'hot' young women, who are dubbed 'Staceys.'"[42]

One such man was the 22-year-old perpetrator of the Isla Vista massacre, who I'm not giving the dignity of naming here. In a video he posted online, he confirmed that, on the Internet, he had found "a forum full of men who are starved of sex, just like me" and that the community had "confirmed many of the theories I had about how wicked and degenerate women really are."[43] So he decided to take revenge against women for failing to sleep with him. On his "day of retribution," he said, "I am going to enter the hottest sorority house at UCSB [the University of California, Santa Barbara] and I will slaughter every single spoiled, stuck-up, blonde slut I see inside there."

In May 2014, he went to the sorority house with the intention of doing just that. Because it was Memorial Day weekend, a lot of the women who lived there weren't around, and the ones who were decided not to answer the door because his knocking sounded so aggressive. So he shot three women outside the dorm, killing two of them. He also went on a more general shooting spree in Isla Vista, California, targeting not just women but also sexually active men, whom he explained in a manifesto that he envied. He murdered six people, injured 14, and then took his own life in an episode that the International Centre for Counter-Terrorism (ICCT) at The Hague described as "male supremacist terrorism."[44]

Kaitlyn Regehr, PhD, an associate professor in digital humanities at University College London, says the Isla Vista attack popularized the incel community. "The colloquial use of the term only emerges in 2014 with the Isla Vista massacre," she told me.

The ICCT noted that, between that attack and February 2020, there were five additional acts of mass violence referencing the Isla Vista perpetrator or incel ideology and two more attempted episodes of mass violence that were stymied. For example, the man who killed ten people in Toronto in 2018 by driving a van onto a sidewalk wrote "the Incel rebellion has already begun!" on Facebook beforehand. "All hail" the Isla Vista attacker, he posted.

Then, in May 2020, a man who police said was part of the incel movement killed one woman and injured two others in a machete attack in Toronto.[45] Also that month, a self-described incel committed a mass shooting in an Arizona shopping mall that injured multiple people.[46] The following month, a 23-year-old Virginia man blew off his hand with a bomb believed to possibly have been intended for use as part of an incel attack targeting cheerleaders.[47] The man who killed five people, including a three-year-old girl, before taking his own life in Plymouth, England, in 2021 also followed incel ideology.[48] And in October 2022, a self-identified incel pled guilty to planning a mass shooting targeting women at a university in Ohio.[49]

Dr. Regehr says that, over the past five years, incel ideology has spread more broadly in pop culture. "Extremist misogyny that was once really segregated to platforms like Reddit forums is now disseminating onto much more popular platforms like TikTok and permeating into youth culture more generally," she told me. "It's much more socially acceptable to throw around incel terminology now."

A lot of this content is "shockingly, shockingly violent," Dr. Regehr says. It's things like jokes about a woman's anatomy looking like roast beef after violent sex. But Dr. Regehr says it's often masked as humor. "We're moving into this new act where that type of dark edgy humor is not that shocking, and that is unique compared to other forms of extremism," she says. "It's the permission that's been granted."

So what Dr. Regehr calls the "incel 1.0" was "typically an individual who was bullied and isolated and who was looking for community so he went online and became more and more isolated and angry." But now, what Dr. Regehr calls the "incel 2.0" is everywhere, she says. "Probably you or I have a friend who is posting these 'funny' sexist memes on their Facebook feed. There's a more general acceptance of overt misogyny that just wasn't present five years ago."

David Futrelle, who runs a blog tracking misogynistic subcultures, told me this kind of online misogyny can only be resulting in more offline abuse of women. In the manosphere, "they talk a lot about wanting to harass women, following women on dark streets at night and making them uneasy," Futrelle says. "I have to believe a certain amount of that is being played out" off social media.

What's more, he says, "this incel ideology creates such resentment of women, and that can't help but bleed out into everyday life and everyday interactions. It's going to poison their relationships and their interactions with women offline."

Futrelle says he thinks the misogyny promoted in these groups also encourages people to push public policies that restrict women's rights and oppose efforts to promote gender equality. Welcome to the world social media has created, where online violence spills over into outright misogyny in our culture—and sometimes deadly abuse.

How has this happened? Social media brings together people who would otherwise have been separated by geography and makes it practically effortless for them to commune with one another. Law professor Cass Sunstein reports that "when like-minded people get together, they often end up thinking a more extreme version of what they thought before they started to talk to one another."[50]

This happens for three reasons: exchanging information strengthens their pre-existing beliefs, validation makes them more confident (which promotes extremism), and they want to be viewed favorably by others.[51]

Dr. Regehr says people also become indoctrinated through an echo chamber effect. "If someone consumes very high doses of this content, it becomes normalized for them and no longer seems wrong," she tells me.

Plus, while they're isolating themselves online, they're becoming more and more disconnected from what's happening offline. "These incels believe that all women are having sex with the same three guys they call Chads and ignoring the rest of men," Futrelle tells me. "It's a reassuring ideology for the people out there who are not having romantic success. They can say, 'it's not my fault, it's the culture's fault, it's that women are too picky and they've been influenced by feminism.' If they would go outside and walk for a few minutes they'd see couples where guys clearly aren't Chads, yet they are somehow getting into relationships with women," he says. But they're too engrossed in the manosphere.

Also remember that the men who participate in these forums don't have to look the women they're abusing in the eye. As we saw in Chapter 3, because of the online disinhibition effect, people say and do things on social media that they'd be ashamed to do face to face. For example, *The Daily Beast* reported that the founder of The Red Pill on Reddit was Robert Fisher, a Republican serving in New Hampshire's House of Representatives. (Fisher denied it.)[52]

Thanks to these social media groups in which men are radicalized, male supremacy is growing. In 2017, the Southern Poverty Law Center designated specific male supremacy groups as hate groups and began monitoring them. "These groups foster and feed into dangerous narratives of hypermasculinity," Kylie Cheung wrote for *Ms.*

"In their glorification of traditional toughness, and in portraying women as oppressive figures and themselves as merely fighting back for their right to be men, violence is not only commodified but also celebrated."[53]

Social media companies don't just allow these kinds of communities and content to live on their networks. They actively promote some of it and profit from it. "What is algorithmically privileged is hate, because hate generates more reactions," Imran Ahmed, chief executive of the Center for Countering Digital Hate, tells me. "We've created an industrial scale economy in which perpetrators and platforms are making bank out of hatred of women."

Take Andrew Tate. When *The Guardian* set up a test account pretending to be a teenage boy, it was "quickly" shown content by Tate—a British-American man who advocates a world in which women stay home and serve men and who has said rape victims "bear responsibility" for being attacked. He talks about choking and hitting women and has been charged with rape and human trafficking[54] himself. He's one of the most popular people on TikTok (a platform that claims not to allow misogyny). In July 2022, more people searched for Tate on Google than for Kim Kardashian or Donald Trump.[55]

Bates, of the Southern Poverty Law Center, told me it's a big mistake to believe that online violence stays online. "It absolutely translates into real-world violence," she told me.

Ahmed told me one way this happens is by changing our society's views of appropriate behavior. Now, this kind of abuse of women is coming to be seen as normal.

"What we've seen for most of human history is the oppression of women and minorities by white men," he says. "It may turn out that what we call modernity was actually a short period in which there were consequences for hatred toward women."

What We Can Do

It doesn't have to be this way. Let's start with online dating. Dating expert Charly Lester told me online dating can be made safer than meeting people offline. Lester founded Lumen, a dating app for people over fifty in the United Kingdom, which used technology that verified the identities of people who signed up for accounts by making them take a selfie in real time. She says the program wouldn't allow people to upload photos from their cameras or hold a photo up to their camera while the selfie was taken, making it harder for people to use fake identities. And she said it could also detect when people were lying about their ages.

Every dating app today should do the same—and also require users to upload government-issued IDs which can be matched against those selfies to more reliably confirm their identities.

But Lester pointed out that a lot of sites are hesitant to implement such requirements because the harder it is to verify, the fewer users they attract. This. is. insane. Users should be demanding safer services—not flocking to ones that offer the most potential matches if the additional users they reach are actually shady characters.

There's also another way online dating companies could deter the use of fake identities: threatening fraudsters. "If you are a felon, sex offender or married, DO NOT use our website," the now defunct dating site True told users. The company said it would sue users if they misrepresented themselves—and did actually follow through and take a registered sex offender to court. (The case was settled.)[56]

Another form of technology Lester said dating sites can use are artificial intelligence products that detect troubling behavior like inappropriate words and evidence of spamming. For example, in 2015 the British dating site Bristlr, which bills itself as "connecting those with beards to those who want to stroke beards" (seriously), launched what it called a "lothario detector" to notify users when they were contacted by a potential match who sent the same message to a lot of people.[57]

Dating apps also need to preserve evidence and share it with law enforcement when crimes are reported.

While I'm telling everyone what to do, NC State should give Aaliyah a full scholarship to finish her studies. Chancellor Randy Woodson, I'm looking at you.

*   *   *

If you're looking to date, consider asking your friends to set you up with their friends—people who they know have things in common with you and aren't catfishers in Cambodia. Or, use dating sites but don't use ones that don't conduct background checks on their users. Don't gain a false sense of security from them—remember that the vast majority of sexual crimes go unreported, so plenty of rapists can clear a background check.[58] But they are a layer of protection against registered sex offenders that you'd be crazy not to avail yourself of.

Meet your dates in public places. Tell people where you're going. Tell your dates you've told people where you're going. And don't be alone with someone until you get to know them well. It's not worth the risk to your safety.

*   *   *

We also need to rebuild our society around women's right to sexual privacy. For all the whining about Big Tech we've heard from Democrats and Republicans lately, Congress has passed exactly two laws regulating the industry in the last *twenty-five years*.[59] It's time for lawmakers to wake up. Congress should pass a law taxing social networks and use the money to fund a massive increase in resources for the FBI to investigate online violence. FBI and local law enforcement agents need to be trained in how to investigate cybercrimes, including gender-based abuse, and be given direct mandates to do so.

We also need a federal law that establishes a right to sexual privacy by making it a felony to share a person's nude images without their express consent. This would help solve the problem Goldberg described of law enforcement being reluctant to take on cases across state lines. What's more, state laws are often too narrow and make these crimes mere misdemeanors, Keats Citron points out, which means a lot of police aren't going to pour resources into investigating them.[60] But if the crime were a felony, the prospect of major prison time could deter potential perpetrators and incentivize law enforcement to go after them.[61]

Jennifer Lawrence, who was also victimized by the hacking of her private images in 2014, told *Vanity Fair* that it should be considered a sex crime. "It is a sexual violation," she said. "It's disgusting."[62] She's right.

In addition, Section 230 of the Communications Decency Act shields site owners from liability for what their users post, with a few exceptions, such as copyrighted material. We need a law amending Section 230 to hold sites liable for hosting intimate images without the consent of the people in them. This would allow victims to sue platforms that refuse to take down nonconsensual porn. Right now, while mainstream sites claim not to allow such content, many of them don't respond to reports from victims, according to Keats Citron[63]—and sites dedicated to hosting "revenge porn" certainly aren't going to do so in the absence of this law (unless they're trying to charge victims for the service).

Keats Citron says a lot of attorneys won't represent victims of nonconsensual porn who can't afford to pay big bucks for their services because they can't recover much money from suing perpetrators unless the perpetrators themselves have money. But if victims could sue social networks—some of the richest companies in the world—more lawyers would take on these cases, so more victims could see justice.[64]

We also need a federal law criminalizing sextortion. While people who sextort children have been prosecuted under federal child pornography laws, sextortionists who target adult women have gotten away with astonishingly light sentences, largely because there isn't an adequate law criminalizing their behavior, according to the Brookings Institution. Brookings has drafted a model statute that provides a smart starting point for lawmakers.[65]

What's more, social media companies need to deplatform content and communities that glorify violence against women, like the Red Pill and incels. Let me directly address the miseducated men who claim they have a First Amendment right to abuse women online: the First Amendment guarantee of free speech applies to what the government does. Private companies like social networks can do whatever they want. (Section 230 of the Communications Decency Act expressly protects their right to moderate content in good faith.)[66] And Keats Citron reminds us that "free speech" is legally restricted all the time—for example, in cases of defamation or when people use speech to make threats, facilitate crimes, or invade privacy.[67] There's no excuse for social networks to allow men to use their platforms to promote hatred and egg one another on until some go out and kill women.

Make no mistake: This is a fight for women's lives. But unlike other issues that affect women, like reproductive rights, we don't have a long history of advocacy on these issues because they're so new. So in order to change things, a lot of us also need to make these problems the fight *of* our lives.

DIGITAL HOUSEWIVES

Brittany Ashley was at Buzzfeed's Golden Globe party at Eveleigh, a hot West Hollywood restaurant. Ashley, who cheekily calls herself "America's lesbian sweetheart," was one of the most well-known actresses on Buzzfeed's YouTube channels, starring in videos that were viewed by millions. But she wasn't there to celebrate with her colleagues. She was there to wait on them.

The harsh reality: Ashley needed to waitress on top of all her other hard work in order to pay her bills. In fact, waitressing was the *primary* way she earned her living. At the time, she says, Buzzfeed was sometimes paying her $50 or $100 per video, sometimes not paying her a cent—all while telling her to lean into her queer identity and then making money as her videos about her identity racked up views.

The party was "absolute hell," Ashley later told me. "I felt super uncomfortable the entire time." But the look on her colleagues' faces when they saw her was familiar. It was the same look she got from other customers when they realized their server was Internet famous.

"You would just watch someone's face be really confused and disappointed and that pity they projected onto me really messed with me," she said.

Welcome to the real world of most social media influencers.

*　*　*

If you read the news, you may have noticed that the media loves to tell stories like that of 27-year-old Andrea Romo. She earned $12.50 per hour working at Lowe's until one day she uploaded a video of her sister deep frying a turkey that became so popular that Snapchat paid her about half a million dollars. Or Maryland high school student Katie Feeney, who was paid over a million dollars by Snapchat in two months for her videos, like one of her hoverboarding in different outfits.[1]

These stories have become the new version of the American dream. So it's no wonder why the majority of American teens would like to be influencers.[2]

But here's the reality: the vast majority—77 percent of influencers on Facebook, YouTube, and Instagram—are women, according to a 2019 study by the influencer marketing platform Klear.[3] And the median salary for a woman influencer is just $10,000, according to a 2022 report by Influencer Marketing Hub.[4] For the record, that's a fraction of the federal poverty level of $30,000 for a family of four in the United States.[5] Kylie Jarrett, PhD, a scholar of media studies, refers to women content creators as "digital housewives," which is fitting because they often earn the same salary as stay-at-home moms: $0.[6]

Of course there are exceptions to the rule: the mega-influencers who reportedly get paid five, six, or even seven figures per post.[7] And we all keep talking about them, which helps mask the reality of a system in which primarily women create content that helps men like Mark Zuckerberg get ridiculously rich by selling ads to the people who view it. Zuck took home over $27 million in compensation in 2022.[8] Meanwhile, many of these women earn little or nothing to support their own families.

Some of the most exploited people of all are Black women and girls who create content, then watch it get appropriated and monetized by others. You might remember the Renegade dance that went viral on TikTok in 2020. It was created by Jalaiah Harmon, a 14-year-old Black girl in Georgia, but popularized by Charli D'Amelio, the white TikToker who was one of the platform's biggest stars, and copied by mega influencers like Kourtney Kardashian and Lizzo.

"I was happy when I saw my dance all over," Jalaiah told *The New York Times*. "But I wanted credit for it."

When she commented on posts asking influencers to tag her, they mostly ignored or ridiculed her, Jalaiah said.[9] Then the NBA invited white TikTokers to perform the dance during its All-Star slam dunk contest. Jalaiah wasn't extended an invite until later on, when her exclusion generated social media outrage.[10]

Similarly, in 2021, Jimmy Fallon invited white TikTok star Addison Rae to perform a series of dances on his show without crediting the original creators. One of the dances, to Cardi B's song "Up," was created by 15-year-old Black TikToker Mya Nicole with her friend Chris Cotter.

When she saw Rae on the show, Mya told ELLE, "I sent it to Chris like, *Dang, that could've been us performing our own dance.*" They were eventually invited on the show via Zoom—but only after, you guessed it, social media outcry."[11] The experience is so common among Black creators that in the summer of 2021 they went on strike to protest the practice of appropriating their work.[12]

After spending three years interviewing more than fifty young women who produce social media content in women-dominated areas like fashion, Cornell professor Brooke Erin Duffy, PhD, concluded that they perform what she calls "aspirational labor." They mostly go unpaid or underpaid but are "remunerated with deferred promises of 'exposure' or 'visibility,'" thinking they might make money in the future. Only that future never seems to come.[13]

*   *   *

On Instagram, Jordan Reid calls herself the "OG"—or original—blogger. Back in the dark ages when influencers were just emerging (circa 2013), *TIME* magazine profiled her as one of the first women who was sponsored by brands for her work.[14] "In the beginning, a big focus was 'look at us and our fabulous New York lifestyle, with champagne, parties, and one girl's boyfriend flew us to St. Barts," Reid told me. "And yeah, I was on unemployment living in a fourth-floor walkup with a hole in the floor."

From the beginning, she says, influencers had to deal with angry "fans" claiming they should get jobs and were being supported by their fathers. "It all rolls off except for when its people saying I've been supported by men, because for a long time I supported my husband when he went to business school," she told me. "What man in a creative job would get that, the automatic assumption that daddy bought you a house?" For the record, she says her parents *didn't* support her.

Another thing that seemed to outrage Reid's followers was that she took money from brands. "I was always seen as shilling out and it's like, I have a baby and a husband and no one will pay me with the fall of print journalism," she remembers.

Influencers sprung up right around the time that major advertisers started redirecting huge parts of their budgets to Facebook and Google instead of newspapers and magazines in the early 2000s—so women like Reid could no longer make decent money from freelance writing for traditional media outlets. Amber Katz, whose blog made her one of the first beauty influencers, told me, "when I write a magazine article today, I'm paid like 50 percent of what I was paid ten years ago—same topic, same kind of story—and you also have to take inflation into account. It's a wild proposition."

But fans are sometimes appalled when influencers are paid for their content by brands—especially if the brand doesn't align with the influencer's carefully curated image. "It was very hard to turn down money even from a Walmart because I had to pay the bills and I just didn't know what the month or year would bring financially," Reid remembers.

Despite the apparent belief of many followers and brands that women's labor doesn't have real monetary value, women content creators don't just work—they do the jobs of many people at once. Jeannette Kaplun, a Latina lifestyle influencer who works full-time as a content creator, has worked with brands like Disney, Target, Procter & Gamble, Exxon, Embassy Suites, and Verizon. She gave me a sense of what it really takes to create content for a client. First, she says, you have to come up with a creative concept, just as you would in an advertising agency. She buys props, pays for music rights, and either hires or does the work of photographers, videographers, makeup artists, hairdressers, and interior designers in order to create photo or video posts.

Once an influencer creates and posts content, her work has only just begun. She has to keep responding to comments on the post and engaging in other conversations on social media in order to keep her follower counts up, so she can get more work in the future.

But Kaplun says she routinely gets "outrageous lowball offers" for her work. Other influencers I talked to also told me brands regularly offer them terrible compensation.

"With men, you pay them," Olivia Howell, a social media manager who has represented Reid and other influencers, told me. "With women, there are all these schemes to get us to work for free."

One way brands try to do this is by offering affiliate links instead of payments, giving influencers special URLs that track the sales they generate and then offering them a percentage of the revenue. "They say, 'if you sell this bathrobe, you can make 15 percent,'" Howell says. "'But we're not going to pay you for your time.' A lot of the big brands do this because they think influencers will hook on with them for their names."

Howell says brands that work with influencers often demand exclusivity, preventing them from also working with their competitors. But they don't like to pay for that exclusivity, either.

Hilary Topper, a triathlon influencer with *A Triathlete's Diary*, told me another scheme brands have come up with is getting influencers to pay *them* to promote their products. As an ambassador for triathlon brands, she has paid companies hundreds of dollars to get discounted apparel, then been responsible for wearing it in trainings and races and creating social media content about it.

Other times, the gear on offer is free—but worth far less than the value of her time. "A shoe company reached out to me and they wanted me to create two YouTube videos, do a Facebook Live, post on Instagram and more in exchange for a *free pair of shoes*," Topper recalled. "And you know, people do it because they think it will make them part of an exclusive club or help them become an influencer."

"There have been other times when I was asked to post something on social in return for free products and all I had to do was pay for the shipping—which was more than the products were worth," Topper told me.

What's more, Reid says, in order to attract and keep fans, "every sponsored post has to be surrounded on both sides of your feed by plenty of unsponsored content so it's not just paid, paid, paid, and that unsponsored content has to be up to the standards of sponsored content. You can't just have mediocre imagery surrounding a single beautiful paid image on your feed and expect brands to be attracted to that. So you have to do a lot more unpaid work than paid."

And the work comes with no income stability—or benefits like health insurance or retirement plans.

When women *do* monetize their work, even in this woman-dominated field, they typically earn far less than men. Women influencers are on average paid $351 per post, while male influencers are paid $459, according to the Klear survey.[15] That means the women they surveyed are paid less than 77 cents for every dollar a man earns for the same kind of work—a wage gap even bigger than the national average of 82 cents.[16] In 2020, HypeAuditor, an influencer analytics firm, surveyed 1,600 Instagram influencers in more than 40 countries and found that men earned an average of $3,051 for a post and story, while women earned an average of $2,040.[17]

Part of the problem, Gabe Dunn, a trans and LGBTQIA+ YouTuber, told me, is content creators tend to start out young and inexperienced in negotiations.

"People have no idea what to ask for and the problem is there's no standard. There's no minimum wage," Dunn told me. "They can just wildly fluctuate. Some big brands will come in and offer a quarter of what a small company paid and you're literally, like, a billion-dollar company."

Dunn told me women content creators often shortchange themselves when they ask for money. When Dunn discusses payments with other influencers, "almost every time I'll say a number and they'll say, 'I literally was going to say half of that' and I'm like, nah, girl."

And even when brands agree to pay influencers, it doesn't mean they'll necessarily see the money anytime soon—or even at all. "I've gotten paid same day and six months later," an influencer who calls herself Brooklyn Active Mama told *The Atlantic*. "You have to be prepared to get paid at any time. It's very difficult for an influencer; if you sign a $2,000 contract, you really never know when you're going to get that money."

In 2018, *The Atlantic* ran an expose on a company called Speakr, which inked deals with content creators on behalf of brands like

23andMe, Disney, Ford, Nissan, Pepsi, Sony, Universal Studios, and Verizon. Speakr never paid some of them. Others were paid partially or months late.

What stops many influencers from publicly exposing this behavior? The fear of scaring away other potential sponsors.[18] Meanwhile, they can't exactly pay their babysitters or landlords with IOUs.

Women of color have it the worst. Kelli Boyer, a running influencer who is Black, says some brands won't work with her at all. She's applied three times to work with one athleticwear company that works with few Black influencers. But when she looks at the white influencers who represent the brand, their content and follower counts don't seem to be different from hers at all.

Part of the problem, she suspects, is "a lot of women of color are not super skinny and we don't fit the mold of what you think of when you think of an elite athlete." Internet trolls make the problem worse. When Boyer and other women of color post pictures of themselves in athleticwear, she says, "the comments we get turn into body shaming, the 'you don't even look good in the brand' kind of stuff. And I think those kinds of comments might be why brands might steer away from bringing in people of color. A brand might say, gosh, the public doesn't seem to respond well to that person, so this person isn't a good ambassador for us."

When brands *do* work with diverse women, they often try to shortchange them. Kaplun told me about a time she attended an event with other women influencers and learned in casual conversation with them that she was being paid *half* of what the brand was paying the other women—even though she was posting in both English and Spanish, and therefore doing double the work.

Because of all this, many content creators say they live on the verge of poverty. And even those who do make bank from brands probably aren't as rich as they'd like us all to think. *Forbes* says the

Kardashian–Jenner family "spent years fighting *Forbes* for higher spots on our annual wealth and celebrity earnings lists" and possibly forged their tax returns to make themselves appear richer than they are. (The family denies the claim.)[19]

But this isn't just a story about the depressingly familiar practice of people devaluing and underpaying women and people of color. It's also about what this kind of work does to the mental health of women influencers—and their families.

Josi Denise, who called herself the "American mama" on her former blog, says that in order to get sponsors to pay her for posts about their products or give her free stuff, she needed a large number of followers. To achieve that, she couldn't write about what she was really facing: postpartum depression, anxiety, and a divorce. If her content wasn't cheery, it wouldn't be shared as much. As a result, mommy influencers "aren't very honest about what's going on in their lives," she says. "I was certainly one of them."[20]

This is understandable when you think about the pressure they face to perform perfect lives. "There's this expectation of women excelling at everything, having the perfect home and the perfect children and the perfect body," Kaplun points out. "Now there's also this huge movement in favor of authenticity and showing your vulnerability and imperfections, and that allows you to connect more deeply with your community. But you have to balance it," she warns. If you want to get work from top brands, you can't be *too* real. After all, who wants to buy products so our lives will look like those of harried women with messy homes and misbehaved kids?

This can leave influencers feeling like actors in their own lives. Reid tells me that "anything from cooking a really nice meal to decorating my living room became content, so it felt performative. I just got tired of pretending to live a life that was exhausting. I so never want to live like that again, where you're photographing your food and your clothing and your kids."

Influencers also face pressure to overshare intimate details of their lives. Deeply personal content is what attracts followers and then brands—or, to be more precise, it's what followers and brands expect of *women*. So women content creators know that these kinds of personal revelations are important for their careers, even if it makes them uncomfortable to expose their inner thoughts, marriages, children, bedroom interiors, health, and other private information to the world.

Baring their private selves also comes with real risks. In 2020, social influencer and model Chrissy Teigen announced that she lost her baby when she was 20 weeks pregnant, since she had already posted that she was expecting. "I feel bad our grief was so public because I made the joy so public," she later wrote in a post on *Medium*. "Stories leading up to this had been chronicled for all. It's hard to look at them now. I was so positive it would be okay. I feel bad that I made you all feel bad. I always will."[21]

All this oversharing also promotes parasocial relationships—the intense, one-way attachments some fans come to have with people in the public eye. "We feel as if we know these people and, indeed, we sort of do—we know how old they were when they had their first kiss, and how long it took them to get over their last break-up, what their bathrooms look like perhaps, and where they're going on holiday next month," Otegha Uwagba writes in *The Guardian*.

Most fans probably realize they aren't actually close with Jennifer Lawrence. But when people are what Uwagba calls "low-level" famous—like popular content creators—followers come to see them more as friends. So they expect influencers to *act* like their friends, such as by responding to personal messages.[22]

Content creators must also walk on eggshells to avoid saying or doing anything their fan-friends don't like. "In their heads as an influencer they trust you and then if you do something they don't like, it's a personal betrayal," Dunn said. "Men don't get the same thing because nobody expects anything of them. As a queer person, the criticism I see people like us get is 'I'm disappointed in you.' No one's ever disappointed in white men."

Dunn told me that they deleted their X (then called Twitter) account—a move that "would have been unimaginable" to them a few years ago—to avoid unintentionally bringing on the outrage of the Internet.

Jordan Reid became less comfortable sharing private information about her children as they grew up, so she has largely stopped working as an influencer. She also worried about the behavior she was modeling for her daughter.

"How do I say to a 13-year-old daughter, 'don't put up content to get likes because it's not healthy, but I do it to pay the rent'?" she said. "It's part of the entire structure of being an influencer. I can't imagine it's great for anyone's mental health or perspective or confidence."

Neither is the way influencers can come to feel about their bodies after spending so much time filtering their images for social media. "I want my daughter to be able to look at herself in the mirror and not be wishing that the mirror would have a filter on it," Kaplun told me. "It distorts your body image. When I look at myself in the mirror, I wish my skin would look smoother, my eyes would look bigger, my mouth would look poutier."

And even when earning money feels empowering to the few women who make solid income from social media content, it can also feel disempowering in the very same breath. In her book *My Body*, model Emily Ratajkowski tells the story of posting a photo of herself in a swimsuit on Instagram while on a paid vacation at an uber-exclusive resort in the Maldives, then watching the post rack up hundreds of thousands of likes and sales for her bikini brand. She liked the money and the power that came with it. She also hated having people judge her body and view it as the measure of her worth.

"I wanted to be able to have my Instagram hustle, selling bikinis and whatever else, while also being respected for my ideas and politics and, well, everything besides my body," she explains.[23] If only.

Part of the job description, after all, is having luscious hair and perfectly smooth legs to promote the products content creators peddle. Dunn told me that, when they came out as nonbinary in 2021, they lost about 40 percent of the brands who sponsored them—from a TV show about women to hair, makeup, nail, and underwear companies.

Here's another reason why women and nonbinary people often rack up likes without being truly liked. Even if they're unpaid or underpaid—or, in the cases of mega-influencers like the Kardashian–Jenners, simply a lot less wealthy than they want us to think—they still enjoy something else that's considered extremely threatening when wielded by women: power. After all, they literally influence the thoughts and behaviors of their often large numbers of followers. Like many women who enjoy power, they're therefore often deemed unlikeable.

As we've seen, there's not much difference between what creative directors in ad agencies (who are overwhelmingly men)[24] and influencers who are sponsored by brands (who are overwhelmingly women) do—other than the fact that the men are usually paid a whole lot more for their work. But how often do you see someone jab a finger in the face of a man who works in advertising at a dinner party and accuse him of being inauthentic and not in his heart of hearts believing in the cosmetics and tampons he peddles?

On the other hand, people complain that influencers are "fake" (hello, authenticity police!) or shilling for money—rather than considering how these women and their work might have worth. For example, when England's National Health Service paid influencers to share information about how to book Covid tests in 2020, the public was outraged. The influencers were called "vacuous media whores." The strategy was deemed "scandalous."

"Because it's women, the respect isn't there, the job's not given the importance it deserves," influencer expert Kat Molesworth says. Not even when they're trying to help save lives.[25]

Follow Me(n)

What about those of us who choose to work in other fields (especially after reading this chapter)? Social media offers us all a way to promote our work, raise our profiles within our professions, and build our networks—which *should* translate to more career opportunities. But the biggest gains from using social media professionally often go to men.

A 2019 study of researchers who study health services and policy found that, although women and men in the field use X (then called Twitter) at similar rates, women are far less influential. Women on average get half as many followers and just over half as many likes and reposts as their male colleagues.[26]

"There must be something implicit going on here in terms of who is seen as most authoritative," Jane Zhu, the lead author of the study who is a physician and assistant professor of medicine at the Oregon Health & Science University, told me. Dr. Zhu says she sees it all the time: her male colleagues are frequently reposted while her posts go ignored.

Other studies back this up. A 2021 survey of doctors found that male physicians were more likely than their women counterparts to receive speaking invitations and scholarship opportunities as a result of their social media use.[27] And a 2020 study of British anesthesiologists who wrote the most visible studies in their field found that, although women and men used most of the social networks studied at similar rates, the women ended up connecting with significantly fewer contacts.[28]

The problem is that people just don't turn to women for expertise in the same way they do to men because we're perceived as less competent. So not only does social media sometimes not allow women to overcome inequities we face offline—it may actually *reinforce* those disparities.

Women are especially invisible on Wikipedia. Less than 20 percent of biographies in English are of women, according to WikiProject Women in Red, a group trying to change that.[29] Anyone can volunteer to write Wikipedia bios, but they're subject to approval by volunteer administrators based on the site's notability criteria.

Jess Wade, PhD, a research fellow at Imperial College London, has written over 1,800 Wikipedia pages for woman and minority scientists and engineers. "It's important for women to be recognized for their work because it's a credibility check in contemporary society," she told me. "Having your information on a really publicly available platform is quite transformative when people are arranging a conference and looking for someone to speak or deciding who to nominate for an award or a fellowship."

Don't discount the career and earnings opportunities we miss out on when we go unrecognized. Take Substack, which allows writers to keep the lion's share of the money made from their writing. In 2020, Anne Helen Petersen, a top writer on the platform, pointed out that women were writing just four of the top twenty-five paid and six of the top twenty-five free Substacks.

But Substack says more than half the writers it gives advances to are women.[30] Why did women rank higher on the free list than the paid list? Petersen posted that women tend to "feel weird & sheepish asking to [be] paid for their labor, *especially* when it's fun, meaningful, or internet labor. We internalize this shit! I certainly did!" What's more, she wrote, "women are also working so much in all corners of their lives that we resist monetizing something (like a newsletter) that might feel pleasurable (and thus turning it explicitly into work) I certainly did!"

What We Can Do

First things first: "We need to make a conscious effort to try to follow people with diverse opinions," Dr. Zhu says. "Follow and support more women. Don't just treat social media like it's pure entertainment but use it to reflect our ongoing efforts for gender equity."

"When I go through a news feed I try to actively like the posts of other women and celebrate their efforts," Dr. Zhu told me. "It's a conscious effort to do that."

Disinformation expert Nina Jankowicz told me she does the same thing—and her feed is more interesting as a result. "Women have a different perspective because we're caretakers in our families and we're also people who are widely discriminated against, so the way we approach issues is different from how a cis white male might approach them," she says.

On my website (Resources, page 234) you'll find a list of feminists to follow—though they're just the tip of the iceberg.

Dr. Zhu also points out that women sometimes hold back from sharing our views because we're less confident than men. "Sometimes I think about posting but then I stop myself and I think maybe it's not that good of an idea," she told me. "Whereas I have male colleagues who will post about anything and everything, and that makes for a more interesting account."

Of course, there's another very valid reason why Dr. Zhu some-times holds back: "I don't want to open myself to really hateful and violent criticism," she told me. "The nature of that is different with visible women than it is with visible men. My women colleagues who are active on social media will say something, and if it doesn't land the right way, they'll get lots of hate."

Palestinian-American feminist activist Linda Sarsour, who you'll hear more from in Chapter 9, told me the same thing. If she hadn't had to take breaks from social media because of Internet trolls, she estimates she'd have hundreds of thousands more followers.

So in order to really fix this problem, we have to make social media a more welcoming place for women (much more from me in Chapter 9 on how tech companies need to crack down on abuse).

Another thing we can all do now is be sure to give women credit when it's due. Dr. Zhu told me she'll sometimes see men share her research—but not attribute it to her. The same also of course goes for original content creators. If you're re-enacting their dances or borrowing their ideas, a shoutout is due.

Also, "we need to just generally recognize and celebrate the women in our lives and in our fields," Dr. Wade says. "I absolutely love seeing the recognition women get after they have a Wikipedia bio. Suddenly just because they're on this platform they're on news channels and TV shows, they're put on these top 10 lists, they're nominated for awards, they're honored and celebrated."

"It can often feel very overwhelming how imbalanced society is," Dr. Wade says, "but we all have this potential to do something really small that can make a transformative difference. If you change one person's perception or one woman's career, you don't know the knock-on effect it will have."

Also use social networks to connect with other women in your field. Dr. Wade points out that "social media is such a powerful platform for uniting women. I've connected with so many extraordinary women scientists internationally. We hang out and plan and strategize and find ways to amplify each other. It's about network building and confidence and tips for surviving your PhD."

Social platforms should also radically expand their pots of money to pay influencers with sizeable followings and help them make money from advertising. After all, these people (who are mostly women) are responsible for the content that makes tech companies like Meta and ByteDance so profitable in the first place. We as users should also send tips and shell out for subscriptions when content creators share material we value.

As for the influencer pay gap, sure, influencers need to negotiate what they're paid. But I'm pretty sick of hearing women who are underpaid told it's their fault for not negotiating. As if that's so simple to do when you work in a culture and industry where it's the norm to underpay women, and where the going rates are shrouded in secrecy, and you don't want to be passed over for opportunities altogether, and maybe you have to find a job with flexibility so you can pick up your kids after school. So how about instead of pointing the finger at the victims of wage inequality, companies stop shortchanging women? Every organization should be analyzing its own internal data to ensure that they're paying everyone equitably.

Here's what influencers can do until that day comes. Content creators of all genders should continue a nascent industry trend of publishing what they're paid. In 2020, an Instagram account called influencerpaygap was set up, posting stories submitted anonymously by influencers to document inequities.[31] And in 2021, an app called F*** You Pay Me was launched to enable creators to share information about their pay and experiences working with brands.[32] If the going rates were better understood, brands couldn't get away with the archaic practice of undercompensating women. Armed with this information, women will be better empowered to negotiate for what they're worth, just as men have long done. And if it were clearer to women how men monetize the same kind of work, they'd realize they shouldn't be offering it up for free.

At least now there's an app for that?

MISINFORMATION FOR MOMMIES

When Margaret Nichols, a forty-year-old meditation teacher in New York City, became pregnant in 2016, she joined a Facebook group called "Homebirth and Waterbirth." She planned to deliver her baby in her West Village home with the help of a midwife and doula—and without pain medication. On her Facebook group, this seemed like a mainstream choice. A subset of that group went even further, choosing unassisted home births.

"The dominant ideology in affluent Instagram circles is definitely a heavy emphasis on being completely natural, with things like unmedicated home birth, organic food, and attachment parenting," Nichols, who is white, told me.

After she went into labor, Nichols stuck to the plan for the first thirty hours. After that, in intense agony and utterly exhausted, she was rushed to a hospital where she got anesthesia and rest, then delivered a healthy boy she named Bo. But, for months afterwards, she felt like a failure, because she hadn't given birth the way the moms on social media said she should.

"My birth story didn't quite work out the way I planned and there was a lot of shame in natural parenting groups around choosing medicalization," she recalls.

Nichols said not managing to deliver her baby "naturally" made her question who she was as a person. "I lost my sense of self," she remembers. "I'm thinking, so I'm not a hippie who can have a home birth in my West Village bathtub, but I'm also not one of those moms going back to some high-powered job. So who am I?"

Although she now realizes her sense of shame for somehow doing motherhood "wrong" contributed to her developing postpartum anxiety, it went undiagnosed at the time. "My anxiety came from this sense of not doing it right and not being able to provide the best for my son," she says.

In the social media mamasphere, mommy influencers peddle the idea of "natural" childbirth, without physicians, medical facilities, or pain medication. Their message is clearly getting through. According to a *TIME* magazine survey, the majority of moms believe "natural" birth is extremely or very important, and 70 percent "felt pressured to do things a certain way."[1]

That's just the start of the pressures many new moms face to raise their kids according to standards set on social media. But when mothers go online seeking information to empower themselves, they often instead end up on the receiving end of misinformation and misogyny. And some of it is *dis*information—content deliberately designed to deceive. This might help explain why, as social media took off between 2000 and 2015, the rate of postpartum depression among women who were hospitalized for childbirth increased by a multiple of *seven*.[2]

* * *

Not everyone buys into the idea that it's the business of other people to know and judge how babies come out of women's bodies.

"In France, the way you give birth doesn't situate you within a value system or define the sort of parent you'll be," Pamela Druckerman writes in *Bringing Up Bébé: One American Mother Discovers the Wisdom of French Parenting.* "It is, for the most part, a way of getting your baby safely from your uterus into your arms."[3]

But much of what #natural childbirth advocates push isn't just guilt and pain-inducing. It can be deadly.

When I started my career as a communicator at the United Nations in 2008, pregnancy and childbirth were the number one killer of women my age in poor countries. Today, they remain one of the leading causes of death among women of childbearing age globally.[4] Knowing this, when I became pregnant, I never considered forgoing a privilege I enjoyed that so many women around the world don't: the option to deliver my baby in a hospital, with the aid of a licensed specialist.

I married an emergency room doctor who delivered more babies than he can count during his medical training. But even he said he'd be terrified to deliver our children at home, because he's seen first-hand how life-threatening complications requiring complex medical interventions can arise without warning. This is why the safest place to deliver a baby is in a hospital, and the safest person to deliver a baby is a physician who is trained in obstetrics.

Babies are three to nine times more likely to die when delivered by midwives as part of planned home births. And, in the United States, over ten times more babies die during home births than as the result of sudden infant death syndrome, or SIDS—the phenomenon in which babies die mysteriously in their sleep.[5] I'm not trying to attack midwives here—the world needs more people who care about helping women. But this is the data.

* * *

Is the medical system flawed? Of course it is.

On the day I delivered my first child, I went to my busy New York hospital only to be told by a nurse that I was emphatically *not* in labor and could not be admitted. She insisted I stand up, change out of my hospital gown, and leave—all things I was physically incapable of doing at that point—and said I could speak to a doctor on my way out. After extensive negotiations, I managed to get admitted for pain management (since I was "not in labor"). My daughter arrived later that morning.

And, by the way, I was probably in a position of unusual privilege because my husband is *a physician who worked in that very hospital.* Quelle surprise: like the rest of the world, members of the medical community frequently don't listen to women the way they should.

After seeing stories on social media about doctors who gaslight their patients—like a video recently posted by a patient who recorded her physician telling her she was not actually experiencing the pain she was experiencing—some women (rightly) conclude something is wrong with the medical system. This also helps explain why they choose midwives over doctors.

Yet no one thinks the solution to the fact that lawyers often don't listen to women is for us to instead be represented in court by people who aren't fully trained in the law. No one thinks the solution to the fact that some car mechanics mansplain and overcharge women is for us to instead find kindly people with less expertise to install our brakes. Likewise, the solution to the fact that the medical establishment doesn't always treat us with respect is not to deprive ourselves of the best medical care. It's to advocate for doctors and nurses to take women's complaints and preferences seriously.

We need to do this individually as patients and collectively as feminists. I delivered my second baby in a different hospital, where my doctors and nurses listened to and acted on my concerns and requests.

Of course, I recognize that I have privileges and choices in selecting my doctors that many women don't. Serena Williams famously told *Vogue* that she had a hard time getting a nurse to believe her when she realized she had developed blood clots after delivering her child.[6] If one of the world's most venerated Black women struggled to be heard, think about what other women of color must go through.

It's a well-documented fact that people of color receive a lower quality of pain care than non-Hispanic white patients.[7] Doctors simply don't take the pain of Black patients as seriously. And, compared to other rich countries, the United States has a shocking record of maternal deaths. Black women die in pregnancy and childbirth at 2.6 times the rate of white women.[8]

But these women are largely not the ones choosing home births. The people attempting home births tend to be women like Nichols, who are sometimes called "crunchy." Non-Hispanic white women are three to four times more likely to deliver at home than women from other racial and ethnic groups.[9]

And they often have privileges beyond their race. When you live in an urban place like Manhattan or the Bay area, you can get to a hospital quickly if you need help—just like Nichols did. In addition, "home births are for essentially healthy people," Karen Jefferson, director of midwifery practice at the American College of Nurse-Midwives, says. Her organization recommends hospital births when there are medical complications or elevated risks, like twins or breech births.

But lots of women don't enjoy these privileges—which is why it's all the more wrong to pressure them to choose home births. Yet on social media home births are often romanticized, and doctors demonized. Promoting the rejection of first-rate medical care is big business, with proponents raking in huge profits from midwife and doula services, websites, workshops, books, and DVDs.[10]

And women are listening. Since social media took off, women who have the option to deliver in hospitals with physicians have increasingly instead chosen home births. Between 2004 and 2017, home births increased by 77 percent in the United States.[11]

Occasionally the devastating outcomes that can accompany them become clear. In 2020, a reality TV star posted on Instagram that her baby had died after suffering catastrophic brain injury during a home birth. There's no need for me to name her here—the grief of losing a child is already so much more than any woman should ever have to bear. But Amy Tuteur, an obstetrician and author of *Push Back: Guilt in the Age of Natural Parenting*, read the mom's description of what happened and told me that, if she had delivered in a hospital, doctors could have almost certainly enabled a different outcome.

Mommy Masochists

Another concept widely promoted to moms on social media is the idea that we should experience unthinkable agony during labor, even though medicine is readily available to reduce it, because giving birth without pain relief is somehow more "natural" and will allow us to better bond with our babies. Writer Jill Filipovic points out that, when it comes to childbirth, "pain has perhaps never been more fetishized—at least not since it was first meted out as punishment for a curious Eve."[12]

One safe, widely available form of pain relief in the United States is an epidural, which involves inserting a needle into mom's spine, putting a catheter into it, and delivering anesthesia. If this sounds painful, I can assure you from personal experience it's negligible compared to the excruciating experience of childbirth. I will always remember the exact moment in time I received my epidural while delivering my first child—5:52 AM—because it was one of the most important moments of my life.

"In French, giving birth without an epidural isn't called 'natural' childbirth. It's called 'giving birth without an epidural,'" Druckerman writes, and the "1 or 2 percent of nonepidural births in Paris are, I'm told, either crazy Americans like me or Frenchwomen who didn't get to the hospital in time."[13]

In the United States, however, Alexander Butwick, MD, a Stanford University anesthesiology professor, points out that there is "a lot of misinformation available online that is more likely to suggest epidurals may not be great."[14] This helps explain why more than 63 percent of women decide before childbirth to *try to avoid pain medication*—yet the vast majority end up getting it in the end. And more than 90 percent of women who get epidurals are happy with them.[15] No wonder: they offer relief from profound agony.

"Personally, I think that the people who invented the epidural should win the Nobel Prize, the Presidential Medal of Freedom, and an Olympic gold medal," Dr. Tuteur writes. "Their contribution to women's well-being has been immeasurable."[16]

As a woman who has benefitted from two of them, I have to disagree. They deserve far more adulation.

What's more, the idea that women should voluntarily forgo relief in order to experience unimaginable pain during a major medical event is twisted. We're not talking about a minor ache here. As Dr. Tuteur explains, "there is a reason why the writers of the Bible imagined that childbirth is a punishment from God. It is widely recognized among specialists in pain management to be the worst pain you are likely ever to experience."[17]

Also keep in mind that there's no big movement to make epidurals safer or better. Rather, women are simply told to decline them. So, apparently, ensuring that women experience profound suffering is *the very point* of withholding pain medicine. Women also report not being offered pain relief by doctors for other unbearably painful gynecological procedures, like cervical biopsies.[18]

To state the obvious, this is a gendered expectation. "No one ever asks if a man is having a 'natural vasectomy,'" comedian Jessi Klein has pointed out.[19]

Momfluencers & Sanctimommies

A lot of this misogyny and misinformation comes from so-called momfluencers. Scroll through the parenting content on many websites, apps, and social networks and it's easy to see that some of the predominant forms of advice they serve up include not just "natural" childbirth but also intensive mothering—a term coined by sociologist Sharon Hays, PhD, to describe the ideas that moms are the ones who should primarily be responsible for taking care of our kids and our lives should revolve around them. According to this philosophy, mothers should constantly cater to our children's needs and desires by selflessly lavishing our time, money, love, and emotional energy on them and raising them according to guidance provided by experts.[20] Similar variations on this theme go by the names natural parenting or attachment parenting. But science simply doesn't support these extreme practices—and there's evidence they have caused significant harm.

Why do some mothers fall for these ideas? Because they're targeted to us when we're uniquely vulnerable and in need of support.

When we give birth, it's not only a baby who is born. So too is a mother. The late psychiatrist Daniel Stern and pediatrician Nadia Bruschweiler-Stern famously said becoming a mom is one of the most dramatic psychological changes we experience in our lives—so much so that we practically become different people as a result. And one universal thing mothers tend to do is seek advice and affirmation from other moms who have more experience.

"Mothers have a profound need, whether conscious or not, for psychological support that expresses itself in the urge to swap information and observe other mothers in action," Drs. Stern and Bruschweiler-Stern wrote in *The Birth of a Mother: How The Motherhood Experience Changes You Forever.*[21]

Let's also remember that a new mother is often isolated. Immediately after giving birth, many women stick close to home while they physically recover, feed their babies, and try to protect their newborns from illnesses which can be deadly in the first weeks of life. Mom is also exhausted and fragile from the physical effects of pregnancy, childbirth, nighttime feedings, and hormonal changes.

I felt all this profoundly after I gave birth to my first child. After spending my twenties and early thirties working in pressure-cooker jobs in the Obama administration and United Nations, it was, to say the least, an adjustment for me to spend weeks in my apartment mostly alone with my baby after my husband went back to work. I was keenly aware of my privilege to have that time with my daughter, who was a joy—but she wasn't able to keep up her end of a conversation. Leaving home for any length of time was tricky at first, when she never went more than two hours without breastfeeding and we were trying to keep her away from germs.

Even though I could afford childcare, I struggled to find it (as so many mothers do). The idea of handing my newborn over to a stranger I found on Care.com was too nerve-wracking. Then there was everything I needed to learn about how to care for a baby, from treating medical problems to pureeing baby food.

Enter the mommy influencers. While we all increasingly turn to the Internet for information, a new mother goes online all the more in search of a community to support her. Of course, decisions about how to birth and raise our children are personal ones. But, as we saw in Chapter 3, the world just *loves* telling women what to do. And the Internet now offers anyone who can access it—which, in affluent countries, is most people—a platform for foisting their views on mothers, regardless of whether they have any scientific or medical expertise. Leah Plunkett, the *Sharenthood* author, told me this has resulted in a dramatic disruption of previous channels for such information: experts with credentials (like pediatricians and scientists) and personal networks of family, close friends, and community members.

What mothers find online are childbirth and parenting ideas that are sometimes extraordinarily inaccurate and dangerous—like those recipes for homemade infant formula that popped up all over social media when there was a nationwide shortage in 2022. There's unfortunately no safe way to make baby formula at home because it needs to have a precise, complex mix of ingredients that can't all be purchased at the grocery store in order to give babies the nutrients they need—but that didn't stop people from trying to convince desperate moms that they had the answers.[22]

For some women, these kinds of posts about pregnancy and parenting may be a meta level of misinformation, since they may have become pregnant in the first place thanks to unreliable information they found on their phones. According to a 2016 study by medical researchers at Columbia University and Mount Sinai, "most available menstrual cycle tracking apps are inaccurate, contain misleading health information, or do not function."[23] But an app's false claims often aren't obvious to the women who rely on them to try to prevent pregnancies.[24]

In 2018, a hospital in Sweden called for health authorities to investigate the Natural Cycles app after thirty-seven women who had used the app to try to avoid pregnancy showed up at its clinic pregnant.[25] How did the Food and Drug Administration respond? By approving Natural Cycles for use in the United States market a few months later.[26]

Then, when women search for abortion information online, they find "resources" like information about underground providers and home recipes that could kill them.[27] A 2021 study of the top search results for "abortion pill" on Google found that only one contained usable, high-quality resources.[28]

But it's often unclear that what we're reading online is downright dangerous. It's hard even for very educated people to figure out what's true and what's false on the Internet, Michael Specter, author of *Denialism: How Irrational Thinking Hinders Scientific Progress, Harms the Planet, and Threatens Our Lives,* told me.

"People who want to put out disinformation are more sophisticated than ever, and it's not that hard to make a really professional looking website," he said. "So if you're just looking at the Internet, it's really difficult to know which websites are made up lies. They're not labeled, they're not ordered in a particular way, and if you're not a researcher, I'm not sure how you go about knowing which is which. It's a huge problem. Bigger than it's probably ever been."

That's partly because "Google creates advertising algorithms, not information algorithms," Safiya Umoja Noble writes in *Algorithms of Oppression: How Search Engines Reinforce Racism.*[29] Google isn't a library or nonprofit organization designed to bring the information that is most accurate or will serve you best to the top of your search results. It's one of the world's richest companies—and it makes its money by bringing pretty much whatever ads the highest bidders want us to see to the top of our screens.

Another reason the Internet allows people with fringe ideas to make it look like their views enjoy wide support is because social platforms like Facebook and search engines like Google are programmed to serve us content that is similar to what we have already viewed. Search just once for information on home births and you may soon have a feed full of articles and recommended groups devoted to the supposed benefits of "natural" childbirth and parenting. And the more we see a message repeated, the more likely we are to believe it's true.

Other sources like mainstream pregnancy websites and the popular apps that most moms (including me) download the second we find out we're expecting can provide helpful information, and the advice they offer up is often vetted by medical professionals. But they typically warn in their terms of service that they shouldn't be relied upon for medical advice—and rightly so. That's because there are so many different complications that can come up during a pregnancy and so many factors of a woman's health that need to be considered when determining what's best, so women really need to get individualized guidance from their doctors.

But, during pregnancy, questions come up all the time: *Is this type of exercise OK? Is this pain I'm experiencing normal? Can I take a hot bath? Can I carry my toddler? Is this medication I need to take safe for my baby?* And it's not like many OB-GYNs patiently sit down for hours going through all these things with their patients. Plus many women can't just jet off for an appointment to see their doctor every time another question or concern pops up. When I showed up for appointments with the OB-GYN who delivered my first daughter, she often kept me in her waiting room for *hours*.

So, when women have questions, they often turn online to the people who are willing to answer them—who typically aren't gynecologists providing individualized answers. They're people with essential oils and midwife services to sell.

A key place where mothers come to believe extreme ideas about childbirth and parenting is in Facebook groups. What happens when someone expresses contrary views? They're often simply kicked out of the group by moderators, leaving the users who remain in the echo chamber with the deeply inaccurate impression that there is widespread consensus on what they're reading. After the 2016 election, Facebook exacerbated this problem by making posts by members of the groups we join more prominent in our feeds. Facebook has also actively encouraged people to join groups. Group memberships on the site quadrupled between February 2017 and April 2019.[30]

Put this all together and it's easy to understand why expecting and new mothers fall for misinformation. Another big source of it are the sanctimommies.

Social media sanctimommies are mothers who promote their own superiority—and, in the process, may subtly shame other women who don't live up to their standards. One of the endless examples I recently came across on Instagram was a photo of complex origami animals a mom had made with her children. Then there was the photo posted by a well-followed mama of a tea party she had set up as a "surprise" for her two daughters. The image of this table was exactly how I'd picture the setup when Princess Charlotte visits Buckingham Palace. The children were eating on what looked like fine china, replete with heart-shaped sugar cubes, cloth napkins, fresh flowers, and small pastries that appeared straight out of a proper Parisian patisserie. The mom claimed she'd pulled the party together in ten minutes with disposable plates (which bore an uncanny resemblance to porcelain), "DIY sugar cubes," "store bought treats," and "grocery store carnations." I couldn't help but wonder: Am I a lesser mom because my daughters and I use a Fisher Price tea set?

In these kinds of posts, of course, kids never spill their tea and burn themselves and have to go to the emergency room before mom can snap pictures for her followers. Children are never tired or misbehaved. They don't refuse to stare at the camera and smile beatifically, keeping perfectly still so mom has time to nab the perfect shot. Their dresses have never been stained or wrinkled from naps or play, they haven't gotten playdough or dirt under their nails, and they never have snot on their faces from melting down because you didn't let them eat cake for lunch. Instead, their dresses are eternally starched and spar-kling—just like their eyes. When I see these shots, I alternately feel badly about myself for not being able to live this kind of life and badly for the kids in them for not being able to be kids.

In the spirit of this book, do me a favor and try to suspend judg-ment on sanctimommies themselves. As we saw in the previous chapter, these women are often exploited by brands and face pres-sure to post aspirational content in order to make money from spon-sors. Let's instead focus on how influencers affect their audience. By mostly showing their shiny, happy (often secretly scripted) moments, sanctimommies promote a culture of perfectionism that can make moms whose homes aren't perennially gleaming and whose kids aren't preternaturally calm, happy, and well-behaved (as in pretty much all of us) feel like failures. But as mainstream social platforms have come to show us more branded content and fewer posts from our friends, this kind of content has become the new normal.[31]

"Moms today have all but turned motherhood into an Olym-pic sport," Gemma Hartley writes in *FED UP: Emotional Labor, Women, and the Way Forward.* "Especially with the new world of social media, which shows many bright and shining moments of motherhood (and little of the tantrums, mess, and general hor-ror) . . . I know I have fallen victim to aspirational motherhood more than once, looking at the clean, carefully curated photographs of family life on Instagram and wondering what I have to do to get my life to look like that. More laundry? More white paint? More parent-ing books?"[32]

What's more, when mommy influencers are paid for the content they produce about brands, that fact—and its implications—is not always as obvious as it should be to their followers. We can't expect people being paid to promote a product to be very critical of it, so that can lead to misleading product evaluations for mothers. But "as moms, we are easy, vulnerable prey because we're all so exhausted and desperate to give the best to our children," Laura Otton, the New York–based psychotherapist, says.

Of course, the philosophy of intensive mothering that these posts promote predates the arrival of social media. But social platforms have turned the pressure up several notches by creating a space for mompetitions. Just as teen girls compare their lives to others, it's practically impossible to follow mainstream mommy influencers—or even our real-life mom friends—without coming across depictions of their apparently perfect parenting.

"The intensive motherhood practiced by the upper classes and broadcast out—whether it's Gwyneth Paltrow's *GOOP* newsletter suggestion for a kid's lunch box of nori-wrapped vegetable sushi or [Mayim] Bialik's advice that you not give a puking kid Gatorade because it has high-fructose corn syrup—gets slowly integrated as the new parenting normal, even for those without the resources, time, desire, or ability to meet these ratcheted-up demands," Filipovic writes.[33]

Ami Shah, a mom and emergency medicine physician who survived residency with my husband, told me that in the Indian American community in which she was raised, it's common for extended family to pitch in with childcare. But the Indian momfluencers she sees on social media don't usually mention getting help from nannies or family members to pull off their charmed lives. "The lives they're portraying wouldn't be possible without a lot of help, or if they don't have help, then without a lot of struggle and messes and tears, and that's not usually acknowledged," she told me. As a physician, this worries her, because "if you're not acknowledging that help on the daily, a mom could be looking at that, and maybe she's experiencing postpartum anxiety or depression and she can't help but compare herself. That could exacerbate a lot of postpartum issues."

When I spoke to Dr. Tuteur, the obstetrician, she pointed out that many moms try to present themselves as intensive mothers on social media because it lets them show off that they're doing a good job. In some ways, she acknowledged, it makes sense for them to seek validation online, since it's pretty tough to get it directly from young kids.

"There's a lot of doubt involved in parenting," she says. "You never know if you're doing it the right way, and it's not like your child is helping you. Your child isn't saying 'thank you for sending me to time out and helping me learn about delayed gratification.' No, they're lying there on the floor screaming at you."

That's precisely why moms turn to other mothers on social media for answers and affirmation—and why so many are happy to oblige with detailed directions. But there isn't a right way to parent every child because each one is unique. Dr. Tuteur says most parents eventually learn this when their kids get older. But, by then, it's a little late.

In the meantime, trying to follow other people's intensive mothering recipes makes life pretty tough for mommies. Dr. Tuteur points out that "by requiring intense around-the-clock effort, they make it nearly impossible for women who want or need something in addition to mothering (a job, a career, free time) to be 'good' mothers."[34] This, of course, prevents women from achieving equality with men in areas like work, since we can't pursue other accomplishments if we're chained to our children.

It also leaves us constantly stressed. "As any mother could tell you, continuous, uninterrupted proximity to infants and small children is extremely draining," says Dr. Tuteur. "No matter—in the cosmology of attachment parenting, the infant's purported need for physical closeness always trumps the mother's need for physical space and the opportunity to recover her equanimity and maintain her mental health."[35]

Unsurprisingly, research finds that buying into these ideas is bad for us. Women who come to believe in intensive mothering experience more stress and depression and are less satisfied with their lives.[36]

Otton, who specializes in working with moms, told me it's also bad for our kids. She says it's healthy for children to experience multiple caregivers as well as solo play time. And kids are better off with moms who get the space they need to take care of themselves and have strong relationships with their partners.

"After a break, you're excited to see your child," she told me. "You are more patient. You are more silly. You are more fun."

Another thing mommy influencers often signal is their economic status. For example, some moms share that they buy pricey European formula or even donor breastmilk, which at a milk bank would cost $40,500 per year, according to Dr. Tuteur's calculations. But Dr. Tuteur says there's no evidence either is better than regular formula for full-term babies. As she sees it, "infant feeding isn't really about what's best for babies; it's about mothers and the curated image they present to their friends and on social media. Commiserating with other high-status mothers over the laboriousness of importing European formula or accessing donor breastmilk is like fretting over the difficulty of finding good servants. It distinguishes you from those who are less well off and that is the point."[37]

In this sense, social media takes age-old social distinctions and ups their visibility. Now, in case it slipped our minds for a hot minute that other moms have nicer homes or kids who are prodigies, we're bombarded with photos of their latest acquisitions and accomplishments while we scroll through our phones in our bed-rooms at night.

And these reminders don't just come from influencers. My close friend Christina, who is Chinese American, told me she tries to avoid momfluencers online, but thanks to the way influencer cul-ture has permeated our society, her friends post the same kinds of self-promotional content—and she admits she can't help but do so herself, sometimes, too.

Christina has become friends with other moms on the Chinese platform WeChat after meeting through her son's Chinese school or their Long Island neighborhood. "They live by the Chinese ideal of providing for your children and pushing your children to the highest standards of growth and performance," Christina told me. So-called tiger moms and the flaunting of wealth have long existed, of course. But now, on her phone, Christina gets a constant stream of updates on the piano recitals and glamorous globetrotting of her friends' kids. "When I see such content, it often makes me feel like I'm depriving my child of opportunities and he's not doing enough outside of school or going to enough wonderful exotic places," she says.

It's therefore not surprising that moms who use social media often end up not only misinformed but envious and unhappy.

What We Can Do

Motherhood doesn't have to be this way.

We need to start by making sure we don't fall victim to misin-formation for mommies. It's clear that we simply can't trust a lot of what we find on the Internet and read on social media. Instead, we've got to devote our attention to people who share sound infor-mation. Visit my website (Resources, page 234) for a list of content creators with credentials to follow for information about pregnancy and parenting, sans sanctimony.

Before acting on or sharing information, do some independent searching online to figure out whether it's accurate. You can expect any claims to be backed up by links to sources that explain the credentials of the people who did the research, its timeframe, and whether it was peer reviewed (it should be). Consider who the information is coming from, how credible the source is, and what their motivations might be. If it's coming from nonexperts (like people who aren't doctors or scientists sharing medical information) or isn't backed up with scientific evidence, alarm bells should be ringing in your head. If other legitimate sources aren't reporting the same thing, the noise should be getting louder. If your source has something to gain from you acting on the information—they're making money when you buy that natural childbirth guide—the sound should be deafening.

Also, "if you are encountering information and feeling yourself getting emotional, that's a good indication you need to do some extra legwork," Jankowicz told me. That's because a lot of fake news is specifically designed to elicit emotional reactions (which, as we've seen, cause people to like and share social media content more).

Jankowicz used a weekly pregnancy guide created by Britain's National Health Service (Resources, page 234).[38] Confused about a source or need more information? Ask your obstetrician, primary care provider, or pediatrician. And check out the websites of the CDC, American College of Obstetricians and Gynecologists, and American Academy of Pediatrics for detailed information and recommendations.

It's also critical for us to choose doctors who will listen to us and act on our needs and concerns. "Women are so conditioned to want people to like us and we feel like if our doctor doesn't like us we might not get the care we need," Dr. Rana Awdish, the pulmonary and critical care physician, told me. "We need to turn the tables on that. Women should make sure their doctors make them feel heard. Our assessment of our needs should be given the same degree of importance as the physician's font of knowledge."

Here's a place where social media can actually be helpful: ask for recommendations of OB-GYNs with whom other women in your community have had good experiences on a local moms group. Dr. Awdish also recommends carefully reading public reviews of physicians and says you can even consider meeting with several doctors before choosing one who you feel confident will be responsive to you.

"It's incredibly time consuming and laborious—and incredibly important," she says. "It's bananas that people do more research on what car to buy than on who is potentially going to do your surgery."

Dr. Shah said residency programs and medical, physician assistant, and nursing schools should also incorporate more training on how medical providers should respond to women's complaints of pain without minimizing them.

Another thing we can all do today is stop participating in mompetitions. If you choose to post pictures of your kids, you don't need to use filters, Photoshop, or professional photographers. It's okay to show messy playrooms in the background (what kid's play space *doesn't* look like a cyclone just blew through?) instead of the fake red barn backdrops used by the family photographers we find on our town's Facebook moms group. The more we start showing what parenting really looks like, the more we'll give other moms permission to do the same. It starts with us.

We also can't let social media sanctimommies make us feel less than. Otton recommends checking in with yourself on how you're feeling after you view different kinds of social media content. "As moms we have this fear of not doing a good enough job for our children because we love them so much," she told me. "So we all have different things we feel insecure about, and in those areas we should only follow people who make us feel validated, inspired, and lifted up."

Otton says if you can view particular momfluencer content and then shrug your shoulder, think that it's nice that that worked out for them and move on with your day, you have a green light to keep consuming it. "But if you're feeling a sense of failure, it's time to unfollow those sorts of people and broaden who you follow to be a diverse, humorous base of women who give you a real picture of what motherhood is like—and they are out there," she says.

Also keep thinking about whether you're getting what you want from the content you consume, Otton says. "Ask yourself, 'how is this serving or not serving me? What do I want to get from this? Am I getting it? Is it helping me?' These answers will change over time."

Of course, you may be more reluctant to unfriend your actual friends. But when you see their posts, remind yourself that, as we saw in Chapter 1, people often share the glamorized versions of their lives. What's more, "we all have a desire to fit in and be accepted and be loved and supported by our peers, and sometimes we think that in order to get love and acceptance and approval we have to do the same thing as other people," Vijayeta Sinh, PhD, a New Jersey–based psychologist and mom, told me. "Remember that we are individuals and can make the choices that are best for us. I often think, yes, it would be nice to have a clean home but I'm not going to sacrifice time with my kids in order to keep my house pristine."

In this world of mompetitions, Otton says it's also important for mothers to remind ourselves that what makes us good moms is the love we have for our children. "It's not the perfection," she says. "A home birth doesn't make you a good mom or a good person. Being on top of your laundry doesn't make you a good person."

We also have to make sure we have a healthy group of mom friends off social media. "Community is not a luxury," Otton warns. "It is a necessity for us to feel happy and healthy. Flat out, hands down, period. Seeing people face-to-face keeps us physically and mentally healthy. It gives us a sense of purpose and belonging and allows us to help others, which is so healthy for us. We need to feel that."

Of course, we'll find plenty of sanctimommies in the real world, too. But if you're lucky like me, you'll also find a group of women like the moms I met at baby yoga after my first daughter was born, who are honest about how hard parenting can be and choose to cheer one another on. We all must be and befriend those people.

As for a lot of what we find on social media, we need to be aware that we're up against the motherload of misinformation. Instead of internalizing ideologies about why women should do things like undergo excruciating, potentially deadly medical events anywhere other than a hospital bed, let's instead put these crazy, dangerous, misogynistic ideas to bed.

HOW ANTI-VAXXERS TARGET WOMEN

On September 18, 2007, actress and comedian Jenny McCarthy—one of the most prominent moms who argues that her child's autism was caused by vaccines—appeared as a guest on *The Oprah Winfrey Show*. In the interview, McCarthy discussed how she obtained information without relying on reputable experts or doctors: by searching on Google. "The University of Google is where I got my degree from," McCarthy explained.[1]

Sadly, the University of Google has some of the most prominent disinformation around.

"Type the word 'vaccination' into Google and one of the first of the fifteen million or so listings that pops up, after the Centers for Disease Control, is the National Vaccine Information Center, an organization that, based on its name, certainly sounds like a federal agency," Michael Specter writes in *Denialism: How Irrational Thinking Hinders Scientific Progress, Harms the Planet, and Threatens Our Lives*. "Actually, that is just the opposite: the NVIC is the most powerful anti-vaccine organization in America."[2]

In the last chapter, we saw how moms are targeted with misinformation about pregnancy and parenting. Another form of parenting disinformation we're up against is flat-out, straight-up lies claiming vaccinations that are critical to our children's health are dangerous. It started with disinformation about routine childhood vaccinations, which fed into the skepticism the majority of

American parents later had about Covid-19 shots. And women are the main targets of anti-vaxxers.

"Anti-vaccine activists tend to aim at women because we make the medical decisions in our families," Dorit Reiss, a law professor at UC College of the Law, San Francisco who has studied the anti-vaccine movement, told me.

Renée DiResta, research manager at the Stanford Internet Observatory, has spent years studying anti-vaccine groups on social media. She told me that, while movement leaders are largely men, "the vast, overwhelming majority of rank-and-file members are women."

A 2019 study found three times more women than men in anti-vaccine groups on Facebook—with women even more over-represented among the most active users.[3] They're often the same moms who are interested in #natural childbirth and parenting, yoga, essential oils, and now, QAnon.[4] (QAnons believe there's a secret cabal of Democrats who worship the devil while trafficking in and consuming the blood of children, Covid-19 was a hoax, Joe Biden didn't win the 2020 election, Democrats are conspiring to take over the world, and only Donald Trump can save us.[5] Seriously.)

As the use of the Internet and social media has exploded since 2000, so has vaccine skepticism. In January 2019, the Royal Society for Public Health in the United Kingdom found that half of parents of children under age two were exposed to inaccurate information about vaccines online[6]—and that was *before* all the conspiracy theories about Covid-19 vaccines began circulating. In the United States, between 2001 and 2017, the number of children who didn't receive any vaccines by age two more than quadrupled, according to the CDC.[7]

Here's the truth: if you don't want your child to die, one of the smartest things you can do is get them vaccinated. Vaccines are "the most powerful public health tool ever invented in order to save human lives," Peter Hotez, co-director of the Texas Children's Hospital Center for Vaccine Development and dean of the National School of Tropical Medicine at Baylor College of Medicine, told me. Before they were introduced, millions of Americans contracted sometimes fatal diseases each year that are now prevented with routine childhood vaccinations.[8]

But that's not what you may learn if you search for vaccine information online. Researchers at the University of San Diego looked at 480 different anti-vaccine websites and found that roughly two-thirds claim that vaccines are dangerous. Two-thirds also link vaccines to autism, even though these contentions are "plain wrong." The vast majority advise people not to trust the government, and 42 percent warn not to trust health practitioners.[9]

Like "natural" childbirth and intensive mothering, the roots of the anti-vaccine movement predate the widespread use of the Internet—but social media put it on steroids. In 1998, the prestigious British medical journal *The Lancet* published a study by gastroenterologist Andrew Wakefield and colleagues, claiming that a small number of children began displaying symptoms of autism shortly after receiving the measles-mumps-rubella (MMR) vaccine. The journalist Brian Deer later reported that Wakefield had failed to disclose that he'd been paid to study those children for a lawsuit against drug manufacturers. Shortly before publication of the study, Wakefield had filed for a patent on an independent measles vaccine that would be in demand if his results were believed because it would be administered separately from inoculations for other diseases.[10] In other words, he was a fraud.

It took twelve years for *The Lancet* to retract the article.[11] Wakefield was also removed from the medical register in the United Kingdom, rendering him unable to practice.[12] One of the numerous later revelations about Wakefield was that he had blood taken from children who were guests at his son's birthday party for research (he compensated them each with 5 pounds).[13]

By then, however, the toothpaste was out of the tube and there was no way of getting it back in. Over the years, other purported experts have piled on. In 2001, an article in the journal *Medical Hypotheses* suggested autism might be caused by thimerosal, an ingredient in some vaccines. The claim was taken up in an entire book edited by none other than Robert F. Kennedy, Jr. Since then, in the United States, thimerosal has been mostly eliminated in vaccines given to children with no corresponding decrease in autism rates.[14]

The next salvo came in 2007, when California pediatrician Robert Sears published *The Vaccine Book: Making the Right Decision for Your Child*, a bestseller which suggests children should not be vaccinated based on schedules recommended by the CDC and American Academy of Pediatrics. The book is based on his unsubstantiated speculation that it could be harmful to receive too many vaccines at once.[15]

"The notion that vaccines could overwhelm the immune system is a fantasy," Paul Offit, a physician and director of the vaccine education center at Children's Hospital of Pennsylvania, told me. That's because the immunological challenge created by vaccines is a minuscule fraction of what a child's body fights every day.

Some now claim maybe the aluminum in vaccines is unsafe, even though research proves the idea baseless.[16] But these ideas are new ways to inculcate unwarranted doubts about vaccines. Ultimately,

Dr. Hotez says, "public engagement with the anti-vaccine movement is a bit like the arcade game of whack-a-mole, in which knocking down the different claims that vaccines cause autism results in a new or alternative allegation."[17]

There's no question that anti-vaxxers are mistaken. Dr. Hotez points out that numerous extremely rigorous, large studies conducted in the United States, Canada, Europe, Australia, and Japan and published in the most prestigious peer reviewed publications have repeatedly documented that there isn't a link between vaccines and autism.[18] In his three decades as a scientist and physician, he says, "I have not seen anything close to this amount of scientific evidence refuting a causal association between an intervention and a medical condition. In my opinion, efforts to study autism and its possible relationship with vaccines rank among the most thorough investigations in all of biomedical science."[19]

Dr. Hotez also says the evidence suggests that autism develops before a baby is born, which means vaccines given after birth *couldn't possibly* be the cause.[20] In fact, at this point, he says, all this research on vaccines is distracting scientists from finding the actual causes of autism.[21] If any vaccine scientist should want to get to the bottom of what causes autism, it would be Dr. Hotez: his own daughter, Rachel, has a severe form of autism, which led him to write an entire book called *Vaccines Did Not Cause Rachel's Autism*.

But parents who buy into this deadly disinformation and choose not to vaccinate their children don't just put their own kids' lives at risk—they also endanger babies, who usually don't receive their first doses of measles vaccines, for example, until they're a year old.[22] Other children who are undergoing treatments like chemotherapy can't be vaccinated, so they're dependent on those around them to get immunized. Otherwise, with their weakened immune systems, they're especially vulnerable if there's an outbreak.[23]

Here's an example of what happens when parents decide not to vaccinate their children. Remember Dr. Bob Sears, of make-your-own-vaccine-schedule fame? In 2008, one of his patients, a seven-year-old boy, returned to California with the measles after a vacation with his family in Switzerland. As Seth Mnookin, author of *The Panic Virus: A True Story of Medicine, Science, and Fear* points out, thanks to this one family's decision, the virus spread to a pediatrician's office, two supermarkets, a swim school, and a charter school. Passengers on a flight to Hawaii had to be quarantined on a military base. Forty-eight children had to be quarantined in their homes (average cost per family: $775). A ten-month-old child was hospitalized and needed medical care for a month. The outbreak cost over $10 million.[24]

Why do anti-vaxxers continue to promote such dangerous ideas despite the devastating potential consequences? Like the natural childbirth industry, Dr. Offit says the anti-vaccine movement is motivated by financial interests. "Anti-vaccine organizations now work hand-in-glove with personal-injury lawyers, many of whom sit on their advisory boards and help them prepare pamphlets that warn of the dangers of vaccines and describe how to collect money," he explains.[25] And, Dr. Offit told me, anti-vaxxers prey on parents' desperate desire to do something for their autistic children by selling them dietary supplements and other dubious products.

Online influencers also sell books, documentaries, essential oils, and access to bootcamps about how to indoctrinate others. According to a 2021 report by the Center for Public Integrity, "although the total value of anti-vaccine businesses is unknown, records indicate that the top influencers alone make up a multimillion-dollar industry." For example, Ty and Charlene Bollinger sell a documentary called "The Truth About Vaccines," for which one mom reported paying around $200. At that rate, the Center points out that the

Bollingers, who said they've sold 25,000 copies, would have made $5 million from this product alone.[26]

Amy Pisani, CEO of the advocacy group Vaccinate Your Family, told me she wonders whether many prominent anti-vaxxers actually believe vaccines are harmful. "We don't think they're authentically against vaccines," she says. "They're just making millions of dollars selling their products."

The content is also a big moneymaker for social media companies. The Center for Countering Digital Hate estimates that anti-vaccination users are worth up to $1 billion each year to these platforms, based on calculations of the amount of money anti-vaxxers spend on ads and the value of selling ads targeted to anti-vaxxers.[27]

Why have so many moms (and dads) clung to a movement instigated by a man who would invite kids to his child's birthday party and then take their blood? And how has this movement that puts children's lives in danger gained such force on social media?

"After their child is diagnosed with autism, mothers go online to look for hope because that's what good mothers do," Reiss says. "Anti-vaccine groups offer hope and treatment," she points out. Never mind that those essential oils and dietary supplements don't work. We all know how hard it is to think clearly when we're worried about our children.

Anti-vaxxers also offer moms a sense of community and belonging. Put yourself in the shoes of a parent whose child has a severe form of autism. They might face social ostracization for the behaviors their child exhibits in public.

"There are no knowing winks when a child won't stop screaming, no 'I've been there' grins [from strangers] when he defecates in public," Mnookin points out. So parents of children with autism might turn to social media to find people who understand what they're going through. Mnookin says that this "sense of being cut off from the world helps to explain why tens of thousands of parents have gravitated to a close-knit community that stretches around the globe. The fact that the community's most vocal and active members believe that vaccines cause autism . . . is of secondary importance—what's paramount is the sense of fellowship and support its members receive."[28]

This same need to overcome isolation can help explain why women become leaders in the movement. Catherine Flores, executive director of the California Immunization Coalition, told me, "stay-at-home mothers have developed camaraderie and found support, along with validation" in online anti-vaxx circles. "Some became leaders and that made them even more interested and interesting to people," she says. "It really builds people up." Think about it: how much other validation does our society give stay-at-home moms?

Pisani told me one way anti-vaxxers grow their movement is by targeting parents whose babies have just died and (falsely) convincing them that vaccines were to blame. One poster child for the movement is Evee Clobes, who according to a medical examiner suffocated and died while sleeping in her mother's bed in 2019, when she was six months old. But shortly after her mom posted about her daughter's death on social media, she was contacted by anti-vaxxers. Evee's mom now says she's convinced the vaccines Evee received 36 hours before she died were responsible for her death. Other babies who died as a result of SIDS or co-sleeping are also used to try to convince parents not to vaccinate their children.[29]

Preying on people when they're in crisis and therefore most vulnerable is a classic move in the conspiracist playbook. For example, a University of Maryland study found that 83 percent of women who were converted to the QAnon conspiracy theory and went on to commit crimes were radicalized after their children were physically and/or sexually abused by a family member or romantic partner.[30]

What's more, humans are more drawn to negative information—like warnings about the dangers of vaccines—than positive information. Why are we wired this way? Probably because paying attention to things like the arrival of a predator kept our ancestors alive. So our brains are primed to look for negative developments. When we find them, we react far more intensely to them than we do to positive news.[31] This can help explain why, online, we share more posts about negative things.[32] A story about a baby who died after getting a vaccine is emotional and can quickly go viral. Meanwhile, we don't talk about the children whose lives were saved by vaccines because there's no sensational story to tell—they never got sick in the first place.

It's hard to penetrate this misinformation with facts because of our filter bubbles on social media. A 2019 study of X (then called Twitter) conversations about vaccines found that anti-vaxxers tend to communicate mainly with other anti-vaxxers, much like the way Republicans interact with other Republicans and Democrats talk to other Dems. The study warned that this clustering makes "it difficult for health organizations to penetrate and counter opinionated information."[33]

Even if the information does get through, few people like to admit (even to themselves) that they're wrong. So, to reconcile that cognitive dissonance, people simply seek out other information to affirm their beliefs.[34]

As we saw in Chapter 5, when like-minded people get together, they become even more confident in their beliefs, which makes them more extreme. And when people can hide behind their screens, they say and do things they'd never have the audacity to do in person. This was a common refrain among the vaccine experts I interviewed.

One anti-vaccine influencer, Mike Adams, known as the "Health Ranger," has compared the people who defend vaccines to Nazi war criminals. When a reporter for the Center for Public Integrity investigated the Bollingers, Adams doxed her and called for his followers to contact her. She received more than 100 messages that were "vulgar, insulting or threatening," according to the Center. One commenter responded to Adams, "I butcher a family as easy as stepping on a roach."[35]

In 2019, just before the coronavirus pandemic began in the United States, the state of Washington declared a public health emergency amid a measles outbreak. What happened when moms turned to Facebook for information in the midst of this crisis? *The Guardian* found that they saw "unscientific, anti-vaccination propaganda." The paper "found that Facebook search results for groups and pages with information about vaccines were dominated by anti-vaccination propaganda, and that YouTube's recommendation algorithm steers viewers from fact-based medical information toward anti-vaccine misinformation."[36]

This is the environment that existed on social media when the Covid-19 pandemic began in early 2020. Parents had been primed to be deeply skeptical of safe, effective, life-saving vaccines by people who had enjoyed license for years to build up their lucrative empires on social networks by peddling conspiracies and their accompanying documentaries and "wellness" products. Mothers were on the frontlines, increasingly getting their information from self-anointed experts on social media instead of the medical community.

Covid Conspiracies

So, when Covid vaccines finally became available, social media continued to serve as a petri dish for deadly misinformation, like the lies that the vaccine had killed over 45,000 people[37] or caused—say it with me now—autism. A 2020 study by the Center for Countering Digital Hate found that anti-vaxxers quickly grew their reach, earning over 58 million followers on social media.[38] And an August 2020 report by Avaaz found that the top ten sources of misinformation were getting nearly four times as many estimated Facebook views as the ten leading health authorities.[39]

As we saw in Chapter 7, on social media, a tiny group of people can make a conspiracy seem true. Another study by the Center for Countering Digital Hate found that 65 percent of the misinformation on the Covid vaccine on Facebook and X (then called Twitter) was disseminated by twelve people. Not 12 million or 12,000. Just twelve![40] They include Robert F. Kennedy, Jr., the Bollingers, and Joseph Mercola, a peddler of dietary supplements and other dubious cures.

Every single one of them directly targeted mothers. A 2022 study of the content of the so-called "disinformation dozen" found that they primarily stuck to themes that mothers who decided against vaccinating their kids were protecting and doting on their children and relying on their intuitions.[41] And, by the way, the majority of these people telling women how to be ideal mothers were *men*.[42]

Anti-vaxxers also glommed on to the comments sections on Facebook posts to sow doubts about accurate information, exploiting a massive vulnerability in the company's software to detect misinformation. According to documents leaked by former Facebook staffer Frances Haugen, one data scientist at the company wrote that the company's capability to detect misinformation in comments was "bad in English, and basically non-existent elsewhere." That helps explain why, according to an internal memo, a staggering roughly 41 percent of English-language comments on posts about vaccines risked discouraging them.[43]

So it's not surprising that using social media is directly linked to vaccine skepticism: people who used social media more than traditional media to get information about Covid-19 were much less likely to say they'd definitely or probably get a Covid vaccine.[44] A May 2021 study found that 81 percent of people who said they definitely wouldn't get Covid vaccines had been exposed to at least one common myth about the vaccine and either believed the myth to be true or weren't sure whether it was true.[45]

Between January 2021 and April 2022, half the people who died of Covid might have survived if they'd chosen to get vaccinated, according to researchers at Brown School of Public Health, Brigham and Women's Hospital, Harvard T.H. Chan School of Public Health, and Microsoft AI for Health. This means that at least 318,000 Covid deaths could have been prevented during this time period alone.[46]

What's more, disinformation expert Nina Jankowicz told me that once women start to believe anti-vaccine conspiracies, they're targeted with more. "Covid or other alternative health misinformation is often the gateway to other conspiracy theories and misinformation," she says. "People say, 'you're into yoga, let's talk about how vaccines are bad.' Then it's 'let's not use any pain medication during birth, don't have support from a doctor during birth.' Beyond that, it's 'the medical system and government are lying to you because they're trafficking children and drinking blood.' There aren't that many steps from a healthy skepticism of the medical system to 'let's overthrow the government,' and that scares me. I've seen it happen."

It happens in two main ways, Jankowicz says. Some women are directly recruited. In an anti-vaxx group, "you make an online 'friend' who adds you to another group or sends you this website and here's all this health misinformation and a little anti-government bit snuck in there," she told me. The other mechanism is through social networks themselves, who realize a woman is into health misinformation and begin to recommend other conspiracies. Like anti-vaxxers, QAnon preys on women's maternal instincts by asking them to "save the children" from an imaginary child exploitation and trafficking ring. That's how the soccer mom next door becomes a "QAmom."[47]

In July 2021, White House officials were so furious about their inability to get social networks to crack down on misinformation about Covid vaccines that President Biden publicly accused them of "killing people"[48] (a claim he later walked back)[49] and surgeon general Vivek Murthy called vaccine misinformation on social media "an urgent threat to public health."[50]

Researchers recently built a model extrapolating current trends which found that anti-vaccination views could become the predominant perspective in the next ten years.[51] The vast majority of parents ignored the advice of the American Academy of Pediatrics to vaccinate their children against Covid. As of April 2023, the majority of children under age 12 hadn't received a single Covid vaccine.[52]

One of the most frightening and apparently effective lies about the Covid vaccine has been targeted directly to women: the canard that it causes infertility. The far-right conspiracy theorist Alex Jones, for example, told followers that if they were vaccinated, "you're not going to be able to have children."[53]

The idea gained credence because its proponents cleverly exploited the way the medical community perpetually ignores women. After getting the Covid vaccine, some women reported changes to their menstrual periods. (Researchers later confirmed that vaccines tended to delay periods by a day.)[54] But because women's periods weren't initially studied as part of clinical trials on the vaccines, there wasn't a way to know whether the reports were true at first.[55]

So anti-vaxxers took advantage of the information gap to make a false claim that would uniquely frighten women and girls. Soon, vaccinated people were being asked not to enter some places—from a private school in Florida to a butcher shop in Ontario, Canada—out of the paranoid fear they would "shed" their virus (this is scientifically impossible) and cause the women around them to have miscarriages or become infertile. Where were people reading this inaccurate information about shedding? On social media, of course.[56]

By June 2021, more than half of people who didn't plan to get vaccinated falsely believed the vaccines could hurt women's fertility.[57] This misinformation especially endangered the lives of pregnant women who chose not to get vaccinated. Pregnant women who contracted Covid were more likely to miscarry, go into labor early, deliver stillborn babies, and die—but, of all the groups at increased risk of severe outcomes from the virus, they seemed to least understand these risks. Shocking numbers of pregnant women remained unvaccinated against Covid in early 2023.[58]

Social networks have tried cracking down on this misinformation. But their efforts haven't begun to match the scale of the problem. Another challenge, DiResta points out, is that anti-vaxxers have tapped into support from far-right groups by making arguments that the government shouldn't be able to mandate vaccines—and such claims often don't run afoul of community standards.[59]

All this vaccine skepticism may be making people more distrustful of medicine, period. A 2022 survey found one in five Americans turn to TikTok before their actual doc for health information, while the majority—65 percent—turn to Google first.[60] This doesn't bode well for mothers, who we all know will be the ones left to care for family members who suffer medical consequences from going without proper treatment.

In the future, expect the primary targets of anti-vaxxers to continue to be mothers. "If and when Covid starts to dissipate, it's not like they're just going to fold up the tent and go home," Dr. Hotez told me. "They're looking around for what's next, and that's going to be stopping mandatory childhood vaccinations."

What We Can Do

What has Congress done so far about vaccine misinformation on social media? Exactly nothing. With legislators asleep at the wheel and even the leader of the free world unable to convince social networks to do more, the burden for not falling prey to sophisticated misinformation about children has been left almost entirely on the shoulders of the people in our society who are already so overburdened with responsibilities: mothers.

In Chapter 7, I talked about how we have to be savvy about spotting misinformation on social media. But, while social networks shouldn't be the arbiters of proper parenting, they should be better about deplatforming vaccine misinformation. As we've seen, a relatively small number of people are responsible for most of the misinformation around topics like vaccines. So finding and removing the bulk of it isn't nearly as complicated as these companies sometimes make it out to be.

Then, to start to correct the damage they've done, social networks must keep prominently amplifying vaccine information from legitimate, credentialed sources. Since the more people see information the more they believe it, social networks should be flooding our feeds with these facts.

Social networks also need to hire more human moderators. Another reason information that violates the community standards of social networks is ubiquitous on these platforms is because machines aren't smart enough to ferret it out. Although Mark Zuckerberg has claimed that artificial intelligence can identify and remove problematic content, documents leaked by Haugen show that's largely untrue. One group of Facebook staffers found that the company's automated systems remove far less than one percent of content in violation of its policies against incitement and violence, for example.[61] On the other hand, Snapchat has human moderators review news content before promoting it. User-generated videos promoted by the company are also reviewed by human moderators before they can be watched by more than twenty-five people.[62] It's a great model for other companies.

Social networks also need to stop exploiting their human moderators, so they can do their jobs properly over the long term. Think people who work for tech companies enjoy fat paychecks and lavish benefits? Think again. Content moderators are often contract employees who work for lousy pay and are sometimes left with lasting trauma after reviewing disturbing content for a living.[63] These people deserve well-paying, permanent jobs with benefits and loads of support—especially given the invaluable service they're doing to social media companies and our society.

Because social networks have been so irresponsible in allowing vaccine misinformation to spread, lawmakers also need to step in. As I have argued for CNN, Congress should pass a law amending Section 230 of the Communications Decency Act—which, as we've seen, protects social networks from responsibility for what their users post—by outlawing content that endangers people's lives (like vaccine misinformation) and gets more than 10,000 shares, comments, or likes.[64] We can't expect social networks to ferret out every nutty thing anyone in the world writes. But we can—and must—hold them responsible for keeping an eye on content that goes viral and making sure it isn't potentially deadly. Social networks that fail to remove these kinds of posts should be slapped with big fines, which would also—perhaps more crucially—create embarrassing public spectacles their executives would be keen to avoid.

Social media companies should also be fined when their algorithms amplify misinformation that endangers lives. We should reasonably expect social networks to ensure that the content they choose to promote isn't dangerous—especially since we know that the way they generate their mega profits is by carefully curating content (for which they often don't compensate creators, by the way) that is designed to keep us glued to our computer screens.

One way these companies have managed to avoid regulation of their algorithms for so long is through classic mansplaining—trying to convince us the way they're programmed is impossibly complex and we couldn't possibly understand. But here's a concept we can make super simple for them: they're responsible for what the products they build do.

Still, given how long it took social networks to wake up to the true impact of vaccine misinformation and other kinds of fake news, we have to believe they'll be slow to act on the next kinds of attempts to misinform us, too. So we all have to get smarter about identifying inaccurate information. Extremism expert Mia Bloom and psychologist Sophia Moskalenko have smartly suggested that libraries offer classes for adults on how to spot fake news. As an added bonus, Bloom and Moskalenko point out that women would meet one another in these classes—which would help foster female friendships offline.[65]

While fact-checking shouldn't become another form of unpaid labor women give our society, we should flag the misinformation we see online for social networks to take down when we can.

Finally, I hope it's clear by now that social media shouldn't be your source of medical information. Unless social networks stop hosting deadly disinformation, it's simply not where we should turn for our answers. Instead, rely on the CDC, your primary care physician, your pediatrician, the American Academy of Pediatrics, and reports published in reliable mainstream media outlets or peer-reviewed academic journals.

As for anti-vaxxers, it's up to us to give them the most devastating response possible in modern times: we should simply ignore them. As we can see, they're not really our friends at all.

THE FLOUNCE

Palestinian-American feminist activist Linda Sarsour has been working with refugee and immigrant women for years, but she came into the national spotlight when she served as one of the co-chairs of the Women's March, which took place the day after Donald Trump took office in January 2017.

"Here I was on this intersectional stage, bringing women and allies together, and the far right was like, 'yeah, that's not going to work,'" Sarsour told me. So people began spreading lies about her, suggesting she was a fundamentalist radical Muslim who hated Jewish people.

The narrative spread like wildfire on social media. Advance Democracy, Inc., a nonprofit public interest research organization, later revealed why: the messaging coming out of the American far right was being amplified by Russian trolls.

The false claims about Sarsour were part of a broader set of posts from fake accounts, posing as conservatives or Black women, for example, claiming they felt left out of the feminist movement—all seeding a familiar narrative that American women are hopelessly divided and at war with one another. But the Russians posted at least 2,642 times about Sarsour alone, according to the Advance Democracy analysis, because they realized messages about her were most effective.[1]

Why? It's not just that she's a woman. It's that she's a *Muslim* woman. "My identity was weaponized because of the acceptability of Islamophobia in America," Sarsour told me. "The Russians figured out it's one of the main types of bigotry in America that is accept-able and there's no consequences for it, so let's go after this Muslim woman and she will be our weapon to undermine this powerful, intersectional women's movement."

Women who are Muslim, Latina, Black, brown, trans, lesbian, and/or nonbinary are the people in our society who come under the greatest social media siege. And here's what it does to them. "When I think back on it, I'll be honest, I'm triggered," Sarsour told me. "I'm triggered by the avalanche of it all. For 20 months straight, my life was under constant attack. I became an Internet fugitive, running from the Internet, choosing to marginalize myself because even if I said 'good morning America,' I would be trolled."

"The trolling escalated to people knowing my whereabouts and showing up in the spaces I'm in and the targeting of my family," Sarsour recalls. "My mom still has voicemail on her landline. She's an old immigrant woman whose second language is English listening to these really hateful things."

Sarsour told me she's tried to correct some of the lies about her, but "the thing about the Internet is if you say something enough times, it must be true." Now, she lives with a cloud over her name that she thinks will stay with her forever. She told me she doesn't think she'd ever be hired in a traditional corporate job. Or even a nonprofit position for which she's eminently qualified. "If I saw a vice president of diversity, equity, and inclusion job at a university and I thought, let me go apply, I'd probably have a really hard time getting that," she says.

Of course, not all users have to deal with online abuse. Social media has basically become a tale of two communities.

"As a straight white guy, I'm not going to get things like the death threats on [X]," Internet security expert Bruce Schneier told me with a shrug.

But, like Sarsour, 38 percent of women have been victims of online violence, according to a 2020 study conducted in fifty-one countries.[2] Justice Department records show that 70 percent of the people who are stalked online are women. (Over 80 percent of defendants are male.)[3] According to Amnesty International, Black, Asian, Latinx, and mixed-race women are 34 percent more likely than white women to be named in abusive or problematic posts. Black women are 84 percent more likely than white women to face this abuse.[4] After Kamala Harris was named as Joe Biden's running mate in 2020, one analysis found that at least 3,000 false claims were shared about her per hour on X (then called Twitter) alone.[5]

Renee Bracey Sherman, a Black reproductive rights activist, told me the online hate she gets is both misogynistic *and* racist. "The violent rhetoric and harassment is doubled in every way," she says. "I don't just get called the c word, I get called the n word and the c word. The threats aren't just violent rape threats, they're violent rape threats with references to slavery or racist violence."

In Chapter 5, I talked about how social media has enabled new kinds of sexual crimes, radicalized men to commit violence against women, and facilitated their introductions to victims. But that's just the start. If you're a woman on social media these days—or even if you never set up a single account—it's hard to keep up with the dizzying kinds of abuse you could face online.

Maybe someone will set up a fake profile using your name and photo and offer people sexual images in exchange for cash.[6] Maybe someone will surreptitiously snap a photo of you bending over in a skirt and post it on an online forum devoted to the genre. Maybe you'll be doxed. Then people can swat you (call the police and claim there's a major crime happening in your home, so a SWAT team storms your house, often in the middle of the night, and could accidentally kill you or your family[7]).

*   *   *

Transgender women also get the motherload of online hate. It was December 2022 when Sunny Laprade, a 22-year-old trans woman, had such a bad stomachache that she had to call out of work. So Sunny, a Brooklyn-based comedian and content creator, made a TikTok saying maybe she was finally getting her period. Sunny knows that, since she doesn't have female reproductive organs, she won't ever really have a menstrual cycle—so this was obviously intended to be a joke. But the conservative accounts Libs of TikTok and PragerU shared her video, presumably to suggest transgender people are deranged. Sunny received such a flood of hateful messages that she took the post down.

There's a term for when tons of trolls all gang up on a single woman. It's called brigading—and it's terrifying. Sunny told me when she reports this kind of abuse to social networks, "either nothing will happen or something will happen 2 months later. But you need something to happen relatively instantaneously for it to have any tangible effect." What's more, Sunny's haters report her to social networks all the time, so she's had her account banned and been restricted from posting in the past.

"I don't do anything controversial, I just exist on the Internet," Sunny told me. "Meanwhile these people known for sending bomb threats to a children's hospital can do whatever they please." (In 2022, after Libs of TikTok started targeting medical workers who care for transgender kids, Boston Children's Hospital received a bomb threat, though the threat has not been directly tied to the group.[8])

On social media, Sunny is also a frequent victim of deadnaming, which is when people use the name a transgender person went by before transitioning. "It's such a fucking fight to get people to recognize me for who I am," she told me. To change her legal name, "I've spent the past couple months going to court multiple times and to the DMV and to the Social Security office and I still have to go to the passport place and where they keep your birth certificate. This all takes time and money, and I still have to pay the rent and maintain my relationships with friends."

After all that, she says, "for someone who has never known me to go through the whole process of googling me to find my deadname just to be mean on social media, that sucks extra. The world is not overwhelmingly kind to trans people, and if I'm having a rough day and I get a notification on my phone that's my deadname, sometimes that's just the last thing, the cherry on a cake made of shit."

All the abuse she takes online also leaves Sunny fearful of her physical safety. When she makes videos, she records with a blank wall behind her and keeps her windows closed, so people can't get clues about her location. "There are crazy people who can get info from my internet presence and hurt me in real material ways or come after my family or something," she told me.

While Sunny is openly transgender, deadnaming can be especially dangerous for people who aren't, Admiral Rachel Levine, a physician who as assistant secretary of health is the highest-ranking openly transgender person in the United States government, told me. "Transgender and nonbinary women are victims of violence and even murder," Dr. Levine said. "If someone is deadnamed and outed, it could literally put their lives at risk. And it can certainly open them up to online bullying, which can lead to depression and suicide."

Erique Zhang, the scholar who studies representations of trans people, told me that attacks like these don't just affect the trans people who experience them. When other people who are coming out of the closet witness these things, it can make them feel that it's not safe to be open about their own identities. "I can see how seeing someone put in harm's way would scare some people off from openly identifying as trans or even deciding to continue to transition," they said.

Zhang also said that the hate toward trans people that is raging online is likely what's fueling a wave of legislative proposals to restrict their rights—from denying people medical care to preventing them from using public restrooms. It's also likely emboldening people to commit physical violence against trans people. According to the Human Rights Campaign, 2021 was the deadliest year on record for people who identify as nonbinary and transgender.[9]

Dr. Levine says the hate is also being fueled by online misinformation. "There are so many claims on social media that there are only two genders, that gender is fixed, that trans individuals are groomers of young people to change their gender identities, that there's a social contagion so when young people hear of trans issues they want to be trans because it's cool, and that gender affirmation treatment is harmful," Dr. Levine told me. "None of it is true. When youth are accepted in their families, communities, and schools and have access to an evidence-based standard of care for gender affirming treatment, they have excellent mental health outcomes."

But a lot of this misinformation is coming from accounts with huge followings, like the ones that targeted Sunny. Zoë Quinn, the game developer you heard from in Chapter 1, says social media platforms are less inclined to ban accounts with lots of followers—even if they spew misinformation and hate—since they bring in so much traffic and revenue. So the interests of social media companies and hateful influencers that Quinn calls "Internet Inquisitors" are sometimes sickeningly aligned.[10]

And Quinn says the reason Internet Inquisitors invest so much time creating content attacking other people is because they make money from it, too. In fact, Quinn says, "you can make a career from online abuse."[11]

The "Short Skirt of the Internet"

Women who dare to share our opinions online are also especially vulnerable to attack. As British journalist Laurie Penny has said, "a woman's opinion is the short skirt of the internet. Having one and flaunting it is somehow asking an amorphous mass of almost-entirely male keyboard-bashers to tell you how they'd like to rape, kill and urinate on you."[12]

If you're not regularly on the receiving end of this kind of vitriol, it might be hard to imagine. "You're telling me you don't have hundreds of men popping into your cubicle in the accounting department of your mid-sized, regional dry-goods distributor to inform you that—hmm—you're too fat to rape, but perhaps they'll saw you up with an electric knife? No? Just me?" writer Lindy West asks. "People who don't spend much time on the Internet are invariably shocked to discover the barbarism—the eager abandonment of the social contract—that so many of us face simply for doing our jobs."[13]

Of course, what we write is merely the pretext for unleashing these men's fury. As Ashley Judd wrote after she was flooded with abusive responses to her post about a March Madness basketball game in 2015, "my tweet was simply the convenient delivery system for a rage toward women that lurks perpetually."[14]

Through early 2021, America's "cyber bully-in-chief"[15] was then-president Donald Trump. Trump's misogyny on social media started long before he was elected president. In 2013, he posted that when the United States military "put men & women together," it should have expected that sexual assaults would happen.[16] From the time he announced his candidacy until X (then called Twitter) suspended his account on January 8, 2021, Trump helped promote social media trolling with thousands of posts directing invective at 850 different targets, according to a *New York Times* analysis.[17] In one post, he referred to Mika Brzezinski, co-host of MSNBC's *Morning Joe*, as "low I.Q. Crazy Mika" and claimed that she had been "bleeding badly from a face-lift."[18]

What happens when women complain about this treatment? Judd neatly sums up the predictable responses we receive from the world: "I brought it on myself. I deserved it. I'm whiny. I'm no fun. I can't take a joke. There are more serious issues in the world. The Internet space isn't real, and doesn't deserve validity and attention as a place where people are abused and suffer. Grow thicker skin, sweetheart. I'm famous. It's part of my job description."[19]

Some men work hard to try to normalize this kind of abuse. Jim Pagels wrote an entire piece for Slate arguing that death threats on X (then called Twitter) shouldn't be taken seriously because the Internet has made them so easy to hurl. Just try to follow that logic. Also, Pagels argues, many of the celebrities who receive these threats are not "being hunted down and attacked . . . on the regular."[20]

Clearly, this piece was written from the privileged position of a man who has never, unlike feminist writer Jessica Valenti, been told by the FBI to flee her home, avoid walking outside alone, and track people who repeatedly show up at her home to protect herself after receiving threats online. Unlike journalist Amanda Hess, Pagels has probably never had to hire a private investigator, miss work to appear in court, post a picture of a stalker who might show up at the front desk of his office, or spend "countless hours" documenting evidence in response to online abuse.[21]

Meanwhile, perpetrators know they can almost always attack women online without fear of consequences. "If someone was misogynistic in my office, I would sack them," Imran Ahmed, head of the Center for Countering Digital Hate, told me. "If I went to the pub and someone started shouting the c word, he'd be kicked out. But online abuse is highly effective because it terrorizes women and nothing happens to [the perpetrator]. Nothing."

As we saw in Chapter 5, this kind of online abuse is making offline spaces less safe for women because, as Ahmed points out, it's reshaping what our society thinks is normal and acceptable. In fact, according to a Pew survey, 5 percent of women on the Internet say they have experienced "physical danger" as a result of something that happened online.[22] And a 2018 study of almost 600 women journalists—almost two-thirds of whom had experienced threats or harassment online—found that more than a quarter had been physically attacked.[23]

The violence spilling over from social media is especially harrowing for women politicians. In 2022, a man broke into then-House of Representatives speaker Nancy Pelosi's home looking for her and brutally attacked her husband, fracturing his skull. She stepped down from party leadership shortly thereafter, telling CNN the episode impacted her decision.[24] Pelosi had begun her career in politics decades before. Her daughter, Alexandra Pelosi, told CNN that the family would never have given its blessing for her mom to enter politics "in this toxic social media environment."[25]

In 2022, men who had planned to kidnap another frequent target of social media vitriol, Michigan Governor Gretchen Whitmer, were convicted of crimes including conspiracy to kidnap, conspiracy to use weapons of mass destruction, and supporting a terrorist act.[26]

Other women in Congress have had their homes vandalized. Representative Alexandria Ocasio-Cortez—who was depicted being murdered in a video posted by one of her male colleagues in the House—has around-the-clock security and switches up where she sleeps at night.[27] British Member of Parliament Virginia Crosbie wears a special jacket to protect her from stabbings when she meets with constituents. "People can turn to social media with impunity," she says.[28]

So make no mistake: Online abuse puts women's lives in danger, despite the fact that clueless men like Pagels are blissfully oblivious to this fact—perhaps simply because it hasn't happened to them.

In many ways, law professor Mary Anne Franks says, online attacks can be worse than in-person abuse. Online, many perpetrators are able to remain anonymous, which makes it difficult to hold them accountable. Social media widens the audience perpetrators get for their abuse and allows them to find more people to join their attacks than they might offline. Whereas in-person harassment often happens in a single place—so at least in theory you can walk out of the bar and your colleagues won't know about it—the abuse you experience online is permanently available for your fellow students, coworkers, clients, and children to see.[29]

According to a 2017 CareerBuilder survey, 70 percent of employers use the social media profiles of job candidates to screen them, and the majority have found information that caused them not to hire an applicant.[30] While an employer can't legally use an applicant's arrest record as the only reason to disqualify her, employers who find other negative (possibly totally untrue or unfair) information posted about a woman online can eliminate her from consideration for a job without her ever knowing.[31]

In fact, the abuse of women online has become so pervasive that it has created market opportunities. Numerous companies now sell insurance to help cover the costs associated with cyberattacks.[32] But this can't, of course, cover the emotional damage women experience.

Cyberbullying victims commonly suffer from PTSD, depression, anxiety, panic attacks, and anorexia.[33]

And in the metaverse—the online world incorporating virtual and augmented reality that Mark Zuckerberg thinks/prays is the future of social media—we can expect things to be worse. In virtual reality, when someone gropes you, you can feel the sensation of it happening.[34]

When social networks are asked *why* they allow this kind of content, they typically say they're protecting free speech. In October 2019, under mounting pressure to better police content on his site, Zuckerberg gave a speech at Georgetown University in which he argued, "I believe we must continue to stand for free expression."[35]

Similarly, X owner Elon Musk has described himself as a "free speech absolutist." (That hasn't stopped him when free speech hasn't served his interests. In 2022, he suggested he could sue activists who called for boycotts of the platform and the company shuttered accounts of journalists who reported critically on him.[36])

Franks says it's "schizophrenic" that, when it comes to freedom of speech, people view cyberspace as a "real" realm and argue that free speech must be protected. But when it comes to cyber harassment, people like Pagels argue the Internet is "not 'really real' and thus [harassment] should not be taken very seriously."[37]

But, by not properly policing content, social networks actually promote the *opposite* of free expression. "Death threats bring nothing to a conversation; nor do attacks on a woman's looks," says video game developer Brianna Wu, who was also targeted during Gamergate. "The value that brings to open speech isn't a gain: it's a huge loss, as many of us learn it's easier to stay silent."[38]

In fact, perhaps the most common piece of advice given to women who are attacked online is "don't feed the trolls." In other words, shut up.[39] When Quinn reported their online harassment, they were told by a judge who declined to issue charges that "if this is the way the Internet is, you should really just get offline."[40] Recall that Quinn—a game developer—*makes their living* online, not to mention the fact that the Internet is now central to political and social life.

So Franks says the online world has become a realm where some groups, like men, experience expanded liberties because they are able to communicate whatever they wish, while women experience a loss of liberties on the Internet as a result of this kind of abuse. In response to online harassment, "women shut down their blogs, avoid websites they formerly frequented, take down social networking profiles, refrain from engaging in online political commentary, and choose not to maintain potentially lucrative or personally rewarding online presences," she points out. She says it has caused women to leave their jobs, schools, and cities and even commit suicide.[41]

Like Sarsour, too many women are forced to respond with the only option sometimes available: fleeing online conversations in order to protect their lives and well-being. After actor Robin Williams committed suicide, trolls sent his daughter Zelda images claiming to show his dead body. She temporarily quit X (then called Twitter).[42]

Model Hailey Bieber said in 2021 that she no longer had an X (then called Twitter) account "because there was never really a time where I would go on there and it didn't feel like it was a very toxic environment." In fact, she said, "the thought of even opening the app gives me such bad anxiety that I feel like I'm gonna throw up."[43]

The rapper Cardi B temporarily left social media in 2019 after people expressed outrage that she was awarded a Grammy. "I used to want this s—t foreva. Ya can have it back!" she posted on Instagram before deactivating her account.[44]

Before taking a break from X (then called Twitter) in 2018, actress Lili Reinhart wrote, "Hate to break it to you online trolls: Spreading your hate and overall negativity online won't make you any less miserable."[45]

"You guys finally did it," actress Sarah Hyland wrote in 2018 before going offline after her teenage cousin was killed by a drunk driver and she was attacked for raising money for her family. "Your horrible negative ignorant words have broken me."[46]

Former *SNL* star Aidy Bryant quit X (then called Twitter) because people kept calling her and the character she played (then-White House press secretary Sarah Huckabee Sanders) pigs. "It's a bad space," she said.[47]

Women's rights advocates often also flee online spaces. In 2016, Jessica Valenti took a public reprieve from social media. The reason, she posted: "This morning I woke up to a rape and death threat directed at my 5 year old daughter. That this is part of my work life is unacceptable."[48]

Reproductive rights advocate Pamela Merritt said that, on X (then called Twitter), "if I'm not in the mood to deal with incoming [abuse], then I don't share my thoughts."

Bracey Sherman said in 2018 that, on X (then called Twitter), "I was dealing with so much hate . . . Someone tweeted at me saying they hoped I would get raped over and over again . . . I threw my phone under the couch and hid in bed. I left social media for 6 weeks."[49]

I could go on with this list. And on. And on. But you get the idea.

And it isn't just high-profile women. A 2020 survey by the rights group Plan International found that being abused or harassed online is the norm, not the exception, for girls today: most girls have experienced it, and 22 percent said they or a friend didn't feel physically safe afterward. The survey also found that 19 percent of girls and young women have either abandoned social media or significantly reduced their use of it after being harassed online, while an additional 12 percent "changed the way they express themselves" as a result.

"Girls are being silenced by a toxic level of harassment," Anne-Birgitte Albrectsen, chief executive of Plan International, said. "Driving girls out of online spaces is hugely disempowering in an increasingly digital world and damages their ability to be seen, heard and become leaders."[50]

A 2018 report by Amnesty International likewise found that 81 percent of women in the United States who had been harassed or abused online changed the way they used social media as a result.[51] According to Amnesty International, "instead of strengthening women's voices, the violence and abuse many women experience on [X, then called Twitter] leads women to self-censor what they post, limit their interactions, and even drives women off" the platform completely.[52]

Publicly leaving social media is now called "the flounce."[53] The origins of the term leave little question that it is women who are doing most of it. According to Urban Dictionary, the word "comes from the original use of gathering up skirts and petticoats and leaving in dramatic, impatient and exaggerated movements."[54] Would we really expect women fleeing rape and death threats to be described as anything but emotional and overwrought?

A passing glance at the demographics of social media platforms makes clear that this is happening way more than a lot of people may realize. While women are much more likely than men to use a lot of mainstream platforms like TikTok, Facebook, Instagram, and Snapchat, we're *less* likely to use platforms like X and Reddit that have become infamous for trolling.[55] You don't need to be a data scientist to see that women are avoiding sites where we're likelier to face abuse.

Also recall how Christine Blasey Ford was excoriated on social media after coming forward with her accusations that she was sexually assaulted by Brett Kavanaugh before he was confirmed to the Supreme Court in 2018—even though she deleted her social media accounts.[56] We'll never know how many other potential victims of Kavanaugh or other men will never come forward because they don't want to set themselves up for a similar digital assault.

And while we know the names of women who have made a point of announcing their exits, we'll never know the identities or thoughts of other women who choose to quietly quit or never enter online conversations to begin with because they don't want to be skewered or fear for their lives. We'll just never know.

Their absence doesn't just rob them of a valuable space for raising the profile of their work, finding opportunities, and participating in public discourse. It affects us all. As West wrote after one troll made a fake account to harass her by imitating her beloved, dead father, "Internet trolling might seem like an issue that only affects a certain subset of people, but that's only true if you believe that living in a world devoid of diverse voices—public discourse shaped primarily by white, heterosexual, able-bodied men—wouldn't profoundly affect your life."[57]

Of course, we'll also never know how many women won't run for office given the violence they see women politicians face on and offline. But this isn't the only advantage trolls give male politicians. Want to know one reason Donald Trump was elected president? Quinn writes that Gamergate "helped solidify the growing connections between online white supremacist movements, misogynist nerds, conspiracy theorists, and dispassionate hoaxers who derive a sense of power from disseminating information." According to Quinn, "they became a real force behind giving Donald Trump the keys to the White House."[58]

Don't underestimate how sinister it is for these kinds of men to silence women. In *Men Explain Things to Me*, Rebecca Solnit argues that "it's a slippery slope" from nonviolent attempts to silence women to violent crimes to achieve the same end. "A man acts on the belief that you have no right to speak and that you don't get to define what's going on," she writes. "That could just mean cutting you off at the dinner table or the conference"—or, today, cyberbullying you into silence. "It could also mean telling you to shut up, or threatening you if you open your mouth, or beating you for speaking, or killing you to silence you forever."[59] They're all on the same continuum.

Trolls Tolerate Trolling

What is the tech world doing in the face of these harrowing threats to women's mental health, reputations, careers, physical safety, and civic participation? Not nearly enough.

To bring you back, Facebook only agreed to better police content promoting rape or domestic violence in 2013 after companies started pulling their advertising dollars over the existence of groups like Fly Kicking Sluts in the Uterus, Kicking your Girlfriend in the Fanny because she won't make you a Sandwich, and Violently Raping Your Friend Just for Laughs.[60]

Most mainstream social networks claim in their community standards that they don't allow serious online hate and violence. But while they may *say* that, they continue to let this kind of content live all over their platforms. In 2022, the Center for Countering Digital Hate studied messages sent to five high-profile women on Instagram. It found that Instagram didn't do anything about 89.7 percent of the accounts that sent women abuse. This seems to have emboldened the perpetrators: half of the users who sent abusive messages went on to send more abuse after Instagram failed to enforce its own rules.[61]

Women also regularly say that when they report abuse to social networks, the platforms don't take action in a timely way—or ever. When your nude photos have just been posted on the Internet or trolls have shared your home address and you fear for the lives of your children, your world is collapsing. You need the content removed immediately. But in 2016 Buzzfeed conducted a survey of more than 2,115 users of X (then called Twitter) who said they'd reported abusive content to the platform. Over 46 percent said the company didn't act on their reports, while 29 percent never heard back. The company issued warnings to the users who posted the offending content just 1 percent of the time and deleted the offending accounts just 2.6 percent of the time.[62]

"Whenever I see content on any platform that might violate the terms of service, I report it," disinformation expert Nina Jankowicz writes in *How to Be a Woman Online: Surviving Abuse and Harassment, and How to Fight Back.* "Generally, these reports disappear into the ether; when the platforms *do* follow up with me, it is usually to tell me something to the effect of 'we're sorry, but we found no violation of terms' in the rape threat you received." Jankowicz says others have told her the same thing in focus groups.[63]

Bloomberg Technology host Emily Chang writes in *Brotopia: Breaking Up the Boys' Club of Silicon Valley* that one troll falsely claimed to be the father of her child, "suggested taking me to a warehouse 'for a whipping,' . . . and tweeted a hard-core pornographic video at me with the words 'Submission Time.'" When she reported the account to X (then called Twitter), she received the following message: "We reviewed your report carefully and found that there was no violation of Twitter's Rules regarding abusive behavior."[64] When Lindy West reported a message to X (then called Twitter) that said "CHOO CHOO MOTH-ERFUCKER THE RAPE TRAIN'S ON ITS WAY. NEXT STOP YOU," she, too, received a response that the message was "currently not violating the Twitter Rules."[65] It isn't hard to find similar complaints.[66]

And women have come to know this. One hundred percent of the women surveyed by Amnesty International who used X (then called Twitter) multiple times per week and didn't report abuse to the platform said it was "not worth the effort."[67]

Quinn, who started a group called Crash Override to help victims, also says "platforms do not treat users equally. . . . If I escalated a report on behalf of a client who was black, less or no action would be taken than in the case of my white clients facing similar problems."[68]

What's more, since users often can't access messages from people they've blocked, it's harder to get evidence to share with law enforcement.[69] Hess also points out that users aren't typically notified when a social network blocks or takes down harmful content about them—even when such posts contain violent threats they have an interest in knowing about so they can try to protect themselves or use it as evidence.[70]

As I'll explore in the next chapter, one thing that can explain why social networks weren't better designed to prevent these problems is that they were largely created by men, who are less likely to face the prospect of this kind of abuse themselves.

Ellen Pao, former interim CEO of Reddit, believes that if women—particularly women of color—had been better represented when social networks like Reddit, Facebook, and X (then called Twitter) were created, they would have been designed from the start to disallow abuse. "I think people would have invested more in tools, would have invested more in community management, would have had different rules, would have taken down more content faster and banned more people in a more consistent way," she says.[71]

But it's not just that social networks were built by men. It's that they were created by a certain kind of man. Before Facebook, Zuck created FaceMash by hacking into websites to get photos of female students at Harvard and then posting the pictures without their consent on a site that invited people to rank how hot they were.[72]

Elon Musk once posted that he'd start a school with the acronym TITS.[73] When Elizabeth Warren said it was wrong for Musk (then the world's richest man) to pay $0 in income taxes, he replied calling her "Senator Karen." "You remind me of when I was a kid and my friend's angry Mom would just randomly yell at everyone for no reason," he wrote.[74]

The social network Truth Social was created by Donald Trump. (Enough said.)

So it's not super surprising that men who troll women themselves have built platforms that allow other men to troll us, too.

Lax Law Enforcement and Laws

But it's not just that victims of online violence often can't count on tech companies for help. They're also often ignored by the very people in our society responsible for protecting us: law enforcement.

Women have plenty of reason not to trust police to begin with. Sexual assault is the second most frequent type of police misconduct, Mikki Kendall writes in *Hood Feminism: Notes From the Women That a Movement Forgot*.[75] And Quinn points out that 22 percent of transgender people say they've been harassed by police officers themselves—so we might forgive them for being skeptical that contacting police will be the solution to their harassment.[76]

Officers often also lack technical knowledge of how to hunt down perpetrators on the Internet.[77] When Quinn tried to report online abuse to San Francisco police, they were told they had to print out their video evidence.[78] How do you print a video?

Then there's the question of whether police can be bothered to care. In the United Kingdom, Caroline Criado-Perez was deluged with rape and death threats on X (then called Twitter) for campaigning to put a woman on British currency after the Bank of England decided to remove Elizabeth Fry from the five pound note, leaving only men (other than the then-Queen) represented on the country's bills.[79] Asked what they were going to do about it, Andy Trotter, a spokesman for the British police, complained that X (then called Twitter) should handle the problem, arguing that police "don't want to be in this arena," as it prevents them from "dealing with something else."[80] (Remarkably, two of Criado-Perez's tormenters were jailed—one for an underwhelming eight weeks and another for twelve[81]—probably because the police felt pressured by a flood of media attention on the case. That's highly unusual. And police shouldn't have to be pressured for women to receive justice.)

Law enforcement agencies in the United States seem to have a similar mentality. Brianna Wu told Jezebel's Anna Merlan that someone threatened to murder her in a video and "this is not just, 'I'm going to kill Brianna,' this is like a multi-minute rant about why they want to murder me, how. Their face is visible in the video. I have their name and testimony from the people who know them and how unbalanced they are. This person lives 15 minutes from my house." Police did not make an arrest.[82]

Contacting the FBI rather than local police is often no more effective. Congresswoman Katherine Clark said that when she reached out to the agency to try to obtain justice for Wu, "frankly, the FBI told us cases of online abuse were not a priority."[83]

But Merlan says there appears to be a notable exception to this rule: when police officers are themselves threatened on social media. Then, all their tired excuses about the Internet not being real, officers not understanding technology, and laws being inadequate to address cybercrimes don't seem to apply. Merlan points out that when someone posted on Facebook that he "Might just go out and kill two cops myself!!!" police had a suspect in a precinct the very same day. When a 17-year-old allegedly posted a photo of a gun pointed at a police car, he was arrested by police in Texas. When another 17-year-old allegedly posted gun emojis that pointed at police emojis with various threats on Facebook, the NYPD arrested him. And when a Colorado man allegedly posted a YouTube comment claiming veterans would kill retired police officers, well, you guessed it. He was arrested by the FBI.[84]

Another reason law enforcement is wrong not to take online abuse seriously is that it could help prevent bigger crimes. Perpetrators of mass shootings, for example (who are almost always men) often have histories of posting misogyny online.[85]

One thing that doesn't help is the dearth of women in law enforcement. Women make up just 12.6 percent of law enforcement officers in the United States, according to the Department of Justice,[86] and just 20 percent of special agents with the FBI.[87]

But even if women report abuse *and* law enforcement takes them seriously, they still can't go after social media platforms, because Section 230 of the Communications Decency Act protects sites from liability for what their users post—with a couple of exceptions, such as cases of copyrighted material. When revisions are proposed to hold sites accountable for the hateful content they host, a lot of people claim it would be impossible to police all the content out there on social media. The only problem with this argument is we know it isn't true. When copyrighted material is shared by users on social media, site operators are quick to take it down because they could otherwise face costly lawsuits.[88] It's simple: our laws are designed to protect Warner Bros., not women.

What We Can Do

Social networks must stop hosting misogyny and other forms of hate. They should start by giving warnings to people who abuse others on their platforms. Then they should give trolls temporary suspensions—and then, if they still don't get in line, trolls should be kicked off sites entirely. Sound naïve to think this could work? We already know it would. Riot Games, maker of the wildly popular game League of Legends, kicked players off games for making negative comments and told them why they were being banished. When these users returned, they engaged in significantly less bad behavior. The policy also turned out to be good for business: League of Legends had 67 million active monthly players when it implemented the policy. Two years later, it had 100 million.[89]

It's pretty darn obvious that expelling trolls makes huge numbers of people feel more comfortable using social networks. Need more evidence? Immediately after X (then called Twitter) shuttered Donald Trump's account in 2021, the number of American adults on social media who said they used the platform *increased by 21 percent,* according to Edison Research. In other words, *millions more people say they used a social network all because the platform got rid of a single troll.*[90]

All it would take would be for a few high-profile people to be deplatformed for other users to realize they can't get away with abuse if they want to stay on these platforms. That would act as a powerful deterrent. Sure, people who were kicked off could skirt the rules and create new accounts under different names, but they would have lost all their friends or followers—an outcome exactly no one wants.

Social networks also need to respond rapidly to abuse reports. As I've said, when someone is the victim of abuse like deadnaming or doxing, their world is falling apart—and they might be in physical danger (or danger of harming themselves). They need help immediately. So social platforms need to dramatically staff up so that every report of community standards violations gets a response within hours—at all hours. And they need to enforce their own community standards, so users never again get responses saying that it's cool for someone to say the rape train is on its way to them.

When a social network's system automatically flags and removes content without a user reporting it—or when the person who reports the abuse isn't the victim and the abuse is taken down—the user who was targeted should be informed so that she is aware of what happened, in case she needs to take other steps to protect herself. And the company should save all evidence of abusive posts it removes in case law enforcement later needs to subpoena them.

Social networks also need to ban deadnaming. It "is *only* ever used for harassment purposes," Quinn writes.[91]

We can also do a lot as users. The Tyler Clementi Foundation—named after a young man who killed himself after his college roommate secretly live-streamed his sexual encounter with a man—asks people to pledge to be "upstanders" and speak up when they witness bullying.[92] Definitely report any abuse you see directly to social networks if you can.

When women are unfairly attacked online, we should also rally around them. You can consider messaging them directly. Quinn suggests that you "consider mentioning something they've said or done that you admired." Also, it can be "helpful to finish off a message with something like, 'I'm not seeking a response, I just wanted to send you a message of support.'" That takes the pressure off the victim, who may feel too burned out to reply."[93]

However, Quinn says that, when responding to online abuse publicly, "*consent is key.*" They point out that some people may not want their abuse made more high profile with lots of comments about it.[94]

Whether or not a woman wants her abusers to be called out online, consider calling out her accomplishments as a different way to buoy her. Quinn writes that "I see how much further stories of bad things happening to us travel than stories about the things we create or make."[95] We can change this.

META MISOGYNY

As a program manager for Apple Maps in Texas, Janneke Parrish worked on a team where everyone above her was male. One of her managers seemed to farm out the most visible, plum assignments to other men, she told me. He called her and other women names like "sweetie."

"At one point there was a training that needed to happen in India, and the manager seemed to be making the decision about whether I would go by asking me about the state of my marriage, whether I had kids and whether I intended to have kids," she told me. "They were deeply sexist questions that got to the mindset he has about women and our limitations."

But it wasn't until she began advocating for the company to continue allowing remote work during the Covid-19 pandemic that she realized she was far from the only woman who was up against this kind of sexism. Janneke told me that, in May 2021, Apple began pushing its workers—who had been working from home since the start of the pandemic the previous year—to come back to the office. So she started collecting stories of how her colleagues would be negatively impacted so they could collectively advocate for the company's so-called "people team" (a.k.a. human resources) to rethink the policy.

Apple has a notoriously secretive and siloed culture, with staffers from different teams rarely communicating with one another, Janneke explained. But when she started talking to colleagues in other parts of the company, she kept hearing about the shocking experiences women were having. So she started gathering those stories, too, and eventually founded a group called #AppleToo with her colleague Cher Scarlett, who had been conducting internal surveys finding that women within the company were being paid less than men for the same work and that men tended to end up with better titles.

Janneke collected over 800 stories. Forty percent of them contained complaints of unequal treatment based on sex, 29 percent contained accounts of sexual harassment, and 7.49 percent contained reports of being sexually assaulted on an Apple campus or in an Apple store, she told me. And 46 percent of the time, the staffers said they approached the "people team" only to have their complaint dismissed or, worse, to be retaliated against, Janneke said.

In 2022, Janneke was fired from Apple. She says the company falsely accused her of leaking a recording of a staff meeting to the media, ordered her to turn in her computer, and then said she was being fired for violating a policy by deleting personal things before surrendering her computer.

"I think they fired me because I was organizing," Janneke told me. "They fired me in hopes of ending this movement in its tracks."

When *The New York Times* asked Apple about what happened to Janneke, a spokesperson said the company doesn't discuss individual personnel matters out of respect for privacy but that it investigates concerns and is "deeply committed to creating and maintaining a positive and inclusive workplace."[1]

That's not what Janneke experienced. "It's a male dominated industry and it continues to espouse masculine coded values," Janneke explained. "The tech industry centers around type A personalities who have a big, assertive, dominant presence in the room. Those are the people who were praised and promoted and who succeeded on my team. But in our society these traits are cultivated in men and not women, so when you select for those traits, you're basically saying you value men more than women."

Another way the culture favors men is through Apple's policy that staffers work in the office at least part of the workweek, Janneke told me. "Remote work is incredible for women who have responsibilities for taking care of other people," she pointed out. "It allows a work schedule that meshes with your other responsibilities. When you insist that the only way you can work as a team is in person, you're inherently saying that those who have other responsibilities can't be part of that team. That's a male coded value because it assumes there is somebody else at home to do the caregiving."

* * *

In this chapter, we'll look at the sexism and misogyny that women who work for tech companies and as social media managers for brands are up against. We'll also see how the absence of the voices of women—who value privacy more than men—can help explain why social networks have been designed to stalk us.

Of course, the meta level of misogyny women are up against in Big Tech isn't even an open secret anymore. It's an established fact. Technology journalist Emily Chang calls their workplaces "Brotopia."

"At tech firms, comments and jokes about sexual behavior, Viagra, porn, and even rape seem to fit right in," Chang writes. According to a 2016 survey, 60 percent of women working in tech experienced sexual harassment or unwanted advances, usually from their supervisors, and 90 percent saw sexist behavior at industry events.[2] It would take a whole different book to tell the stories of all the women like Janneke who say they've experienced sexual harassment and/or gender discrimination—and sometimes retaliation for reporting it—at other major tech firms (hello Google,[3] Microsoft,[4] Facebook,[5] Twitter,[6] Tinder,[7] Reddit,[8] and Pinterest[9]).

That's if they're hired at all. Even though women are over-represented in the professional labor market, women hold just 27 percent of professional computing jobs, according to the National Center for Women & Information Technology.[10] Just 4.7 percent of Silicon Valley's firms with the highest revenue were led by women in 2020, according to law firm Fenwick & West. For the record, that's lower than the (abysmal) 6 percent of S&P 500 companies led by women.[11]

In 2021, before Elon Musk bought X (then called Twitter) and laid off much of its workforce, women held less than 31 percent of technical roles and less than 40 percent of leadership roles at the company.[12] Over at Facebook, as of June 2021, women held less than 25 percent of technical roles and less than 36 percent of leadership roles.[13]

Women are also devalued in their pay. A 2019 Glassdoor study found that, while the average pay gap between men and women in the United States is 4.9 percent, it's well over double that—11.6 percent—in computer programming.[14]

Unsurprisingly, many women flee tech jobs. Forty-three percent of new moms who work in STEM careers full time leave their jobs after having kids, according to a 2019 study.[15]

Then there's the racism women in tech contend with on top of the sexism and misogyny. April Curley, who is Black, recruited candidates from historically Black colleges and universities to work for Google from 2014 to 2020. "I watched so many of the Black women I recruited looked over for promotion and leadership opportunities," she told me.

April also says she and other Black women were made to feel like they didn't belong in the company. On multiple occasions, she was asked by men to restock items in the micro kitchen in her New York office, even though her badge clearly identified her as a nonservice employee, she told me.

April had a close friend who took the bus to campus from San Francisco and told her that, numerous times, other Google employees asked to see her badge to confirm she was a fellow staffer.

"I would hear directly from the [Black] employees I had recruited that they would have their badges checked while they were working on the campus," she told me. "It's part of the culture at Google."

April says she was fired in 2020 after speaking out against the way Google treats Black employees. She's now suing the company for discrimination.[16] (Google didn't respond to a request for comment about the lawsuit by *The New York Times*.[17])

April also told me she knows of a dozen other Black women staffers who have taken medical leave after experiencing harassment and other forms of discrimination at the company.

This culture explains a lot about the products tech companies build. As I said in Chapter 9, it makes sense that men who think they can mistreat women with impunity would build products that allow others to mistreat women with impunity. It makes sense that men with high salaries and low worries would forget to think about how people with far less privilege in life—like women who are vulnerable to the nonconsensual sharing of their nude images—might be harmed by their products. It makes sense that men who don't think they need to have women represented in the development process would build products that don't reflect the priorities of women. A 2013 study, for example, found that women take privacy violations much more seriously than men.[18] But, as we'll discuss later in this chapter, Big Tech has programmed their products to stalk us.

A lot of tech companies say they're trying to hire more women. In recent years, there have been signs that they might become more attractive places for women to work, as companies have allowed more remote work and gotten rid of perks like free food that encouraged people to live at work—a lifestyle that is obviously incompatible with the kinds of caregiving many women do.[19] But we've also seen that these companies can regress: after Elon Musk bought X (then called Twitter) in 2022, he fired a ton of his workforce, including a lot of staffers responsible for safety, and workers filed a class-action lawsuit claiming he'd axed a greater percentage of women than men.[20]

And even when tech companies try to do the right thing, women staffers still have to contend with sometimes-abusive colleagues. When companies gave parents time off to care for out-of-school kids during Covid-19, some staffers came up against ugly criticism from their colleagues who felt they weren't pulling enough weight while they kept their children alive.[21] What working mom feels welcome in a place like that?

The Pink-Collar Jobs of Tech

Another place where women bump up against shockingly sexist treatment is in jobs that involve managing a company or other organization's social media channels. These kinds of positions are often designed with women specifically in mind—and come with far less remuneration and respect than similar jobs held by men.

In 2017, Brooke Erin Duffy and Becca Schwartz studied job postings for social media managers. They found that the ads used the kind of language typically used to describe women. "In addition to stated calls for 'passion' and 'love,' the ads emphasized a positive demeanor," they reported. "Feminized language was frequently deployed: 'upbeat,' 'kind-hearted,' able to 'promote a positive and enthusiastic work environment,' and possessing a 'warm, enthusiastic personality.'" Overall, the typical worker companies sought was "sociable, emotive, and flexible"—all stereotypically feminine qualities.[22]

This makes sense, when you think about it. After all, social media managers look after their organizations' relationships with the public. It's a kind of emotional labor, so it would be surprising if people *didn't* look to women to perform it.

So the job has become very gendered: 81.2 percent of social media managers identify as female and 17.3 percent identify as male (1.5 percent self-define), according to the salary reporting site PayScale.[23]

A wide body of research shows that when women enter a field in large numbers, professionals in the field end up being perceived as less valuable and getting paid less.[24] Keidra Chaney, a digital strategist who advocates for equitable online communities for disabled and other marginalized people, told me that in social media's early days, social media manager positions were often considered tech or tech-adjacent jobs. But now, they're often considered communication jobs—with huge implications for their pay and prestige. In 2020, the average salary in the male-dominated tech sector was $146,000.[25] By contrast, the average salary for a social media manager is under $55,000, according to PayScale.[26]

But Cassie Olivos, vice president of content and social quality at the Internet marketing company Scorpion (and, I can't help but brag, a former student of mine), told me that people in these jobs often have to understand search engine optimization and data management and analysis. They frequently code. They produce and edit videos and use design tools to create images. Many build tech products, like tools to schedule content to be posted at particular times. All of these things require tech skills—so it's wrong that the (mostly) women who work in this profession aren't compensated in line with the (mostly) men who work in tech.

It's especially outrageous when you consider the value of a social media manager's work. "Strategic use of social media has been credited for influencing elections, harnessed to transform fledgling start-ups into billion-dollar companies, and used as a form of warfare," writer Jessi Hempel observed in Wired. "But this influence doesn't translate into a higher paycheck or more internal power." That's, of course, because social media management positions have become "the digital version of the pink collar job."[27]

Another hallmark of the presence of women on the Internet is, of course, heightened judgement (ahem, Chapter 3) and abuse (see Chapters 5 and 9)—which social media managers report receiving in spades. Alana Hope Levinson, a former engagement editor for Talking Points Memo, has written that when she held the job she lived in fear because she was hyper-aware that a single slipup could make her a topic of national conversation. The worry kept her in a "near-constant state of anxiety," she says. Annie Shields, engagement editor at *The Nation*, once wrote a typo on Facebook that triggered hundreds of mean comments. "The criticism is over the top," Shields said.[28]

Stalking

Of course, all this sexism and misogyny isn't just felt by the women who work for or on social networks. It also deeply affects us as users. As we saw in Chapter 9, one reason why tech companies don't do a better job of protecting women on their platforms is probably because they were mostly built by and continue to be run largely by men. The lack of women's influence in tech companies can also help explain why the bros who run Silicon Valley are stalking us.

When we use social apps, nearly everything we do is tracked by social networks that learn deeply intimate things about us from our online behavior, can keep records of them forever, and share what they know with shadowy third parties whose identities we don't even know. Al Gore pretty much summed things up when he said we now "have a stalker economy."[29]

Shoshana Zuboff, PhD, author of *The Age of Surveillance Capitalism: The Fight for a Human Future at the New Frontier of Power,* calls what tech companies do "the pervasive strip search of our lives." We ostensibly agree to this when we sign up for "free" services like Instagram and Gmail. Wait, you didn't read the fine print when you accepted their terms of service? Of course you didn't: a 2008 study found that reading all the privacy policies we receive each year would take 76 days. Today, as apps have become even more prevalent in our lives, that number can only be bigger. So companies benefit from the agreements being too long and complicated for us to understand. What's more, experts have named these terms of service "contracts of adhesion" because our only options are to accept them or to not use these platforms at all—which would hold us back in our social lives, careers, and ability to participate in public discourse.[30]

When you use apps on your cell phone, they often track your physical location—and there aren't laws to stop them from selling this information to third parties.[31] This information is supposedly anonymized, but with enough data points, the people who get their hands on it can—and sometimes do—identify people. Security expert Bruce Schneier reports that, by looking at the times, dates, and locations of just four places an American turns up, it's possible to identify 95 percent of us.[32]

What's more, on sites like dating apps, users answer the most personal of questions. When you set up a profile on OKCupid, you're asked everything from whether you've ever used psychedelic drugs to whether you'd consider an open marriage.[33] If you think you're disclosing in confidence, think again. Dating apps share what you reveal to them with countless other companies. OkCupid says it may share your information with over 300 different companies—and, of course, there's no telling what those third parties might go on to do with it.[34] Now picture information on your HIV status and sexual proclivities that you shared on a dating app hacked or purchased by a foreign government and used to blackmail you into working for them. Or used by criminals to extort money from you.

And if you use Gmail for your email, Google has a record of every search you've ever conducted while logged in—and there's no way for you to force the company to delete it. This record is "more intimate than if you'd sent Google your diary," Schneier writes in *Data and Goliath: The Hidden Battles to Collect Your Data and Control Your World*.[35] The company also searches all of your Gmail messages, using keywords "to more intimately understand you," Schneier warns.[36] Even if you don't use Google's search engine, it tracks websites you visit because so many sites use Google Analytics. And even if you don't use Gmail, Google has records of any communications you have with other people who use Gmail.[37]

Of course, all this stalking is ostensibly done to provide you the service of (chillingly) targeted ads for the exact products and services you'll want. In my family, my husband usually handles the vacation bookings. This means that when he starts planning a getaway for us to Turks & Caicos, I immediately start getting Facebook ads for local hotels. Now imagine a domestic violence victim searching for flights to escape her abusive boyfriend. The Facebook ads her partner sees next may be a dead giveaway. And I mean that literally. He might kill her.

Plenty of other apps access your search history, contacts, calendar, and other personal information.[38] And, of course, our intimate information is also carefully surveilled by the so-called "Internet of Things"—devices with sensors supposedly designed to improve our lives, like fitness apps that record information about our health and "smart" home products that know when we come and go from our homes and what we do inside of them.

All of this is creepy enough. But things get even scarier when you realize that companies can—and do—combine data sets from different places to reveal even more personal things about you. This can help explain how brokers sell lists of the names of rape victims, for example.[39]

"Who can buy access to data-broker dossiers? Anyone—your neighbor, your ex, your former high school classmate," Danielle Keats Citron writes in *The Fight for Privacy: Protecting Dignity, Identity and Love in the Digital Age*.[40] Think about what might happen if this data is purchased by a man who suspects his wife is cheating on him. Or subpoenaed by authorities prosecuting illegal abortions. Sound crazy? After *Roe v. Wade* was overturned in 2022, a company began selling location data for people who had visited abortion clinics, which also indicated where they went afterward (presumably, in many cases, home).[41]

What's more, with these troves of private information, these companies may know things about us that we may not have even realized about ourselves—and one thing they can do with all this information is psychologically manipulate us. In 2012, Facebook ran a small study which found it could adjust its algorithm to manipulate our moods. When people were shown happier posts, they wrote happier posts themselves. The reverse was true for sadder updates.

Schneier warns that marketers are well aware that women perceive themselves as less attractive on Mondays and when they're depressed. He also says companies have started building tools to read our moods.[42] Imagine the possibilities for manipulating the content we see to prey on our deepest vulnerabilities. As women, we can be sure we're major targets for these kinds of efforts, for a simple reason: we do the vast majority of the consumer purchasing in our society.[43]

Even when you think your data isn't being stored, it often isn't true. For example, Snapchat photos are supposed to disappear shortly after we send them and we're supposed to be notified if someone screenshots a snap we send. So users had a rude awakening in 2014 when thousands of images sent through the site were hacked and then posted online. They were obtained from a third-party app called SnapSaved.com, which allowed users to save the pictures they received without the senders knowing.[44]

In 2021, Apple finally gave users the option to tell apps not to track us and share information about what we do online. An overwhelming 94 percent of Americans opted not to be digitally stalked.[45] But a study later that year by former Apple engineers found that when users asked Apple to automatically deny new tracking requests, Apple often didn't honor that request, and when companies were asked not to track users across other sites, they frequently didn't comply.[46] There's also nothing to stop new leadership at Apple—which came under intense pressure from Facebook for the policy—from changing it in the future.

Google said it would give users the same option by 2023. But in 2022, the District of Columbia and several states sued Google, claiming the company was tricking users into using location tracking services by falsely claiming apps wouldn't work properly without it and continuing to collect data on users' locations even after they disabled location tracking. Google denied the claims,[47] but settled a separate lawsuit with the state of Arizona over claims it deceptively tracked location data for $85 *million*.[48]

Plus, who knows how many companies still have the data they gathered before we had these privacy options—and what they'll do with it? Companies like Facebook, Apple, and Google, let's remember, have the content of our emails. They have our pictures and videos. They have our text messages and phone records. They have our calendars.[49] And companies like Google and Meta are still piling up mounds of data about what we're doing on their sites, even if we limit the ability of others to do so.[50]

Why have we all been so quick to hand this over to them? Ciarán Mc Mahon, PhD, points out in *The Psychology of Social Media* that the privacy options sites offer users—like allowing us to restrict access to our posts only to "friends"—give us the illusion that we're protecting ourselves, while obscuring the availability of this data to tech companies themselves (and, from them, to data brokers, and from there, who knows).[51]

What's more, even when we realize what's happening, "there is a kind of prisoner's dilemma at play in social media," Dr. Mc Mahon writes. "If everyone resisted sharing their private information with these services, then they would have to find some way of operating without it. But because we seem to have a compelling desire to see each other's personal information, we divulge our own as part of a plea bargain."[52]

And the United States doesn't have federal laws that protect our digital data. All we've got are laws protecting the ways very specific types of information—like healthcare, student, and financial data—can be used.[53]

Why aren't lawmakers protecting us? Politicians rely on this data *themselves* in their election campaigns.[54] Technology companies wield enormous influence through political campaign contributions and top-flight lobbyists. And Schneier points out that governments often compel tech companies to share the data they collect as part of law enforcement and anti-terrorism efforts. So "governments don't really want to limit their own access to data by crippling the corporate hand that feeds them."[55]

What happens when law enforcement gets its hands on our social media data? Eva Galperin, director of cybersecurity at the nonprofit Electronic Frontier Foundation, told me that "emails and social media messages and Google searches have all been used as evidence that someone has had an abortion in cases where people have been prosecuted for pregnancy outcomes."

Just ask Nebraska teenager Celeste Burgess, who was charged with multiple crimes (along with her mom) in 2022 after she reportedly exchanged messages with her mother over Facebook suggesting she had taken abortion pills. Law enforcement served Meta with a search warrant for their messages, and the company handed them over within two days.[56]

Galperin warns that the information social networks make public about us is also a useful tool for people who stalk women physically. Social networks typically make your social graph—your list of friends and contacts—public by default. That means a deranged ex-boyfriend can identify and contact these people to try to learn your whereabouts by telling them he's concerned about your mental state and wants to make sure you're OK.

None of this is OK.

What We Can Do

The United States needs a federal data privacy law. Under Europe's General Data Protection Regulation, companies can't just sneak consent to collect people's sensitive data into mile-long take-it-or-leave it privacy policies. Users have to be asked to consent to it.[57] We need a similar law that requires companies to ask our permission before collecting or selling our digital data. Lawmakers should also give us the right to tell tech companies and data brokers to delete and not act upon any information they've already collected about us.

Of course, if we do this, companies would lose some revenue. Don't cry too hard for them—Meta and other tech companies make obscene profits, and they could still sell ads. But without the creepy level of micro-targeting social media companies currently offer advertisers based on all the intimate data they're collecting about us—which allows them to show ads on social media to people of a particular age and political affiliation with a history of buying a particular product in a particular community, for example—advertisers might start spreading out some of their spending in other places. That would be good for us, too—it might mean advertisers would go back to funding community and national media outlets so they can invest in reporting on issues that are critical to our lives.

But it might also mean that, to earn revenue, social networks would charge us fees to use their products, and some people wouldn't be able to afford to pay. The best-case scenario would be for nonprofit social networks to crop up: apps devoted to serving our interests rather than stalking us to enrich shareholders. Keats Citron has called, for example, for period tracking apps to be developed by reproductive justice organizations and dating apps for the LGBTQ community to be developed by advocacy groups.[58] Just imagine how differently they'd treat women.

Also, social networks shouldn't wait for these laws to stop stalking us and sharing their intelligence on us. We're living in a time of unprecedented "techlash," as people become increasingly conscious of the dark side of social media. Ending these practices would be a way for tech companies to start to earn back our trust (which is pretty critical if they want us to keep using their products) and distinguish themselves from the competition.

Galperin says social networks should also hide our social graphs by default.

It should go without saying that tech companies should hire more women, pay and treat them equitably, and banish bro culture. Since it seems necessary to spell this out for them, we have firsthand experience of what it's like to be a woman on the Internet, so we're pretty well positioned to help develop platforms and policies that work for women.

Another big thing that would help would be for tech staffers to band together and collectively stop tolerating discrimination against their women colleagues. For example, in 2021, thousands of employees of the videogame maker Activision signed a letter and walked out of their jobs to protest allegations of bro culture, sexism, and abuse at the company. Staffers also spoke out publicly on social media. "The actions at Activision may signal a new phase, where a critical mass of the industry's own workers are indicating they will no longer tolerate such behavior," *The New York Times* reported.[59] Make this statement true.

As for users, we need to protect ourselves online. Remember: this isn't just about preventing companies from surveilling you (though that's certainly reason enough). As we saw in Chapter 5, it's also about preventing people from hacking you and accessing your intimate images, or turning on your web cam and capturing the pictures themselves.

Nina Jankowicz recommends using a password manager to generate a unique password for each website you use, so a hacker can't guess one of your passwords and then log in to lots of other sites using it. Enable two-factor authentication so when you try to log in to a site, the site double-checks that it's you by sending you a text, code on an app, or phone call (or you could have a physical security key that generates a code). Shell out for an email service that doesn't read your emails, like Proton Mail. Use a virtual private network (VPN) to route your Internet traffic through a secondary server, so your online activity can't be tracked. If you're vulnerable to being doxed, pay a service like DeleteMe to remove your home address and other personal information from the Internet.[60]

Don't use public wi-fi—it's not worth the risk of being hacked.

Keep a post-it or band aid over your computer camera when you're not using it, so hackers can't record you.

Update the settings on your phone and apps to limit which apps can access your location.

By now I probably don't have to tell you not to post pictures of your front door that show your address on social media or take those quizzes that ask things like the names of concerts you've attended—an easy way to get answers to security questions that can be used to hack your accounts.[61]

If you're communicating sensitive information—planning an abortion, for example—Galperin, of the Electronic Frontier Foundation, suggests using Signal, which is end-to-end encrypted, so the company can't hand your messages over to law enforcement because it can't access them in the first place—and keep the disappearing messages feature turned on. (WhatsApp is also end-to-end encrypted so it's better than using Facebook Messenger, she says, but Meta retains metadata for WhatsApp—like records of what numbers you messaged—which can still be very revealing).

Ultimately, we need to keep raising our voices—using the very platforms Silicon Valley has given us—to demand that social networks give us a serious status update.

THE #FEMINIST FALLACY

In early 2019, Gillette posted an online video called "We Believe: The Best Men Can Be," which called on men to stop bullying and sexual harassment.

Men responded to this proposition by saying they'd boycott the brand. "Comments on the video are largely negative, with viewers saying they will never buy Gillette products again or that the advert was 'feminist propaganda,'" the BBC reported.[1]

"I'm researching every product made by Proctor & Gamble, throwing any I have in the trash, and never buying any of them again until everyone involved in this ad from top to bottom is fired and the company issues a public apology," a user named JoeS3678 posted on X (then called Twitter).[2]

When I talked to Rondell Wescott, executive producer of the video, he explained that Procter & Gamble had asked the Grey advertising agency's New York office to create a concept that would speak to the #MeToo movement that was roiling the culture at the time. The reaction wasn't exactly what they'd expected.

Wescott showed me clips of men responding to the video by flushing Gillette razors down the toilet and smashing their shaving cream cans with a bat. And he told me the film's director received threats against her family and career.

"People were like, how dare we have a female director tell men what to do?" he remembers. "This didn't just become the most disliked ad of the year on YouTube. It became the most disliked ad *of all time.*"

Remember: this wasn't a video that called for women to have equal opportunities—or anything else that some men might perceive as taking privileges away from them. It simply called on men not to let people be *physically attacked.*

"Whereas a lot of ads ask women to improve themselves and explain how to be a better mom or friend, men are not really challenged in that same way in our popular culture," Kasey Windels, PhD, an associate professor of advertising at the University of Florida, told me. "So calling attention to toxic masculinity and asking for reflection and change really backfired in a big way."

Wescott says he's never seen another brand try to send this message to men in an ad ever again.

Instead, campaigns by brands telling women what to do—or "femvertising," short for "female empowerment advertising"[3]—have been one of the predominant ways "feminism" has been represented on social media in recent years. These days it feels like peak femvertising has passed—but we're just beginning to reckon with the backlash against feminism it has helped usher in, circumscribing the rights of millions of women and girls. And, on social media, we can expect brands to keep deploying the same tactics they've used in femvertisements in the future, trying to convince women that the path to empowerment is through products rather than fighting the patriarchy.

*   *   *

Here's how it started. In 2004, Dove launched its Campaign for Real Beauty. The company announced it had commissioned research which found that only 2 percent of women around the world think of themselves as beautiful and set out to change that (never mind that Dove learned of this "global" phenomenon from an analysis that did not include a single woman in Africa or in any Asian country other than Japan).[4] Initial ads featured billboards that asked strangers to stare at the bodies of women who were allegedly not professional models and phone in to vote whether they were "grey or gorgeous," "fat or fab."[5] (If you've made it this far in this book, I probably don't have to explain to you that judging women based on their bodies rather than their brains is a profoundly antifeminist— not feminist—act.)

Over the years, Dove has stuck with the theme. In 2013, it released an online video showing what happened when women were asked to describe their appearances to an artist who sketched them. Then strangers described the same women to artists. The sketches, unsurprisingly, revealed that strangers find women to be much more beautiful than they describe themselves to be.[6] The campaign quickly went viral and within a month became the most watched video ad ever.[7] Dove's 2022 campaign warned girls and their parents about toxic beauty advice girls see on social media.[8]

The company's appropriation of feminism—using it in the service of sales rather than to address the structural problems women face—proved astonishingly profitable: over the first ten years of the campaign, Dove's sales increased from $2.5 billion to $4 billion.[9]

Seeing its success, other companies were soon spinning out similar campaigns. Pantene launched a 2013 campaign in the Philippines showing the double standards women face. When a man leads, he's the "boss," whereas a woman is "bossy." A man is "persuasive," while a woman is "pushy."[10] The company followed up the next year with a #ShineStrong campaign showing that women frequently say sorry in situations when men don't apologize.[11]

Always launched its #LikeAGirl campaign in 2014 to show how girls lose their confidence when they hit puberty. Videos showed what happened when boys and older girls were asked to run like a girl: they helplessly flailed their arms and legs.[12]

"It's like, wow, OK, here's an ad that isn't shaming women or explicitly telling them they're doing something wrong," Andi Zeisler, cofounder of Bitch Media, told me. "They were clearing a very low bar and yet people still lost their minds. Trade publications couldn't shut up about it, there were whole conferences about it. The ad industry got very high on its own supply."

Soon femvertisements were ubiquitous. A 2019 study found over 100 different examples.[13] They're still all over social media.

And if you don't want to practice feminism by purchasing Pantene hydrating glow shampoo with baobab essence, you can buy "feminist" or "girl power" products across the Internet. In early 2023, there were over 100,000 of them for sale on etsy.

Now women wear feminist t-shirts and think they're somehow advancing the cause. It's part of a movement dean of the Annenberg School for Communication Sarah Banet-Weiser, PhD, calls "popular feminism."[14] The phrase seems to be everywhere.

Femvertisements encourage us to fall for something I call the #feminist fallacy. In 1990, sociologist Marjorie Ferguson, PhD, called the "feminist fallacy" the misconception that women's increased visibility in the media would lead to more real-world power for women.[15] Today, popular feminism campaigns on social media have left us with the modern myth that the portrayal of feminism on the Internet will somehow lead to an improvement of the lives of women offline. Instead, in many ways, the opposite has happened.

That's partly because these campaigns keep the focus on our bodies. Dove's campaigns aren't telling us to fight for our rights. They don't suggest that it's what's inside that counts. They encourage us (and everyone around us) to keep looking at our bodies—just (a little) differently.

After all, most of the women they show are still conventionally attractive, Dr. Windels pointed out. "We are seeing people who are beautiful in every way except they are not a size 2, so that means they are relatable to us regular people," she says. "And we're seeing a very specific version of femininity in which women tailor their bodies to be their most beautiful, sexual, available-to-men versions of themselves."

By the way, it turns out Dove photoshopped the women featured in the Real Beauty campaign. (No, I'm not making this up. I really couldn't.)[16]

It's great for women to know they shouldn't compare themselves to flawless supermodels. But the new standards these campaigns set aren't exactly revolutionary. In fact, even the companies that create them don't buy into their own messages. While running its Real Beauty campaign, Dove has continued to sell "firming cream" designed to reduce cellulite. (Everyone has cellulite. It's not caused by being overweight.[17]) And Dove's parent company Unilever has kept right on selling Glow & Lovely—a rebranded form of its skin-whitening cream formerly called Fair & Lovely.[18] For the first ten years of the Real Beauty campaign, Unilever also sold Slim-Fast products designed to help people diet and lose weight.[19]

What's more, Dr. Windels pointed out, at the same time as Dove has been running these women's empowerment campaigns, Unilever, its parent company, has been running ads for other brands like Axe and Lynx that suggest, "hey men, spray on this spray and thin, gorgeous, haven't-eaten-in-a-week women are going to flock to you and throw themselves at you wearing bras and underwear." So, in the end, the company's commitment to challenging the shocking beauty standards women are up against didn't extend beyond its bottom line.

"I don't think advertising is meant to do anything but what it says on the tin," Zeisler told me. "It's trying to get you to buy stuff."

But more than 70 percent of poor people in America are women and children.[20] They can't buy their way to empowerment. That probably helps explain why, as Dr. Banet-Weiser points out, the women featured in femvertising are often part of "a particular race and class—typically white and wealthy enough to purchase the latest trends and a smart phone."[21]

It's more than a little ironic for companies like Dove and Pantene that have long sold beauty products by capitalizing on women's insecurities to now tell us that our insecurities are our *own faults* and *we* need to do the changing by rethinking how we see ourselves. But that's not the half of it. Dr. Windels points out that femvertisements are all about what women need to do individually: Buy the right products. Feel confident. Be our best selves. Instead of changing the structures and systems that hold us back.

"They do a really excellent job of drawing on the ideals of feminism, stripping away all the parts that are political and make us reach for collective action, and selling it back to us," Dr. Windels told me. "But us not feeling empowered isn't really what's keeping women from achieving equality. That's things like the glass ceiling, men being seen as leaders while women aren't, and women being penalized for having children while dads get promotions."

Dr. Windels says we won't solve women's problems until we address these things—but the good feelings these online videos give us may stop us from doing the harder work that needs to happen in order to change our society.

Keeping us busy blaming and trying to change ourselves instead is awfully convenient for a lot of people. "To paraphrase James Baldwin, to be aware of what is happening in this world is to be in an almost perpetual state of rage," Mikki Kendall writes in *Hood Feminism*.[22] If we used social media to talk about our real problems, we might demand that the auto industry stop making cars designed to save the lives of men instead of women. Women are 73 percent more likely than men to be severely injured in car crashes and 17 percent more likely to die in them, because crash test dummies have been mostly designed to protect the body of the average man in the 1970s[23]. We might demand that companies stop expecting professionals to put in more than 40 hours of work per week—a barefaced form of misogyny that assumes workers can be available round the clock because women are home to take care of the house and children, and largely helps explain why American women earn 82 cents for every dollar earned by men.[24] We might even ask for things like more toilet stalls in public places, since women spend more time in the bathroom because we get our periods, experience pregnancy, and are more likely to bring kids with us.[25]

Of course, if we really wanted to talk about how to solve our problems, we might also mention what men need to do. We live in a world where nearly one in three women has experienced sexual violence or violence from a partner, according to UN Women. The numbers are so staggering that the pope recently referred to them as "almost satanic."[26] But, as we've established, you're not likely to see another viral video telling men to stop assaulting their girlfriends and wives.

And if women weren't so focused on fixing ourselves, we might call on companies that claim to be all about empowering women to bring receipts. "If you're going to have a message of female empowerment, your organization should have equality for men and women," Dr. Windels argues. "You should have an equal number of men and women on the corporate board, on the executive level, and all the way down and those men and women should make equal salaries for their equal contributions. I don't know that any organization does that currently."

But instead of complaining, in recent years many of us have been watching and sharing viral videos these companies make telling us to feel beautiful, be confident, and buy triple-moisture body wash.

I'll admit that femvertising is a massive improvement from the messages brands used to send. In the 1980s, a lot of ads featured white, anorexic, half-naked women. The fact that we see a bit more diversity and slightly larger body sizes *is* progress. And because they're online, we can talk back. When Dove released a 2017 ad for body wash that appeared to show a Black woman turning white, social media (rightly) erupted in outrage. The company apologized.[27]

But the problem is that while I see some serious commentary on feminist issues online thanks to the people I follow, it's certainly not among the most popular content shared on social media. Remember that Dove's Sketches video was one of the most watched videos on the Internet at the time it was released. It wasn't in competition with others about rape culture or the way unpredictable, last-minute shift scheduling makes it impossible for moms working in retail and food service jobs to arrange childcare.[28]

Backlash

What's more, femvertising hasn't just *not* empowered women. It has also triggered a tidal wave of backlash that has stripped us of some of our power and rights.

"Every time there's a prominent feminist movement, it's followed by an equally prominent backlash," Zeisler told me. "In our culture there's a way in which any sort of issue becomes repellent to people when it hits a certain saturation point. Right now we're seeing a backlash that's structurally similar to the 1980s, where people are like, 'there's too much feminism in the culture.' They're saying, 'I'm tired of hearing about this subject and in fact I'm so tired of hearing about it that it's annoying me and making me not like it.'"

The effects of this are clear. Donald Trump was elected president in 2016 after video footage emerged of him bragging that he could sexually assault women with impunity.[29] "Trump presents himself (and his supporters see him) as being on a recuperative mission, a pursuit to restore patriarchy, to repair injuries caused by women, to return capacity to men," Dr. Banet-Weiser writes in *Empowered: Popular Feminism and Popular Misogyny*.[30]

Brett Kavanaugh was confirmed to the Supreme Court in 2018 after being credibly accused of sexual assault.[31] *Roe v. Wade*, the Supreme Court decision that protected women's right to abortion in the United States, was overturned in 2022.[32]

The number of high school girls who said they'd been forced to have sex increased by nearly 17 percent between 2011 and 2021, according to the CDC's Youth Risk Behavior Survey.[33]

In 2022, Erin Griffith pointed out in *The New York Times* that bro culture is back in Silicon Valley.[34] Some of the men pushed out of Hollywood by the #MeToo movement are also back.[35] When Amber Heard accused Johnny Depp of domestic and sexual violence, social media rallied to support him. The week before the verdict in a 2022 trial in which they both claimed they'd been victims of defamation, #IStandWithAmberHeard racked up 8.2 million views on TikTok. #JusticeForJohnnyDepp got 15 *billion*.[36]

Shocking numbers of people say they think feminism has done more harm than good. As Michelle Goldberg recently declared in *The New York Times*, "the future isn't female anymore."[37]

"We are the first generation in American history to have to tell the next generation they have less rights than us," Linda Sarsour told me.

Of course, this is partly thanks to a decades-long fight against feminism bankrolled by right-wing groups. But part of it is also a reaction to what people have seen on social media.

"This backlash amounts to feminism fatigue," Zeisler says. "But that's not the fault of feminists, that's the fault of the people who amplified the signal so they could make money."

Similarly, in *Terrorizing Gender: Transgender Visibility and the Surveillance Practices of the U.S. Security State*, Mia Fischer, PhD, argues that contrary to popular belief, the increased visibility of transgender people on social media and other forms of media hasn't made our society more tolerant. It's had the opposite effect: it "has actually resulted in a conservative backlash, with increased surveillance and regulation of trans people." That helps explain the wave of recent legislation targeting their rights and violence against transgender people, Dr. Fischer says.[38]

Meanwhile, all the problems women face, all the reasons we need *real* feminism, still exist. But what happens when we try to talk about them?

"Social media has turned feminism into a pariah," Sarsour tells me. "When people are not saying 'let's be confident and ask for a raise' but we're challenging systems and holding corporations or people in power accountable, people who don't support our rights are really attracted to these posts. It's an invitation for being harassed and mocked by trolls in ways that are really detrimental to progress and also to the mental health of these women."

Activism Versus Slacktivism

The other problem is how what we see on social media distracts us, which can prevent us from focusing on the harder work of advancing feminism. We're constantly checking out the latest memes and updates on our ex's tropical vacation with another woman and what our high school friends cooked for dinner. We're also preoccupied selecting the right filters for our own posts. It keeps us busy with a never-ending circus that would have exceeded the wildest imaginations of ancient Roman rulers.

This is why, as writer Jia Tolentino puts it, the Internet can "feel like a shunt diverting our energy *away* from action, leaving the real-world sphere to the people who already control it, keeping us busy figuring out the precisely correct way of explaining our lives."[39]

While serious commentary on issues does exist, it's not front and center on most people's feeds. In recent years, many of the sites that focused on issues that actually matter to women—like The Hairpin, the Feministing blog, and Bitch Media—have shuttered.[40]

But Zeisler tells me we can still advance the feminist movement online. "The term intersectional feminism [the idea that you can't talk about a woman's experience without taking her race, class, and other factors into account] has been around for a couple decades, but it was really demystified by social media and the conversations happening there," she points out. "So education is possible if you really want to learn and contribute less and listen more." (Credit check: the term intersectionality was coined by Kimberlé Crenshaw, a Black feminist legal scholar.[41])

Renee Bracey Sherman told me she remembers taking a feminism class in college with a white professor who insisted that Beyoncé's song "Single Ladies (Put a Ring on It)" was antifeminist. Back then, Bracey Sherman wasn't on social media, but she thinks if she had been she would have had the language to push back on that professor's beliefs more. Now, she says, she loves following Black feminists online who dissect the deeper meanings in Beyoncé's songs. And, she says, talking about feminism through pop culture can be an onramp for people. "People can learn a bit, learn a little more, and go from there," she says.

What about online feminist activism? We've seen that social media can be a formidable tool. Take the Women's March. It began with a single Facebook post. On election night 2016, Theresa Shook—a retired grandma in Hawaii—created a Facebook event for a protest online. Others were thinking the same thing and joined forces. The rest is history—literally.[42] It was the biggest single-day protest ever held in the United States, according to the History Channel.[43]

And after Lauren Smith-Fields, a 23-year-old Black woman, died on a Bumble date with a 37-year-old white man in Connecticut in 2021, a detective told her mom that the man was "a really nice guy." Police didn't initially collect evidence from Smith-Fields' apartment, where she died, according to her mom's lawyer. But after sustained social media outrage, the police opened an investigation.[44]

Sarah Jackson, PhD, Moya Bailey, PhD, and Brooke Foucault-Welles, PhD, write in *#Hashtag Activism* about the ways that women who have been excluded from mainstream media and culture have managed to shape the public conversation by using hashtags. For example, when the Komen Foundation announced they were cutting off funds for breast cancer screening at Planned Parenthood and people responded with outrage on social media, the foundation changed its decision. Three Black women—Alicia Garza, Patrisse Cullors, and Opal Tometi—started the Black Lives Matter movement, and it took off online, changing public attitudes by raising awareness of the injustices Black people face. Other hashtags like #WhyIStayed, #GirlsLikeUs, and #FastTailedGirls have raised public awareness of problems like victim blaming, abuse against transgender people, and the sexualization of Black girls. And the #MeToo movement can only have made men more fearful of being held responsible—very publicly—for sexual abuse.[45]

When I spoke to Dr. Jackson, she pointed out that social media has allowed women to come together and show that so many of us are having the same experiences with things like street harassment. "Speaking in that collective voice is an important strategy because it's always central to shifting public opinion," she told me. But, she said, "there's a risk of over-essentializing experiences. We need to recognize the differences experienced by women of different races and sexual identities."

Take the #MeToo movement. Yes, we heard from women in Hollywood and the media and politics and fashion. But how many stories did you hear of women janitors, farmworkers, and domestic workers? Bernice Yeung, who shares these women's experiences in her book *In a Day's Work: The Fight to End Sexual Violence Against America's Most Vulnerable Workers*, told me that "some of the women reacted to the #MeToo movement by saying, 'we've been dealing with this for so long, when we said something how come no one responded this way?' Some definitely felt frustrated that they weren't initially heard."

Part of the problem is their social media reach, she said. "I know a lot of the workers are on social media, but they're sometimes not on platforms in English or posting in English and they don't have the same platform as Alyssa Milano where their post might be read by millions and reacted to by millions, so they're just not being seen," she said.

But while these women are often being ignored, as we've seen, other heavily shared content about the supposed problems with "feminism" is being written by Russian trolls who know how to craft an inflammatory post to go viral.[46]

Another problem is that when we talk about issues on social media, we think we've done something about them. Tolentino calls these kinds of virtue signaling posts, where women collectively react with outrage to events like the Isla Vista massacre or the #MeToo movement, "performative solidarity." We say what we're against but not what we're for, then we move on with our lives and don't do anything more to change things.

Tolentino says "the most mainstream gestures of solidarity are pure representation, like viral reposts or avatar photos with cause-related filters, and meanwhile the *actual* mechanisms through which political solidarity is enacted, like strikes and boycotts, still exist on the fringe."[47]

It's not that these kinds of posts are meaningless. They can help shape public opinion—and changing perceptions is usually the first step toward changing public policy. But the next step often requires putting on our shoes and going offline to protest, attend town halls, vote. We don't always do that part.

What happens when women propose taking action—like when a senator singlehandedly kills a bill that would have provided the childcare America's moms desperately need, and someone posts suggesting we all bring our kids to cry outside his yacht? Do we grab our baby carriers and go? Nope, too often we laugh, hit like, and keep scrolling, looking for our next lark.

What We Can Do

We've all got to start practicing instead of purchasing feminism. Here's how we can do it.

"The future of issues we care about depends on which voices are amplified, which calls to action are amplified, and which are maligned and marginalized," Sarsour told me. The good news is that social media allows us to have a say in this. So we need to actively seek out, follow, like, and share the content of people who post about issues that matter to women collectively. If we want sites like Women's eNews to survive, we have to read and share their stories. Visit my website, www.karaalaimo.com, for a list of feminists to follow.

Social media also offers ways of pushing back on misogyny. "Conservative narratives say feminists are sad and angry and have no husbands," Bracey Sherman says. "Social media gives us a way to say yeah, some of us don't have kids and husbands and guess what?

Our lives are fucking amazing. It exposes people to something new and different but also creates a counternarrative to whatever conservatives are saying about us."

It's up to us to follow these diverse voices. "Widening the reach of who you are following and paying attention to is super important," Senti Sojwal, cofounder of the Asian American Feminist Collective, told me. "With the rise in anti-Asian violence, I would hope people are turning for assessment and commentary to Asian-American organizers and political institutions focused on liberating our communities and anti-violence activists. I hope you're not just turning to the most visible feminists out there."

Feminists with larger followings can amplify the voices of women who don't enjoy big platforms, Yeung pointed out. She says the best way to do this is often by developing relationships and trust in real life, then moving into the virtual world and helping create spaces where women can tell their stories.

Bracey Sherman says she gets frustrated when people with power, money, and influence tell her they are following and learning from her—but don't give her credit or fund her work. "Feminists should be talking about who they are learning from," she says.

We also have to speak out on social media about issues and how they affect us. But it's not enough to complain. We have to explicitly call on people to change things. Post and tag senators and businesses telling them exactly what you want them to do.

As we've seen, so-called hashtag activism can call out and change the behavior of individuals and groups. It can also raise consciousness of issues and the structures we need to dismantle. We all just need to grab our phones and do a whole lot more of it.

On social media we can also change the terms of conversations. The top Google results when you search Elon Musk or Donald

Trump might all be different versions of the same story about the latest outrageous thing they did or said to try to control the narrative, but we can post about what's most relevant rather than most recent—like their ugly brands of misogyny.[48]

While we have to take the conversation about feminism back from brands, we should also demand more from them. When corporations tell women we have to solve our problems, let's all reply and tell them to try taking a look at the people who are actually holding us back. When they tell us our worth is tied up in our bodies, let's clap back and tell them we've had enough. One thing we can all learn from the Gillette video is that brands are easily spooked. Throw some serious shade on one company for airbrushing their "real" women or telling us the secret to empowerment is shampoo, and the whole industry might be scared to commit the same sin.

While we're absolutely up against goliaths when we take on corporations, don't lose sight of the fact that calling them out *can sometimes work*. Google didn't exactly put out a press release thanking Safiya Umoja Noble, PhD, for pointing out that its top search results for "Black girls" were often porn sites—but it did quietly fix the problem.[49] What's more, one of the reasons major tech companies reportedly didn't jump in first to launch products with generative artificial intelligence—the kinds of tools that create content for us— was because they knew it can spew sexism and other offensive material.[50] While these concerns also haven't stopped companies from developing the technology, this does tell us that the outrage they've heard about sexism on their platforms in the past has been heard and is at least making them try to act more responsibly. This is proof of why we have to keep the pressure on.

We also have to take the fight to the nonvirtual world. Sarsour tells me the tougher bonds to forge—between Jewish and Muslim women, or women who are faithful and those who aren't religious, for example—are often better built offline. "The reason I have empathy for people in other communities is not because I'm a naturally empathetic person," she says. "It's because I have people from these communities who I love. I've been to their homes, I've broken bread with them, I know their children. Getting to know people is something we've lost because of social media. Everyone is behind a screen. We need to meet people. Get coffee. Listen to their story and that's how you build relationships."

This is why social media posts alone probably aren't going to change the world. "This can't just be virtue signaling online, 'this discrimination needs to end,' end post, and that's the tweet," Dr. Jones, the Farmingdale sociology professor, told me. "It needs to be backed up with some kind of direct action."

So donate to Planned Parenthood. Volunteer at your local rape crisis center. Vote like your life depends on it. (It does.) Phone bank to help elect women who will fight for other women to office. Better yet, run for office. And the next time someone organizes that sit in with screaming babies outside the yacht of a senator who is standing in our way, grab your kid. Go. Don't just sit there and keep scrolling while you're getting screwed over.

HOW TO BE SAVVY ON SOCIAL MEDIA

By now it's sickeningly clear that being a woman or girl makes us even more vulnerable to harm on social media. For some women and girls like Vivian, social media displaces the deep friendships we need in order to be happy and promotes dangerous body dissatisfaction and eating disorders. Social networks encourage us to focus on our appearances and invite the world to judge us. They expose us to a slew of new dangers—like introductions to catfishers trying to steal our money or serial rapists who find their victims on dating apps, as well as sextortionists who now sexually abuse women without ever having to leave their homes. Social media also serves us up misinformation that can harm our mental health and encourages us to make potentially deadly medical decisions. Many of the women who try to make a living on social media are exploited, while women who work in tech companies are up against shocking sexism, sexual abuse, misogyny, and racism. Women in other professions who try to use social media to burnish their professional reputations often get fewer followers and opportunities as a result than men. The trolling women experience has become so toxic that many women are fleeing social media altogether, leaving them deprived of opportunities to bolster their careers, keep up with friends, and generally participate in our society. And social media has been used to feed us a form of feminism that involves blaming ourselves while worshiping the very corporations who perpetuate our problems. Now everyone's so sick of these representations of women's supposed empowerment that the backlash has begun—leaving us in a world that is in many ways far uglier and more dangerous for women than it was before social networks arrived on the scene.

It's absolutely on lawmakers and tech companies to fix a lot of these problems. But, in the meantime, we've got to make sure we stay safe on social media and look out for our moms, daughters, and friends. Here's a reminder of how to be savvy on social media—and, even better, how to use your platforms to empower yourself and other women.

Using Social Media Yourself

1. Pay attention to how much time you spend online, Laura Otton, the psychotherapist, says. Would you be better off using the time to work out, read a book, pursue a hobby? Or sleep, even? Social platforms are designed to hack our attention, with addictive features like notifications when we get likes or comments and bottomless feeds that never send us the signal that maybe it's time to sign off.
2. Think about how the people you follow are making you feel. If it's less than, it's time to swap them out for people who make you laugh, mamas with messy homes, or women who preach body positivity.
3. Watch what you post. Are you authenticity policing a woman? Criticizing her in ways you wouldn't if she were a white cisgender man? Commenting on her appearance or other attributes that wouldn't be noteworthy if she were a man? Shaming her for something that might be a totally inaccurate representation of her true character?

4. Watch what your family and friends post. If it's sexist or misogynistic, call them in for a respectful offline conversation. Tell them why you think it's wrong. But resist the urge to give sexist strangers your most devastating comebacks. That will only up the algorithmic rankings of their posts and encourage social networks to show us all more toxic content. Better to report posts that violate the community standards of social networks so platforms can (hopefully) take them down.

5. If you see a woman attacked online, don't jump in to defend her unless you know she wants you to. But do report the abuse to the social network it's happening on. Then try to support the woman by posting something positive about her—like comments about the value of her work. You can also consider sending her a personal message of support, but tell her you don't expect a reply.

6. If you meet someone online—on a dating app or otherwise—be very, very wary the person could be a cyber scammer. Ask to speak to them via video chat so you can see who is behind the screen. If you're meeting up in person, do so in a very public place, tell people where you're going, and make sure the person you're meeting knows that your loved ones know where you are. Meet their family, friends, and colleagues to verify their identity and confirm they're good people. Don't trust or be alone with the person until you're certain you'll be safe. Don't use dating sites that don't do background checks, but also don't put too much faith in men whose results come up clear. Most rapists don't have criminal records.

7. If you're looking for a romantic partner online, take my friend Kate's advice: Be very specific about what you're looking for in your profile. Don't be afraid to say it. Good people who are looking for a relationship won't be scared away by a woman who is also looking for a partner. Spend time reading profiles

of potential dates carefully. If they haven't put much effort into them, it's a sign they're probably not serious. Weird spelling or grammar mistakes could be the sign of a foreign catfisher—or of someone who is just careless about dating. If you're looking for someone who is willing to commit, don't put up with people who string you along. Move on and meet people who do seem interested in pursuing an offline relationship. Don't take rejection personally (or, better yet, take it as a referendum on *them*, not you). And, of course, don't weed out potentially great matches based on race or for other superficial reasons. After you've done your filtering for the right reasons, take dating historian Zoe Strimpel's advice to "hold your nose and play a numbers game."

8. Do not use social media as a source of medical information. Full stop. There's way too much disinformation out there. Instead turn to your doctor and medical authorities like the CDC, American Academy of Pediatrics, and American College of Obstetricians and Gynecologists.

9. Remember that a lot of the information circulating on social media is not just fake, but deliberately designed to prey on women's deepest vulnerabilities. Before acting on anything you find on social media, conduct independent research to see if legitimate sources are also reporting that it's true. Look at the source, consider whether it's credible (does it come from people with legitimate credentials?) and think about what their motivations might be. Also keep Nina Jankowicz's advice in the back of your head: if you're having an emotional reaction to something, your guard should really go up that it may have been designed to misinform or manipulate you.

10. Protect your personal information. Use different, secure passwords for every single website. Don't answer questions or quizzes

online that give away answers to common security questions. Don't post personal information like your address on social networks. Consider using a VPN so websites can't track you. Think about paying for an email service that doesn't read the contents of your emails. If you need to share sensitive information, use Signal so the company can't access your messages.

11. Share your work with the world so it's visible. And boost other women! Make it a point to share, like, follow, and comment on other women's posts. Remember Linda Sarsour's words: "The future of issues we care about depends on which voices are amplified, which calls to action are amplified, and which are maligned and marginalized." So, like Dr. Zhu, use social media as a tool in the fight for gender equality. And anytime you learn something from a woman, be sure to give her public credit for it.

12. Create and share posts about issues women face. If we all do more of this, social networks will boost this kind of content in their algorithms. But don't just post empty messages of outrage or support. @ the lawmakers and corporate executives you want to take action and be specific about what you demand that they do. And remember that while online action can be great for raising awareness and connecting with like-minded people, to get things to change, we often have to combine our social media activism with offline work. I'm here for this. I hope you are, too.

13. When sharenting, take Nina Jankowicz's advice to create a Facebook list or use "close friends" on Instagram. Only share photos and updates with close friends and family and never, ever post pictures of your children undressed. Consider referring to your kids by pet names or initials. Post anonymously or

use a pseudonym when seeking resources like therapy or medical treatment for your child. And don't share anything that might send your daughter's future presidential campaign into a tailspin.

Helping Your Children Navigate Social Media

1. Talk to your kids' friends' parents while they're young and try to get on the same page about delaying when they start using social media, since it will be hard to enforce a no social media policy if all your children's friends are online.
2. Talk to your kids about the pressures and dangers they'll face on social media, from peers who ask them to sext to professional sextortionists—and how they can best handle them.
3. Discuss your family's values and how you can all display them online (hints: Spread kindness. Support others. Watch out for friends who might be in trouble. Don't value anyone—including yourself—for their appearances).
4. Make sure your kids know other people's lives aren't half as glamorous as they may appear on Instagram.
5. Make sure your kids know what they post can be used against them in very different contexts in the future.
6. Teach your kids to say no when they're not comfortable in a situation.
7. Make sure your kids receive comprehensive sex education, including porn literacy, so when they're inevitably exposed to online porn, they don't take the wrong lessons from it.
8. When they're old enough to use social media, help your kids find positive role models to follow and join healthy communities where they can develop their interests and identities.

9. Watch for signs your kids are not OK and get professional help if they need it.

10. Be a good role model by putting away your own phone and not oversharing on social media yourself.

11. Above all, make sure your children know they can come to you for help with any situation they face online without fear of punishment. No messing around here. Their lives may depend on it.

RESOURCES

Feminists to Follow

Visit my website, www.karaalaimo.com, for a list of feminists to follow and content creators with credentials who share information about pregnancy and parenting.

Have a Medical Question?

Please consult your doctor, not social media.

You can also check out the websites of the Centers for Disease Control and Prevention (www.cdc.gov), American College of Obstetricians and Gynecologists (www.acog.org), and American Academy of Pediatrics (www.aap.org) for medical guidance from credentialed experts.

As you read in Chapter 5, Britain's National Health Service has a weekly pregnancy guide. It's available at www.nhs.uk/pregnancy /week-by-week/

Helping Your Kids Use Social Media

The website of Common Sense Media, www.commonsensemedia. org, offers guides to help your kids navigate social media.

If You Experience an Online Crime

If you're the victim of an online crime, please strongly consider reporting it to the FBI. You can fill out an online form on the agency's Internet Crime Complaint Center.

If you're the victim of nonconsensual pornography, go to the Cyber Civil Rights Initiative website. The organization offers a 24-7 crisis helpline for victims (844-878-2274), a guide explaining how to report the material to major social platforms (be sure to document evidence first), a list of attorneys who will help for free or on a low-cost basis, and more resources.

And if your child has been the victim of sextortion or other exploitation, contact the National Center for Missing and Exploited Children (their 24-hour hotline is 1-800-843-5678).

I'm a professor. You didn't really think I'd let you go without recommending more books, did you?

- For more on the misogyny women are up against in our society, I highly recommend Kate Manne's powerful book *Entitled: How Male Privilege Hurts Women*
- John Palfrey and Urs Gasser's *The Connected Parent: An Expert Guide to Parenting in a Digital World* offers helpful tips for handling your kids' use of social media, as does Devorah Heitner's *Growing Up in Public: Coming of Age in a Digital World*
- Danielle Keats Citron's *The Fight for Online Privacy: Protecting Dignity, Identity and Love in the Digital Age* is an important book about why we need a right to sexual privacy and how laws can be designed to protect it
- Carrie Goldberg discusses gendered violence women experience online in her book *Nobody's Victim: Fighting Psychos, Stalkers, Pervs, and Trolls*

- Nina Jankowicz's book *How to Be a Woman Online: Surviving Abuse and Harassment, and How to Fight Back* contains a lot of helpful tips for protecting your privacy and safety online
- Zoë Quinn's book *Crash Override: How Gamergate (Nearly) Destroyed My Life, and How We Can Win the Fight Against Online Hate* is a powerful firsthand account of their experience with online hate and how we can stop it
- For more on the problems with "natural" childbirth and parenting, I recommend Dr. Amy Tuteur's book *Push Back: Guilt in the Age of Natural Parenting*

REFERENCES

Introduction

1   Kelly, Yvonne, Afshin Zilanawala, Cara Booker, and Amanda Sacker. "Social Media Use and Adolescent Mental Health: Findings from the UK Millennium Cohort Study." *EClinicalMedicine* 6 (2019): 59–68. https://www.thelancet.com/journals/eclinm/article/PIIS2589 -5370(18)30060-9/fulltext

2   "Public Attitudes About Today's Dating Landscape." *Pew Research Center*, August 14, 2020. https://www.pewresearch.org/social -trends/2020/08/20/public-attitudes-about-todays-dating-landscape /psdt_08-19-20_dating-relationships-03-9/

3   "Emerging New Threat in Online Dating." National Crime Agency, February 7, 2016. https://nationalcrimeagency.gov.uk/who-we-are /publications/607-nca-scas-online-dating-report-2016/file

4   Cousins, Keith, Hillary Flynn, and Elizabeth Naismith Picciani. "Tinder Lets Known Sex Offenders Use the App. It's Not the Only One." *Pro-Publica*, December 2, 2019. https://www.propublica.org/article/tinder -lets-known-sex-offenders-use-the-app-its-not-the-only-one

5   Harris, Kamala. *The Truths We Hold: An American Journey*. New York: Penguin, 2019, p. 264.

6   DiBranco, Alex. "Male Supremacist Terrorism as a Rising Threat." *ICCT*, February 10, 2020. https://www.icct.nl/index.php/publication /male-supremacist-terrorism-rising-threat

7   Jarrett, Kylie. *Feminism, Labour and Digital Media: The Digital House-wife*. Routledge, 2017.

8   Zhu, Jane M., Arthur P. Pelullo, and Sayed Hassan. "Gender Differences in Twitter Use and Influence Among Health Policy and Health Services Researchers." *JAMA International Medicine* 179, no. 12 (October 14, 2019): 1726–1729. https://jamanetwork.com/journals/jamainternalmedicine/article-abstract/2753117; Woitowich, Nicole C., Vineet M. Arora, and Tricia Pendergrast. "Gender Differences in Physician Use of Social Media for Professional Advancement." *JAMA Network Open* 4, no. 5 (2021). https://jamanetwork.com/journals/jamanetworkopen/fullarticle/2779868

9   "Measuring the Prevalence of Online Violence Against Women." *Economist Intelligence Unit*, March 1, 2021. https://onlineviolencewomen.eiu.com/

10   "Troll Patrol Findings." Amnesty International, April 4, 2018. https://decoders.amnesty.org/projects/troll-patrol/findings

11   "The Klear Influencer Marketing Rate Card." *Klear*, 2019. https://klear.com/KlearRateCard.pdf

12   McCarthy, Niall. "Where U.S. Tech Workers Get Paid the Most." *Statista*, June 17, 2020. https://www.statista.com/chart/22030/average-tech-worker-salary-in-us-cities/; "Average Social Media Manager Salary." *PayScale*, 2021. https://www.payscale.com/research/US/Job=Social_Media_Manager/Salary

13   "Violence Targeting Women in Politics: Trends in Targets, Types, and Perpetrators of Political Violence." *ReliefWeb*, December 8, 2021. https://reliefweb.int/report/world/violence-targeting-women-politics-trends-targets-types-and-perpetrators-political

14   Grose, Jessica. "Nikki Haley's Résumé Is Perfect. It Might Not Matter." *The New York Times*, March 11, 2023. https://www.nytimes.com/2023/03/11/opinion/nikki-haley.html

Chapter 1: Girl Meets Instagram

1   Plunkett, Leah. *Sharenthood: Why We Should Think Before We Talk About Our Kids Online.* Cambridge: MIT Press, 2019, p. xviii.

2 "Youth Risk Behavior Survey Data Summary & Trends Report: 2011–2021." CDC, 2023. https://www.cdc.gov/healthyyouth/data/yrbs/pdf/YRBS_Data-Summary-Trends_Report2023_508.pdf

3 Garcia, Sandra E. "Baby Tate Turns Hate Into Positivity." *The New York Times*, December 1, 2021. https://www.nytimes.com/2021/12/01/style/baby-tate.html

4 Durkin, Sarah J. and Susan J. Paxton. "Predictors of Vulnerability to Reduced Body Image Satisfaction and Psychological Wellbeing in Response to Exposure to Idealized Female Media Images in Adolescent Girls." *Journal of Psychosomatic Research* 53, no. 5 (2002): 995–1005.

5 Kolata, Gina. "New Drugs Could Help Treat Obesity. Could They End the Stigma, Too?" *The New York Times*, May 11, 2021. https://www.nytimes.com/2021/05/11/health/obesity-drugs.html

6 Howard, Jacqueline. "What's the Average Age When Kids Get a Social Media Account?" *CNN Health*, June 22, 2018. https://www.cnn.com/2018/06/22/health/social-media-for-kids-parent-curve/index.html

7 Twenge, Jean. "Why Teen Depression Rates are Rising Faster for Girls than Boys." *The Conversation*, January 16, 2020. https://theconversation.com/why-teen-depression-rates-are-rising-faster-for-girls-than-boys-129732

8 "Brain Maturity Extends Well Beyond Teen Years." *NPR*, October 10, 2011. https://www.npr.org/templates/story/story.php?storyId=141164708

9 Shipman, Claire, Katty Kay, and JillEllyn Riley. "How Puberty Kills Girls' Confidence." *The Atlantic*, September 20, 2018. https://www.theatlantic.com/family/archive/2018/09/puberty-girls-confidence/563804/

10 Perry, Tod. "It's Getting Harder to Deny the Damage that Social Media is Doing to Teenage Girls." *Upworthy*, February 28, 2022. https://www.upworthy.com/its-getting-harder-to-deny-the-damage-that-social-media-is-doing-to-teenage-girls?rebelltitem=3#rebelltitem3

11 Franco, Marisa G. "How the Science of Attachment Can Help You Make and Keep Friends." Podcast audio. *Ten Percent Happier*,

February 20, 2023. https://www.tenpercent.com/podcast-episode/marisa-g-franco-561

12 Quinn, Zoë. *Crash Override: How Gamergate (Nearly) Destroyed My Life, and How We Can Win the Fight Against Online Hate.* New York: PublicAffairs, 2017, pp. 2, 3, 16, 19, 92, 165, 196.

13 Quinn, Zoë. *Crash Override: How Gamergate (Nearly) Destroyed My Life, and How We Can Win the Fight Against Online Hate.* New York: PublicAffairs, 2017, p. 5.

14 Quinn, Zoë. *Crash Override: How Gamergate (Nearly) Destroyed My Life, and How We Can Win the Fight Against Online Hate.* New York: PublicAffairs, 2017, pp. 26–27, 32, 39.

15 Zuboff, Shoshana. *The Age of Surveillance Capitalism: The Fight for a Human Future at the New Frontier of Power.* New York: PublicAffairs, 2019, p. 461.

16 Krasnova, Hanna, Helena Wenninger, Thomas Widjaja, and Peter Buxmann. "Envy on Facebook: A Hidden Threat to Users' Life Satisfaction?" *BORIS*, (2013). https://boris.unibe.ch/47080/1/WI%202013%20Final%20Submission%20Krasnova.pdf

17 Center for Countering Digital Hate. "Deadly by Design: TikTok Pushes Harmful Content Promoting Eating Disorders and Self-Harm into Young Users' Feeds." December 15, 2022. https://counterhate.com/research/deadly-by-design

18 O'Sullivan, Donnie, Clare Duffy, and Sarah Jorgensen. "Instagram Promoted Pages Glorifying Eating Disorders to Teen Accounts." *CNN Business*, October 4, 2021. https://www.cnn.com/2021/10/04/tech/instagram-facebook-eating-disorders/index.html

19 Center for Countering Digital Hate. "Deadly by Design: TikTok Pushes Harmful Content Promoting Eating Disorders and Self-Harm Into Young Users' Feeds." December 15, 2022. https://counterhate.com/research/deadly-by-design

20 Garcia, Sandra E. "Baby Tate Turns Hate Into Positivity." *The New York Times*, December 1, 2021. https://www.nytimes.com/2021/12/01/style/baby-tate.html

21 "Instagram Ranked Worst for Young People's Mental Health." *Royal Society for Public Health*, May 19, 2017. https://www.rsph.org.uk /about-us/news/instagram-ranked-worst-for-young-people-s-mental -health.html

22 Vogels, Emily A., Risa Gelles-Watnick, and Navid Massarat. "Teens, Social Media and Technology 2022." *Pew Research Center*, August 10, 2022. https://www.pewresearch.org/internet/2022/08/10/teens-social -media-and-technology-2022/

23 Kamenetz, Anya. "Facebook's Own Data Is Not As Conclusive as You Think About Teens and Mental Health." *NPR*, October 6, 2021. https:// www.npr.org/2021/10/06/1043138622/facebook-instagram-teens -mental-health

24 Wells, Georgia, Jeff Horwitz, and Deepa Seetharaman. "Facebook Knows Instagram Is Toxic for Teen Girls, Company Documents Show." *Wall Street Journal*, September 14, 2021. https://www.wsj.com /articles/facebook-knows-instagram-is-toxic-for-teen-girls-company -documents-show-11631620739

25 Anderson, Monica and Jingjing Jiang. "Teens, Social Media and Technology 2018." *Pew Research Center: Internet, Science & Tech*, May 31, 2018. https://www.pewresearch.org/internet/2018/05/31/teens-social -media-technology-2018/

26 Chua, Trudy Hui Hui and Leanne Chang. "Follow Me and Like My Beautiful Selfies: Singapore Teenage Girls' Engagement in Self-presentation and Peer Comparison on Social Media." *Computers in Human Behavior* 55 (2016): 190–197. https://doi.org/10.1016 /j.chb.2015.09.011

27 Sales, Nancy Jo. *American Girls: Social Media and the Secret Lives of Teenagers*. New York: Alfred A. Knopf, 2016, pp. 61–63.

28 Erikson, Erik H. *Identity and the Life Cycle*. W. W. Norton & Company, 1994.

29 Zuboff, Shoshana. *The Age of Surveillance Capitalism: The Fight for a Human Future at the New Frontier of Power*. New York: PublicAffairs, 2019, pp. 455–456.

30 "Youth Risk Behavior Survey Data Summary & Trends Report: 2011–2021." CDC, 2023. https://www.cdc.gov/healthyyouth/data/yrbs/pdf/YRBS_Data-Summary-Trends_Report2023_508.pdf

31 Mercado, Melissa C., Kristin Holland, and Ruth W. Leemis. "Trends in Emergency Department Visits for Nonfatal Self-Inflicted Injuries Among Youth Aged 10 to 24 Years in the United States, 2001–2015." *JAMA* 318, no. 19 (2017): 1931–1933. https://jamanetwork.com/journals/jama/fullarticle/2664031

32 "QuickStats: Suicide Rates for Teens Aged 15–19 years, by Sex—United States 1975–2015." *MMWR Morbidity Mortal Weekly Report* 66, no. 816. CDC, 2017. https://www.cdc.gov/mmwr/volumes/66/wr/mm6630a6.html

33 Orben, Amy, Andrew K. Przybylski, Sarah-Jayne Blakemore, and Rogier A. Kievit. "Windows of Developmental Sensitivity to Social Media." *Nature Communications* 13, no. 1649 (March 2022). https://www.nature.com/articles/s41467-022-29296-3

34 Alaimo, Kara. "In the Age of Internet Fame, Children Need Protection." *CNN*, August 4, 2019. https://www.cnn.com/2019/08/04/opinions/protections-for-child-internet-stars-opinion-alaimo/index.html

35 Levine, Alexandra S. "How TikTok Live Became 'A Strip Club Filled With 15-Year-Olds'." *Forbes*, April 27, 2022. https://www.forbes.com/sites/alexandralevine/2022/04/27/how-tiktok-live-became-a-strip-club-filled-with-15-year-olds/?sh=1b49d98a62d7

36 Williamson, Elizabeth. "A Child's TikTok Stardom Opens Doors. Then a Gunman Arrives." *The New York Times*, February 17, 2022. https://www.nytimes.com/2022/02/17/us/politics/tiktok-ava-majury.html

37 Manago, Adriana M., L. Monique Ward, Kristi M. Lemm, Lauren Reed, and Rita Seabrook. "Facebook Involvement, Objectified Body Consciousness, Body Shame, and Sexual Assertiveness in College Women and Men." *Sex Roles* 72 (2015): 1–14. https://link.springer.com/article/10.1007/s11199-014-0441-1

38 Sales, Nancy Jo. *American Girls: Social Media and The Secret Lives of Teenagers*. New York: Alfred A. Knopf, 2016, p. 134.

39 "Sexualization of Girls Is Linked to Common Mental Health Problems in Girls and Women—Eating Disorders, Low Self-Esteem, and Depression; An APA Task Force Reports." *American Psychological Association*, 2007. https://www.apa.org/news/press/releases/2007/02/sexualization

40 Mori, Camille, Jessica E. Cooke, Jeff R. Temple, Ly Anh, Lu Yu, Nina Anderson, Christina Rash, and Sheri Madigan. "The Prevalence of Sexting Behaviors Among Emerging Adults: A Meta-Analysis." *Archives of Sexual Behavior* 49 (2020): 1103–1119. https://www.proquest.com/docview/2387920622?pq-origsite=gscholar&fromopenview=true

41 "Social Media Fails Women: Transforming Social Media Policies for a Feminist Future." *UltraViolet*. https://weareultraviolet.org/wp-content/uploads/2021/11/Social-media-fails-women.pdf

42 Feldman, Amy E. "For Teens, Sexting Can Be a Crime." *The Wall Street Journal*, November 19, 2020. https://www.wsj.com/articles/for-teens-sexting-can-be-a-crime-11605801722

43 Goldberg, Carrie. *Nobody's Victim: Fighting Psychos, Stalkers, Pervs, and Trolls*. New York: Plume, 2019, p. 67.

44 Sales, Nancy Jo. *American Girls: Social Media and The Secret Lives of Teenagers*. New York: Alfred A. Knopf, 2016, p. 60.

45 Rothman, Emily F., Jonathon J. Beckmeyer, Debby Herbenick, Tsung-Chieh Fu, Brian Dodge, and J. Dennis Fortenberry. "The Prevalence of Using Pornography for Information About How to Have Sex: Findings From a Nationally Representative Survey of U.S. Adolescents and Young Adults." *Archives of Sexual Behavior* 50 (2021): 629–646. https://link.springer.com/article/10.1007%2Fs10508-020-01877-7

46 Jones, Maggie. "What Teenagers Are Learning From Online Porn." *The New York Times*, February 7, 2018. https://www.nytimes.com/2018/02/07/magazine/teenagers-learning-online-porn-literacy-sex-education.html

47   Orenstein, Peggy. "If You Ignore Porn, You Aren't Teaching Sex Ed." *The New York Times,* June 14, 2021. https://www.nytimes.com/2021/06/14/opinion/sex-ed-curriculum-pornography.html

48   Orenstein, Peggy. *Boys & Sex: Young Men on Hookups, Love, Porn, Consent, and Navigating the New Masculinity.* New York: Harper, 2020, p. 48.

49   Bartelt, Elizabeth, Debby Herbenick, Tsung-Chieh Fu, Bryant Paul, Ronna Gradus, Jill Bauer, and Rashida Jones. "Feeling Scared During Sex: Findings From a U.S. Probability Sample of Women and Men Ages 14 to 60." *Journal of Sex & Marital Therapy* 45, no. 5 (2019): 424–439. https://www.tandfonline.com/doi/full/10.1080/0092623X.2018.1549634

50   Wright, Paul J., Robert S. Tokunaga, and Ashley Kraus. "A Meta-Analysis of Pornography Consumption and Actual Acts of Sexual Aggression in General Population Studies." *Journal of Communication* 66, no. 1 (2016): 183–205. https://doi.org/10.1111/jcom.12201

51   Brosi, Matthew W., John D. Foubert, and R. Sean Bannon. "Pornography Viewing Among Fraternity Men: Effects on Bystander Intervention, Rape Myth Acceptance and Behavioral Intent to Commit Sexual Assault." *Sexual Health & Compulsivity* 18, no. 4 (2011): 212–231. https://www.tandfonline.com/doi/abs/10.1080/10720162.2011.625552

52   "The State of Gender Equality for U.S. Adolescents." *Plan International,* September 12, 2018. https://planusa-org-staging.s3.amazonaws.com/public/uploads/2021/04/state-of-gender-equality-summary-2018.pdf

53   Safronova, Valeriya. "A Private-School Sex Educator Defends Her Methods." *The New York Times,* July 7, 2021. https://www.nytimes.com/2021/07/07/style/sex-educator-methods-defense.html

54   Jankowicz, Nina. *How to Be a Woman Online: Surviving Abuse and Harassment, and How to Fight Back.* New York: Bloomsbury Academic, 2022, p. 14.

55   Mosseri, Adam. "Pausing 'Instagram Kids' and Building Parental Supervision Tools." *Instagram,* September 27, 2021. https://about.instagram.com/blog/announcements/pausing-instagram-kids

56 boyd, danah. *It's Complicated: The Social Lives of Networked Teens.* New Haven: Yale University Press, 2014, pp. 21–22.

57 boyd, danah. *It's Complicated: The Social Lives of Networked Teens.* New Haven: Yale University Press, 2014, p. 22.

58 Gobin, Keisha C., Sarah E. McComb, and Jennifer S. Mills. "Testing a Self-compassion Micro-intervention Before Appearance-based Social Media Use: Implications for Body Image." *Body Image* 40 (December 11, 2021): 200–206. https://pubmed.ncbi.nlm.nih.gov/34990896/

59 Jenco, Melissa. "AAP Endorses New Recommendations on Sleep Times." *American Academy of Pediatrics*, June 13, 2016. https://publications.aap.org/aapnews/news/6630/AAP-endorses-new-recommendations-on-sleep-times

60 Bloom, Mia and Sophia Moskalenko. *Pastels and Pedophiles: Inside the Mind of QAnon.* Stanford: Stanford University Press, 2021, p. 125.

61 Wells, Georgia, Jeff Horwitz, and Deepa Seetharaman. "Facebook Knows Instagram Is Toxic for Teen Girls, Company Documents Show." *Wall Street Journal*, September 14, 2021. https://www.wsj.com/articles/facebook-knows-instagram-is-toxic-for-teen-girls-company-documents-show-11631620739

Chapter 2: The Face in the Filter

1 "Social Intelligence Report: Adobe Digital Index Q4 2013." Yumpu.com. https://www.yumpu.com/en/document/read/40527196/adi-socialintelreport-q413

2 Salm, Lauren. "70% Of Employers Are Snooping Candidates' Social Media Profiles." *CareerBuilder*, June 15, 2017. https://www.careerbuilder.com/advice/social-media-survey-2017

3 Grant, Katie. "Female Job Applicants Far More Likely to Be Judged on Appearance, Study Finds." *Independent*, January 6, 2016. https://www.independent.co.uk/news/business/news/female-job-applicants-far-more-likely-to-be-judged-on-appearance-study-finds-a6799856.html

4   Fardouly, Jasmine and Lenny R. Vartanian. "Social Media and Body Image Concerns: Current Research and Future Directions." *Current Opinion in Psychology* 9 (2015): 1–5. https://www.sciencedirect.com /science/article/pii/S2352250X15002249

5   Fardouly, Jasmine, Brydie K. Willburger, and Lenny R. Vartanian. "Instagram Use and Young Women's Body Image Concerns and Self-objectification: Testing Mediational Pathways." *New Media and Society* 20, no. 4 (2018): 1380–1395. http://www2.psy.unsw.edu.au /Users/lvartanian/Publications/Fardouly,%20Willburger,%20%26 %20Vartanian%20(2018).pdf

6   Manago, Adriana M., L. Monique Ward, Kristi M. Lemm, Lauren Reed, and Rita Seabrook. "Facebook Involvement, Objectified Body Consciousness, Body Shame, and Sexual Assertiveness in College Women and Men." *Sex Roles* 72 (2015): 1–14. https://link.springer .com/content/pdf/10.1007/s11199-014-0441-1.pdf

7   "Plastic Surgery Statistics Report." *American Society of Plastic Surgeons,* 2020. https://www.plasticsurgery.org/documents/News/Statistics/2020 /plastic-surgery-statistics-full-report-2020.pdf

8   "The Aesthetic Society Releases Annual Statistics Revealing Significant Increases in Face, Breast and Body in 2021." *PR Newswire*, April 11, 2022. https://www.prnewswire.com/news-releases/the-aesthetic -society-releases-annual-statistics-revealing-significant-increases-in -face-breast-and-body-in-2021-301522417.html

9   Cramer, Renée. *Pregnant With the Stars: Watching and Wanting the Celebrity Baby Bump.* Stanford: Stanford University Press, 2016, p. 53.

10 Marcus, Stephanie. "Barbara Walters Tells Kardashian Family: 'You Have No Talent'." *HuffPost*, March 12, 2015. https://www.huffpost .com/entry/barbara-walters-tells-kardashian-family—you-have-no -talent_n_1151089

11 Kulish, Nicholas. "When Influencers Make Fools of Themselves." *The New York Times*, February 24, 2021. https://www.nytimes.com/2021 /02/24/magazine/when-influencers-make-fools-of-themselves.html

12 Motseki, Mpho and Toks Oyedemi. "Social Media and the Cultural Ideology of Beauty Among Young Black Women in South Africa." *Journal for Community Communication and Information Impact* 22 (2017). https://doi.org/10.18820/24150525/Comm.v22.11

13 Tatlow, Didi Kirsten. "On Social Media in China, Size 0 Doesn't Make the Cut." *The New York Times*, March 18, 2016. https://www.nytimes.com/2016/03/19/world/asia/china-paper-waist-challenge.html

14 Donato, Al. "Snapchat Controversy Arises Over 'Whitewashing' Beauty Filters." *HuffPost*, May 17, 2016. https://www.huffpost.com/archive/ca/entry/snapchat-controversy-arises-over-whitewashing-beauty-filters_n_10011062

15 ScienceDaily. "90% of Young Women Report Using a Filter or Editing their Photos Before Posting." March 8, 2021. https://www.sciencedaily.com/releases/2021/03/210308111852.htm

16 Julian, Kate. "Why Are Young People Having So Little Sex?" *The Atlantic*, December 2018. https://www.theatlantic.com/magazine/archive/2018/12/the-sex-recession/573949/

17 Wolf, Naomi. *The Beauty Myth: How Images of Beauty Are Used Against Women*. New York: William Morrow and Company, 1991, pp. 14–15.

18 Wolf, Naomi. *The Beauty Myth: How Images of Beauty Are Used Against Women*. New York: William Morrow and Company, 1991, pp. 18–19.

19 Sanders, Linley. "Hillary Clinton's Campaign Hair and Makeup Took 600 Hours Because the World Is Sexist." *Newsweek*, September 27, 2017. https://www.newsweek.com/hillary-clinton-spent-600-hours-campaign-makeup-because-gender-expectations-672514

20 Dahl, Melissa. "Stop Obsessing: Women Spend 2 Weeks a Year on Their Appearance, TODAY Survey Shows." *TODAY*, February 24, 2014. https://www.today.com/health/stop-obsessing-women-spend-2-weeks-year-their-appearance-today-2D12104866

21 Maher, Sanam. *A Woman Like Her: The Story Behind the Honor Killing of a Social Media Star*. Brooklyn: Melville House, 2018, pp. xii, 66, 82.

22 Maher, Sanam. *A Woman Like Her: The Story Behind the Honor Killing of a Social Media Star.* Brooklyn: Melville House, 2018, pp. 79–83.

23 McNamee, Roger. *Zucked: Waking Up to the Facebook Catastrophe.* New York: Penguin Press, 2019, p. 88.

24 Maher, Sanam. *A Woman Like Her: The Story Behind the Honor Killing of a Social Media Star.* Brooklyn: Melville House, 2018, p. 81.

25 Maher, Sanam. *A Woman Like Her: The Story Behind the Honor Killing of a Social Media Star.* Brooklyn: Melville House, 2018, pp. 17, 175.

26 Hess, Amanda. "The Latest Celebrity Diet? Cyberbullying." *The New York Times,* October 12, 2016. https://www.nytimes.com/2016/10/13/arts/celebrities-twitter-instagram-cyberbullying-kardashian-swift.html

27 Schiffer, Jessica. "You May Not Want to Get Your Beauty Tips From TikTok." *The New York Times,* June 15, 2021. https://www.nytimes.com/2021/06/15/style/you-may-not-want-to-get-your-beauty-tips-from-tiktok.html

28 MacMillan, Amanda. "Why Friends May Be More Important Than Family." *TIME,* June 7, 2017. https://time.com/collection/guide-to-happiness/4809325/friends-friendship-health-family/

Chapter 3: Social Media and Women's "Perpetual State of Wrongness"

1 Russian, Ale. "Amal Clooney Calls for Vigilance Against ISIS in U.N. Speech: 'Don't Let ISIS Get Away With Genocide.'" *People,* March 9, 2017. https://people.com/human-interest/watch-amal-clooney-address-un-isis/

2 Mikkelson, David. "Is This a Photograph of Jill Biden in 'Fishnet Stockings'?" *Snopes,* April 5, 2021. https://www.snopes.com/fact-check/jill-biden-fishnet-stockings/

3 "Jill Biden Wore a Pair of Fishnet Tights, and Twitter Broke." *Glamour,* April 5, 2021. https://www.glamour.com/story/jill-biden-wore-a-pair-of-fishnet-tights-and-twitter-broke

4   Wanshel, Elyse. "Jill Biden's Outfit Prompts Deluge of Sexist Jokes on Twitter." *HuffPost*, April 5, 2021. https://www.huffpost.com/entry /jill-biden-outfit-twitter-sexism_n_606b3b3dc5b68872efe96a61

5   Filipovic, Jill. *The H-Spot: The Feminist Pursuit of Happiness.* New York: Nation Books, 2017, p. 254.

6   Solnit, Rebecca. *Recollections of My Nonexistence.* New York: Penguin Books, 2020, p 80.

7   Sales, Nancy Jo. *American Girls: Social Media and The Secret Lives of Teenagers.* New York: Alfred A. Knopf, 2016, p. 165.

8   Hartley, Gemma. *FED UP: Emotional Labor, Women, and the Way Forward.* New York: HarperOne, 2018, p. 151.

9   Manne, Kate. *Down Girl: The Logic of Misogyny.* New York: Oxford University Press, 2018, pp. 251–257, 267.

10 Serano, Julia. *Whipping Girl: A Transsexual Woman on Sexism and the Scapegoating of Femininity.* Berkeley: Seal Press, 2016, p. 32.

11 "Parental Leave Systems." *OECD*, December 2022. https://www .oecd.org/els/soc/PF2_1_Parental_leave_systems.pdf

12 Miller, Claire C. "How Other Nations Pay for Child Care. The U.S. Is an Outlier." *The New York Times*, October 6, 2021. https://www .nytimes.com/2021/10/06/upshot/child-care-biden.html

13 McGough, Matt, Krutika Amin, Nirmita Panchal, and Cynthia Cox. "Child and Teen Firearm Mortality in the U.S. and Peer Countries." *KFF*, July 8, 2022. https://www.kff.org/global-health-policy /issue-brief/child-and-teen-firearm-mortality-in-the-u-s-and-peer -countries/

14 Fry, Richard, Carolina Aragão, Kiley Hurst, and Kim Parker. "In a Growing Share of U.S. Marriages, Husbands and Wives Earn About the Same." *Pew Research Center*, April 13, 2023. https://www .pewresearch.org/social-trends/2023/04/13/in-a-growing-share-of-u-s -marriages-husbands-and-wives-earn-about-the-same/

15 Fry, Richard, Carolina Aragão, Kiley Hurst, and Kim Parker. "In a Growing Share of U.S. Marriages, Husbands and Wives Earn About

the Same." *Pew Research Center*, April 13, 2023. https://www
.pewresearch.org/social-trends/2023/04/13/in-a-growing-share-of
-u-s-marriages-husbands-and-wives-earn-about-the-same/

16 Hartley, Gemma. *FED UP: Emotional Labor, Women, and the Way
Forward*. New York: HarperOne, 2018, p. 67.

17 Hartley, Gemma. *FED UP: Emotional Labor, Women, and the Way
Forward*. New York: HarperOne, 2018, p. 36.

18 Lockman, Darcy. *All the Rage: Mothers, Fathers, and the Myth of Equal
Partnership*. New York: Harper, 2019, p. 147.

19 Manne, Kate. *Entitled: How Male Privilege Hurts Women*. New York:
Crown, 2021, pp. 78–80.

20 Jaschik, Scott. "Graded on Looks." *Inside Higher Ed*, January 4, 2016.
https://www.insidehighered.com/news/2016/01/05/new-study-finds
-women-who-are-not-considered-attractive-receive-lower-grades

21 Commisso, Melissa and Lisa Finkelstein. "Physical Attractiveness
Bias in Employee Termination." *Journal of Applied Social Psychology*
42, no. 12 (November 2012). https://onlinelibrary.wiley.com/doi
/abs/10.1111/j.1559-1816.2012.00970.x

22 Quast, Lisa. "Thin Is In For Executive Women: How Weight Discrimination Contributes to the Glass Ceiling." *Forbes*, August 6, 2012.
https://www.forbes.com/sites/lisaquast/2012/08/06/thin-is-in-for
-executive-women-as-weight-discrimination-contributes-to-glass
-ceiling/?sh=83ca6fb412c0

23 Fisman, Raymond, Sheena S. Iyengar, Emir Kamenica, and Itamar
Simonson. "Gender Differences in Mate Selection: Evidence From a
Speed Dating Experiment." *The Quarterly Journal of Economics* 121,
no. 2 (May 2006): 673–697. https://academic.oup.com/qje/article
-abstract/121/2/673/1884033

24 Duffy, Brooke Erin. "Meghan Markle and the Long History of Authenticity Policing." *Vox*, March 11, 2021. https://www.vox.com/the-goods
/22323961/meghan-markle-fakery-piers-morgan-authenticity

25 Keats Citron, Danielle. *Hate Crimes in Cyberspace*. Cambridge:
Harvard University Press, 2014, p. 58.

26 Suler, John. "The Online Disinhibition Effect." *CyberPsychology & Behavior* 7, no. 3 (2004): 321–326. http://drleannawolfe.com/Suler -TheOnlineDisinhibitionEffect-2004.pdf

27 Orenstein, Peggy. *Boys & Sex: Young Men on Hookups, Love, Porn, Consent, and Navigating the New Masculinity.* New York: Harper, 2020, p. 32.

28 Manne, Kate. *Down Girl: The Logic of Misogyny.* New York: Oxford University Press, 2018, p. 88.

29 Searcey, Dionne. *In Pursuit of Disobedient Women: A Memoir of Love, Rebellion, and Family, Far Away.* New York: Ballantine, 2020, p. 221.

30 Manne, Kate. *Down Girl: The Logic of Misogyny.* New York: Oxford University Press, 2018, p. 33.

31 Alaimo, Kara. "With Golf Retweet, Trump Blunders into the 'Strei-sand Effect'." *CNN*, September 18, 2017. https://www.cnn.com /2017/09/17/opinions/trump-golf-ball-clinton-alaimo/index.html

32 Scheff, Sue. *Shame Nation: The Global Epidemic of Online Hate.* Naperville: Sourcebooks, 2017, p. 22.

33 Lewinsky, Monica. "The Price of Shame." Filmed 2015 at TED2015, Video. https://www.ted.com/talks/monica_lewinsky_the_price_of _shame/transcript?language=en#t-1333371

34 Preidt, Robert. "'Mommy-shaming' Is Common, Survey Reveals." *CBS News*, June 20, 2017. https://www.cbsnews.com/news/mommy -shaming-is-common-parenting-poll-reveals/

35 Abrahamson, Rachel Paula. "Meghan Markle Gets Mom-shamed for the Way She Holds Son Archie." *Today*, July 11, 2019. https://www.today.com /parents/meghan-markle-criticized-way-she-holds-son-archie-t158159; Spina, Ellie. "'That's Not How You Hold a Baby': Emily Ratajkowski Criticized for 'Careless' Photos." *Yahoo*, July 7, 2021. https://www.yahoo .com/lifestyle/emily-ratajkowski-mom-shamed-new-photos-175022595 .html

36 McGough, Matt, Krutika Amin, Nirmita Panchal, and Cynthia Cox. "Child and Teen Firearm Mortality in the U.S. and Peer Countries."

     KFF, July 8, 2022. https://www.kff.org/global-health-policy/issue-brief/child-and-teen-firearm-mortality-in-the-u-s-and-peer-countries/

37 Gutowitz, Jessica. "'Mom Shaming' Is Further Exacerbated by Social Media." *Pipe Dream*, November 14, 2019. https://www.bupipedream.com/opinions/112577/mom-shaming-is-further-exacerbated-by-social-media/

38 Keats Citron, Danielle. *The Fight for Privacy: Protecting Dignity, Identity and Love in the Digital Age*. New York: W. W. Norton & Company, 2022, p. 54.

39 Alaimo, Kara. "Social-Media Shaming Is Good (in Moderation)." *Bloomberg*, December 4, 2017. https://www.bloomberg.com/opinion/articles/2017-12-04/social-media-shaming-is-good-in-moderation

40 Lewinsky, Monica. "The Price of Shame." Filmed 2015 at TED2015, Video. https://www.ted.com/talks/monica_lewinsky_the_price_of_shame/transcript?language=en#t-1333371

41 Lewinsky, Monica. "The Price of Shame." Filmed 2015 at TED2015, Video. https://www.ted.com/talks/monica_lewinsky_the_price_of_shame/transcript?language=en#t-1333371

42 "The Changing World of Digital in 2023." *We Are Social*, January 26, 2023. https://wearesocial.com/us/blog/2023/01/the-changing-world-of-digital-in-2023/

43 Duffy, Brooke Erin. "Meghan Markle and the Long History of Authenticity Policing." *Vox*, March 11, 2021. https://www.vox.com/the-goods/22323961/meghan-markle-fakery-piers-morgan-authenticity

44 Bennett, Jessica. "What if Instead of Calling People Out, We Called Them In?" *The New York Times*, November 19, 2020. https://www.nytimes.com/2020/11/19/style/loretta-ross-smith-college-cancel-culture.html

Chapter 4: Plenty of Catfish

1   Quirk, Mollie. "Welcome to the Textationship—The Ultimate Time Wasting Dating Trend." *Huffington Post*, April 10, 2023. https://www.huffingtonpost.co.uk/entry/welcome-to-the

-textationship-the-ultimate-time-wasting-dating-trend_uk
_642ed16fe4b0859acb92d4a1

2   "Public Attitudes About Today's Dating Landscape." *Pew Research Center*, August 14, 2020. https://www.pewresearch.org /social-trends/2020/08/20/public-attitudes-about-todays-dating -landscape/psdt_08-19-20_dating-relationships-03-9

3   "Partnered LGB Adults Are Far More Likely Than Their Straight Counterparts to Have Met Their Partner Online." *Pew Research Center*, August 14, 2020. https://www.pewresearch.org/social -trends/2020/08/20/nearly-half-of-u-s-adults-say-dating-has-gotten -harder-for-most-people-in-the-last-10-years/psdt_08-19-20_dating -relationships-00-2/

4   Brown, Anna. "Nearly Half of U.S. Adults Say Dating Has Gotten Harder for Most People in the Last 10 Years." *Pew Research Center*, August 20, 2020. https://www.pewsocialtrends.org/wp-content /uploads/sites/3/2020/08/PSDT_08.20.20.dating-relationships.final_ .pdf

5   Saini, Angela. *Inferior: How Science Got Women Wrong—and the New Research That's Rewriting the Story.* Boston: Beacon Press, 2017, p. 127.

6   "Breadcrumbing." *Urban Dictionary*, March 15, 2018. https://www .urbandictionary.com/define.php?term=Breadcrumbing

7   Sales, Nancy Jo. *Nothing Personal: My Secret Life in the Dating App Inferno.* New York: Hachette, 2021, p. 41.

8   Feliciano, Cynthia, Belinda Robnett, and Golnaz Komaie. "Gendered Racial Exclusion Among White Internet Daters." *Social Science Research* 38, no. 1 (2009): 39–54. https://www.sciencedirect.com /science/article/abs/pii/S0049089X0800104X

9   Curington, Celeste Vaughan, Jennifer H. Lundquist, and Ken-Hou Lin. *The Dating Divide: Race and Desire in the Era of Online Romance.* Oakland: University of California Press, 2021, p. 5.

10 Curington, Celeste Vaughan, Jennifer H. Lundquist, and Ken-Hou Lin. *The Dating Divide: Race and Desire in the Era of Online Romance.* Oakland: University of California Press, 2021, pp. 13, 67.

11 Majaski, Christina. "Most Men Judge Pictures First When Swiping on Dating Apps." *AskMen*, April 3, 2019. https://www.askmen.com/news /dating/most-men-judge-pictures-first-when-swiping-on-dating -apps.html

12 Julian, Kate. "Why Are Young People Having So Little Sex?" *The Atlantic,* December 15, 2018. https://www.theatlantic.com/magazine /archive/2018/12/the-sex-recession/573949/

13 Eastwick, Paul W., Eli J. Finkel, Benjamin R. Karney, Harry T. Reis, and Susan Sprecher. "Online Dating: A Critical Analysis from the Perspective of Psychological Science." *Psychological Science in the Public Interest* 13, no. 1 (2012): 3–66. https://journals.sagepub.com/stoken /rbtfl/cK9EB6/4zQ0AM/full

14 Eastwick, Paul W., Eli J. Finkel, Benjamin R. Karney, Harry T. Reis, and Susan Sprecher. "Online Dating: A Critical Analysis From the Perspective of Psychological Science." *Psychological Science in the Public Interest* 13, 1 (2012): 3–66. https://journals.sagepub.com /stoken/rbtfl/cK9EB6/4zQ0AM/full

15 Coren, Victoria. "The Curse of True Love." *The Guardian,* October 14, 2006. https://www.theguardian.com/commentisfree/2006/oct/15 /comment.victoriacoren

16 Slater, Dan. "A Million First Dates." *The Atlantic,* February 15, 2013. https://www.theatlantic.com/magazine/archive/2013/01/a-million -first-dates/309195/

17 Rosenfeld, Michael J. "Are Tinder and Dating Apps Changing Dating and Mating in the U.S.?" In *Families and Technology,* edited by Jennifer Van Hook, Susan M. McHale, and Valarie King, 103–117. Springer, 2018.

18 Vogels, Emily A. "10 Facts About Americans and Online Dating." *Pew Research Center,* February 6, 2020. https://www.pewresearch.org /fact-tank/2020/02/06/10-facts-about-americans-and-online-dating/

19 Bonos, Lisa and Emily Guskin. "It's Not Just You: New Data Shows More Than Half of Young People in America Don't Have a Romantic Partner." *The Washington Post,* March 21, 2019. https://www

.washingtonpost.com/lifestyle/2019/03/21/its-not-just-you-new-data
-shows-more-than-half-young-people-america-dont-have-romantic-
partner/

20 Fry, Richard and Kim Parker. "Rising Share of U.S. Adults Are Living
    Without a Spouse or Partner." *Pew Research Center's Social & Demo-
    graphic Trends Project*, October 5, 2021. https://www.pewresearch.org
    /social-trends/2021/10/05/rising-share-of-u-s-adults-are-living
    -without-a-spouse-or-partner/

21 Galvin, Gaby. "U.S. Marriage Rate Hits Historic Low." *U.S. News*,
    April 29, 2020. https://www.usnews.com/news/healthiest-communities
    /articles/2020-04-29/us-marriage-rate-drops-to-record-low

22 Chappell, Bill. "The 2021 Rise in U.S. Births Is Likely a Baby Blip, Not a
    Boom." *NPR*, July 19, 2022. https://www.npr.org/2022/07/19/1112259628
    /us-birth-rate-increase-replacement

23 Brown, Anna. "Nearly Half of U.S. Adults Say Dating Has Gotten Harder
    for Most People in the Last 10 Years." *Pew Research Center*, August 20,
    2020. https://www.pewsocialtrends.org/wp-content/uploads/sites/3/2020
    /08/PSDT_08.20.20.dating-relationships.final_.pdf

24 Brown, Anna. "Nearly Half of U.S. Adults Say Dating Has Gotten Harder
    for Most People in the Last 10 Years." *Pew Research Center*, August 20,
    2020. https://www.pewsocialtrends.org/wp-content/uploads/sites/3/2020
    /08/PSDT_08.20.20.dating-relationships.final_.pdf

25 Fletcher, Emma. "Reports of Romance Scams Hit Record Highs in
    2021." Federal Trade Commission, February 10, 2022. https://www.ftc
    .gov/news-events/data-visualizations/data-spotlight/2022/02/reports
    -romance-scams-hit-record-highs-2021

26 Podkul, Cezary and Cindy Liu. "Human Trafficking's Newest Abuse:
    Forcing Victims Into Cyberscamming." *ProPublica*, September 3, 2022.
    https://www.propublica.org/article/human-traffickers-force-victims
    -into-cyberscamming

27 Roose, Kevin. "Crypto Scammers' New Target: Dating Apps." *The
    New York Times*, February 21, 2022. https://www.nytimes.com/2022
    /02/21/technology/crypto-scammers-new-target-dating-apps.html

28 Podkul, Cezary and Cindy Liu. "Human Trafficking's Newest Abuse: Forcing Victims Into Cyberscamming." *ProPublica*, September 3, 2022. https://www.propublica.org/article/human-traffickers-force-victims-into-cyberscamming

29 Chan, Stella, Zoe Sottile, and Josh Campbell. "Family of Alleged 'Catfish' Killer's Victims Says Be Careful, Talk to Your Children About Predators." *CNN*, November 30, 2022. https://www.cnn.com/2022/11/30/us/riverside-murders-catfishing-victims-family/index.html

30 Brumberg, Joan Jacobs. *The Body Project: An Intimate History of American Girls*. New York: Vintage Books, 1997, p. 212.

31 Finkel, Eli J., Paul W. Eastwick, Benjamin R. Karney, Harry T. Reis, and Susan Sprecher. "Online Dating: A Critical Analysis From the Perspective of Psychological Science." *Psychological Science in the Public Interest* 13, no. 1 (March 7, 2012). https://journals.sagepub.com/stoken/rbtfl/cK9EB6/4zQ0AM/full

Chapter 5: Sex Crimes and Murder in the Time of Social Media

1 Brown, Joel. "Raleigh Rape Survivor Speaks Out After Filing Suit Against Tinder, Snapchat." *ABC11*, January 10, 2020. https://abc11.com/amp/snapchat-tinder-lawsuit-aaliyah-palmer/5836719/

2 Cousins, Keith, Hillary Flynn, and Elizabeth Naismith Picciani. "Tinder Lets Known Sex Offenders Use the App. It's Not the Only One." *ProPublica*, December 2, 2019. https://www.propublica.org/article/tinder-lets-known-sex-offenders-use-the-app-its-not-the-only-one

3 "Emerging New Threat in Online Dating." National Crime Agency, February 7, 2016. https://nationalcrimeagency.gov.uk/who-we-are/publications/607-nca-scas-online-dating-report-2016/file

4 Valentine, Julie L., Leslie W. Miles, Kristen Mella Hamblin, and Aubrey Worthen Gibbons. "Dating App Facilitated Sexual Assault: A Retrospective Review of Sexual Assault Medical Forensic Examination Charts." *Journal of Interpersonal Violence* 38, no. 9–10 (October 2022). https://doi.org/10.1177/08862605221130390

5　Manganis, Julie. "Accused Rapist Released." *The Salem News*, May 3, 2018. https://www.salemnews.com/news/local_news/accused-rapist-released/article_405267c8-3d05-5c07-87a4-4351327c7e56.html

6　Cousins, Keith, Hillary Flynn, and Elizabeth Naismith Picciani. "Tinder Lets Known Sex Offenders Use the App. It's Not the Only One." *ProPublica*, December 2, 2019. https://www.propublica.org/article/tinder-lets-known-sex-offenders-use-the-app-its-not-the-only-one

7　Solnit, Rebecca. *Recollections of My Nonexistence*. New York: Penguin Books, 2020, p. 49.

8　Forristal, Lauren. "Match Expands Background Checks to Two More Dating Apps." *TechCrunch*, July 13, 2022. https://techcrunch.com/2022/07/13/match-expands-tinders-free-background-checks-to-two-more-dating-apps

9　Cousins, Keith, Hillary Flynn, and Elizabeth Naismith Picciani. "Tinder Lets Known Sex Offenders Use the App. It's Not the Only One." *ProPublica*, December 2, 2019. https://www.propublica.org/article/tinder-lets-known-sex-offenders-use-the-app-its-not-the-only-one

10　"The Criminal Justice System: Statistics." RAINN. https://www.rainn.org/statistics/criminal-justice-system

11　Edwards, Brian and Elizabeth Naismith Picciani. "Tinder and OkCupid Could Soon Let You Background Check Your Date –for a Price." *ProPublica*, March 18, 2021. https://www.propublica.org/article/tinder-and-okcupid-could-soon-let-you-background-check-your-date-for-a-price

12　Peterson, Kolbie. "Utah Man Sentenced in 2020 Killing of Ashlyn Black." *The Salt Lake Tribune*, February 23, 2022. https://www.sltrib.com/news/2022/02/22/utah-man-sentenced/

13　"Grace Millane Murder: Jesse Kempson Guilty of Attacking Two More Women." *BBC News*, December 21, 2020. https://www.bbc.com/news/uk-england-essex-55346213

14　Southall, Ashley. "He Used Tinder to Hunt the Women He Raped and Killed, Police Say." *The New York Times*, July 30, 2018. https://www.nytimes.com/2018/07/30/nyregion/murder-tinder-uber-nurse-queens-nyc.html

15 Green, Sara Jean. "Man Sentenced to More Than 27 Years for Killing, Dismemberment of Renton Nurse and Mother." *The Seattle Times*, January 5, 2018. https://www.seattletimes.com/seattle-news/crime/man-sentenced-to-27-years-for-killing-dismemberment-of-renton-nurse-and-mother/

16 Goldberg, Carrie. *Nobody's Victim: Fighting Psychos, Stalkers, Pervs, and Trolls.* New York: Plume, 2019, pp. 2–3, 112–113.

17 Harris, Kamala. *The Truths We Hold: An American Journey.* New York, Penguin, 2019, p. 264.

18 Blackmon, Michael. "A Hacker Responsible for 2014's 'Celebgate' Is Going to Prison for 8 Months." *BuzzFeed News*, August 30, 2018. https://www.buzzfeednews.com/article/michaelblackmon/celebgate-hacking-fappening-jail-prison

19 Heard, Amber. "Are We All Celebrities Now?" *The New York Times*, November 4, 2019. https://www.nytimes.com/2019/11/04/opinion/amber-heard-revenge-porn.html

20 Stasko, Emily C. and Pamela A. Geller. "Reframing Sexting as a Positive Relationship Behavior." *American Psychological Association* (2015): 6–9. https://www.apa.org/news/press/releases/2015/08/reframing-sexting.pdf

21 Gonzalez, Michelle. "Nonconsensual Porn: A Common Offense." *Cyber Civil Rights Initiative*, June 12, 2017. https://www.cybercivilrights.org/2017-natl-ncp-research-results/

22 Keats Citron, Danielle. *The Fight for Privacy: Protecting Dignity, Identity and Love in the Digital Age.* New York: W. W. Norton & Company, 2022, pp. 39–40.

23 Keats Citron, Danielle. *Hate Crimes in Cyberspace.* Cambridge: Harvard University Press, 2014, p. 17.

24 Bennett, Jessica. "The Nudes Aren't Going Away. Katie Hill's OK With That." *The New York Times,* August 8, 2020. https://www.nytimes.com/2020/08/08/style/katie-hill-she-will-rise-revenge-porn.html

25 Keats Citron, Danielle. *Hate Crimes in Cyberspace.* Cambridge: Harvard University Press, 2014, p. 122.

26 Keats Citron, Danielle. *Hate Crimes in Cyberspace.* Cambridge: Harvard University Press, 2014, p. 147.

27 Hill, Katie. *She Will Rise: Becoming a Warrior in the Battle for True Equality.* New York: Grand Central Publishing, 2020, p. 30.

28 Keats Citron, Danielle. *Hate Crimes in Cyberspace.* Cambridge: Harvard University Press, 2014, p. 25.

29 Wittes, Benjamin, Cody Poplin, Quinta Jurecic, and Clara Spera. "Sextortion: Cybersecurity, Teenagers, and Remote Sexual Assault." *Brookings*, May 2016. https://www.brookings.edu/wp-content/uploads/2016/05/sextortion1-1.pdf

30 Jurecic, Quinta, Clara Spera, Benjamin Wittes, and Cody Poplin. "Sextortion: The Problem and Solutions." *Brookings*, May 11, 2016. https://www.brookings.edu/blog/techtank/2016/05/11/sextortion-the-problem-and-solutions/

31 Dean, Michelle. "The Story of Amanda Todd." *The New Yorker,* October 18, 2012. https://www.newyorker.com/culture/culture-desk/the-story-of-amanda-todd; Scheff, Sue. *Shame Nation: The Global Epidemic of Online Hate.* Naperville: Sourcebooks, 2017, pp. 216–218.

32 Wittes, Benjamin, Cody Poplin, Quinta Jurecic, and Clara Spera. "Sextortion: Cybersecurity, Teenagers, and Remote Sexual Assault." *Brookings*, May 2016. https://www.brookings.edu/wp-content/uploads/2016/05/sextortion1-1.pdf

33 Jurecic, Quinta, Clara Spera, Benjamin Wittes, and Cody Poplin. "Sextortion: The Problem and Solutions." *Brookings*, May 2016. https://www.brookings.edu/blog/techtank/2016/05/11/sextortion-the-problem-and-solutions/

34 Olson, Parmy. *We Are Anonymous: Inside the Hacker World of LulzSec, Anonymous, and the Global Cyber Insurgency.* New York: Back Bay Books, 2013, pp. 29–30, 377–378.

35 "Fraping." *Urban Dictionary,* January 24, 2010. https://www.urbandictionary.com/define.php?term=Fraping

36 Malone Kircher, Madison and Callie Holtermann. "How Is Everyone Making Those A.I. Selfies?" *The New York Times*, December 7, 2022. https://www.nytimes.com/2022/12/07/style/lensa-ai-selfies.html

37 "8 Dead in Atlanta Spa Shootings, With Fears of Anti-Asian Bias." *The New York Times*, March 17, 2021. https://www.nytimes.com /live/2021/03/17/us/shooting-atlanta-acworth

38 Southall, Ashley, Ali Watkins, and Jeffrey E. Singer. "Screams That 'Went Quiet': Prosecutors' Account of Chinatown Killing." *The New York Times*, February 14, 2022. https://www.nytimes.com/2022/02/14 /nyregion/suspect-christina-yuna-lee-murder.html

39 Bacarisse, Bonnie. "The Republican Lawmaker Who Secretly Created Reddit's Women-Hating 'Red Pill'." *The Daily Beast*, May 5, 2017. https://www.thedailybeast.com/the-republican-lawmaker-who -secretly-created-reddits-women-hating-red-pill

40 Lin, Jie Liang. "Antifeminism Online MGTOW (Men Going Their Own Way): Ethnographic Perspectives Across Global Online and Offline Spaces." *ResearchGate*, January 2017. https://www.research-gate.net/publication/314158167_Antifeminism_Online_MGTOW _Men_Going_Their_Own_Way_Ethnographic_Perspectives _Across_Global_Online_and_Offline_Spaces

41 Taylor, Jim. "The Woman Who Founded the 'Incel' Movement." *BBC*, August 30, 2018. https://www.bbc.com/news/world-us-canada -45284455

42 Manne, Kate. *Entitled: How Male Privilege Hurts Women*. New York: Crown, 2021, p. 17.

43 Quinn, Zoë. *Crash Override: How Gamergate (Nearly) Destroyed My Life, And How We Can Win the Fight Against Online Hate*. New York: PublicAffairs, 2017, p. 47.

44 Manne, Kate. *Entitled: How Male Privilege Hurts Women*. New York: Crown, 2021, pp. 14–15; DiBranco, Alex. "Male Supremacist Terrorism as a Rising Threat." *ICCT*, February 10, 2020. https://www.icct.nl /index.php/publication/male-supremacist-terrorism-rising-threat

45 Cecco, Leyland. "Canada Police Say Machete Killing Was 'Incel' Terror Attack." *The Guardian*, May 19, 2020. https://www.theguardian .com/world/2020/may/19/toronto-attack-incel-terrorism-canada -police

46 Miller, Jax. "Self-Proclaimed 'Incel' Gets 44 Years After Filming Himself Committing Arizona Mall Shooting." *Yahoo*, July 12, 2022. https://finance.yahoo.com/news/self-proclaimed-incel-gets-44-173954738.html

47 Mack, David. "The FBI Says a Guy Blew His Hand Off With a Bomb Possibly Planned for an Attack on 'Hot Cheerleaders'." *BuzzFeed News*, June 7, 2020. https://www.buzzfeednews.com/article/davidmack/incel-bomber-blows-hand-off-cheerleaders

48 Morris, Steven. "Plymouth Shooter Fascinated by Serial Killers and 'Incel' Culture, Inquest Hears." *The Guardian*, January 18, 2023. https://www.theguardian.com/uk-news/2023/jan/18/plymouth-shooter-jake-davison-fascinated-by-mass-shootings-and-incel-culture-inquest-hears

49 "Ohio Man Pleads Guilty to Attempting Hate Crime: Defendant Plotted to Conduct Mass Shooting of Women." U.S. Department of Justice, October 11, 2022. https://www.justice.gov/opa/pr/ohio-man-pleads-guilty-attempting-hate-crime

50 Sunstein, Cass R. *On Rumors: How Falsehoods Spread, Why We Believe Them, and What Can Be Done.* Princeton: Princeton University Press, 2014, p. 6.

51 Sunstein, Cass R. *On Rumors: How Falsehoods Spread, Why We Believe Them, and What Can Be Done.* Princeton: Princeton University Press, 2014, pp. 36–40.

52 Bacarisse, Bonnie. "The Republican Lawmaker Who Secretly Created Reddit's Women-Hating 'Red Pill'." *The Daily Beast*, May 5, 2017. https://www.thedailybeast.com/the-republican-lawmaker-who-secretly-created-reddits-women-hating-red-pill

53 Cheung, Kylie. "Male Supremacy Organizations Are Now on SPLC's List of Hate Groups." *Ms. Magazine*, February 26, 2018. https://msmagazine.com/2018/02/26/southern-poverty-law-center-will-track-male-supremacy-groups/

54 Faguy, Ana. "Andrew Tate Leaves Jail for House Arrest After Human Trafficking Charges." *Forbes*, March 31, 2023. https://www.forbes.

com/sites/anafaguy/2023/03/31/andrew-tate-leaves-jail-for-house
-arrest-after-human-trafficking-charges/?sh=6c2c00ae749c

55 Dias, Shanti. "Inside the Violent, Misogynistic World of TikTok's New
Star, Andrew Tate." *The Guardian*, August 6, 2022. https://www
.theguardian.com/technology/2022/aug/06/andrew-tate-violent
-misogynistic-world-of-tiktok-new-star

56 Cousins, Keith, Hillary Flynn, and Elizabeth Naismith Picciani. "Tinder Lets Known Sex Offenders Use the App. It's Not the Only One."
ProPublica, December 2, 2019. https://www.propublica.org/article/
tinder-lets-known-sex-offenders-use-the-app-its-not-the-only-one

57 Edmunds, Simon. "Beard Dating App Bristlr Adds 'Lothario Detector'." *Global Dating Insights*, April 27, 2015. https://www.global-
datinginsights.com/news/27042015-beard-dating-app-bristlr-adds
-lothario-detector/

58 "The Criminal Justice System: Statistics." RAINN, 2021. https://www.
rainn.org/statistics/criminal-justice-system

59 Kang, Cecilia. "As Europe Approves New Tech Laws, the U.S. Falls Further Behind." *The New York Times*, April 22, 2022. https://www
.nytimes.com/2022/04/22/technology/tech-regulation-europe-us.html

60 Keats Citron, Danielle. *The Fight for Privacy: Protecting Dignity, Identity and Love in the Digital Age.* New York: W. W. Norton & Company,
2022, p. 94.

61 Keats Citron, Danielle. *The Fight for Privacy: Protecting Dignity, Identity and Love in the Digital Age.* New York: W. W. Norton & Company,
2022, p. 143.

62 Vanity Fair. "Cover Exclusive: Jennifer Lawrence Calls Photo Hacking
a 'Sex Crime'." *Vanity Fair*, October 7, 2014. https://www.vanityfair
.com/hollywood/2014/10/jennifer-lawrence-cover

63 Keats Citron, Danielle. *The Fight for Privacy: Protecting Dignity, Identity and Love in the Digital Age.* New York: W. W. Norton & Company,
2022, p. 90.

64 Keats Citron, Danielle. *The Fight for Privacy: Protecting Dignity, Identity and Love in the Digital Age.* New York: W. W. Norton & Company,
2022, p. 138.

65 Wittes, Benjamin, Cody Poplin, Quita Jurecic, and Clara Spera. "Closing the Sextortion Sentencing Gap: A Legislative Proposal." *Brookings*, May 2016. https://www.brookings.edu/research/closing-the-sextortion-sentencing-gap-a-legislative-proposal

66 Keats Citron, Danielle. *The Fight for Privacy: Protecting Dignity, Identity and Love in the Digital Age*. New York: W. W. Norton & Company, 2022, p. 149.

67 Keats Citron, Danielle. *Hate Crimes in Cyberspace*. Cambridge: Harvard University Press, 2014, pp. 190–191.

Chapter 6: Digital Housewives

1 Lorenz, Taylor. "Snapchat Wants You to Post. It's Willing to Pay Millions." *The New York Times*, January 15, 2021. https://www.nytimes.com/2021/01/15/style/snapchat-spotlight.html

2 "The Influencer Report: Engaging Gen Z and Millenials." *Morning Consult*, 2019. https://morningconsult.com/wp-content/uploads/2019/11/The-Influencer-Report-Engaging-Gen-Z-and-Millennials.pdf

3 "The Klear Influencer Marketing Rate Card." *Klear*, 2019. https://klear.com/KlearRateCard.pdf

4 Geyser, Werner. "Creator Earnings: Benchmark Report 2022." *Influencer MarketingHub*, August 2, 2022. https://influencermarketinghub.com/creator-earnings-benchmark-report/

5 "Poverty Guidelines." Office of the Assistant Secretary for Planning and Evaluation, 2023. https://aspe.hhs.gov/topics/poverty-economic-mobility/poverty-guidelines

6 Jarrett, Kylie. *Feminism, Labour and Digital Media: The Digital Housewife*. Routledge, 2017.

7 Geyser, Warner. "20 of Instagram's Highest Paid Stars in 2023." *Influencer MarketingHub*. February 1, 2023. https://influencermarketinghub.com/instagram-highest-paid/

8 Kunert, Paul. "Meta's Zuckerberg Paid $27M in 'Other' Compensation for 2022." *The Register*, April 18, 2023. https://www.theregister.com/2023/04/18/metas_zuckerberg_paid_27m_in/

9   Lorenz, Taylor. "The Original Renegade." *The New York Times,* February 13, 2020. https://www.nytimes.com/2020/02/13/style/the-original-renegade.html

10 "Girl Behind Renegade TikTok Dance Reclaims Spotlight at NBA All-Star Game." *CBC Kids News,* February 18, 2020. https://www.cbc.ca/kidsnews/post/girl-behind-renegade-tiktok-dance-steals-spotlight-at-nba-all-star-game

11 Penrose, Nerisha. "TikTok Was Built on the Backs of Black Creators. Why Can't They Get Any Credit?" *ELLE,* April 29, 2021. https://www.elle.com/culture/a36178170/black-tiktok-creators-mya-nicole-chris-cotter-addison-rae-jimmy-fallon/

12 Pruitt-Young, Sharon. "Black TikTok Creators Are on Strike to Protest a Lack of Credit for Their Work." *NPR,* July 1, 2021. https://www.npr.org/2021/07/01/1011899328/black-tiktok-creators-are-on-strike-to-protest-a-lack-of-credit-for-their-work

13 Duffy, Brooke Erin. *(Not) Getting Paid to Do What You Love: Gender, Social Media, and Aspirational Work.* New Haven: Yale University Press, 2017, p. x.

14 Wolverson, Roya. "The Human Billboard." *TIME,* April 5, 2013. http://content.time.com/time/subscriber/article/0,33009,2140224,00.html

15 "The Klear Influencer Marketing Rate Card." *Klear,* 2019. https://klear.com/KlearRateCard.pdf

16 Aragão, Carolina. "Gender Pay Gap in U.S. Hasn't Changed Much in Two Decades." *Pew Research Center,* March 1, 2023. https://www.pewresearch.org/fact-tank/2023/03/01/gender-pay-gap-facts/

17 Komok, Anna. "Does the Pay Gap Exist on Instagram? Remuneration of Male vs Female creators." *Hype-Journal,* January 9, 2020. https://hypeauditor.com/blog/does-the-pay-gap-exist-on-instagram-remuneration-of-male-vs-female-creators/

18 Lorenz, Taylor. "When a Sponsored Facebook Post Doesn't Pay Off." *The Atlantic,* December 26, 2018. https://www.theatlantic.com/technology/archive/2018/12/massive-influencer-management-platform-has-been-stiffing-people-payments/578767/

19 Peterson-Withorn, Chase. "Inside Kylie Jenner's Web of Lies—and Why She's No Longer a Billionaire." *Forbes*, June 1, 2020. https://www.forbes.com/sites/chasewithorn/2020/05/29/inside-kylie-jennerss-web-of-lies-and-why-shes-no-longer-a-billionaire/?sh=1751780525f7

20 Dawson, Mackenzie. "My Mommy Blog Ruined My Life." *New York Post*, May 29, 2016. https://nypost.com/2016/05/29/my-mommy-blog-ruined-my-life/

21 Teigen, Chrissy. "Hi." *Medium*, October 27, 2020. https://chrissyteigen.medium.com/hi-2e45e6faf764

22 Uwagba, Otegha. "Too Close for Comfort: The Pitfalls of Parasocial Relationships." *The Guardian*, February 13, 2022. https://www.theguardian.com/media/2022/feb/13/too-close-for-comfort-the-pitfalls-of-parasocial-relationships

23 Ratajkowski, Emily. *My Body*. New York: Metropolitan Books, 2021, pp. 88–89.

24 Altman, Mara. "Yes, Marketing Is Still Sexist." *The New York Times*, August 26, 2021. https://www.nytimes.com/2021/08/26/us/marketing-industry-sexism-brandsplaining.html

25 Tait, Amelia. "'Influencers Are Being Taken Advantage Of': The Social Media Stars Turning to Unions." *The Guardian*, October 10, 2020. https://www.theguardian.com/media/2020/oct/10/influencers-are-being-taken-advantage-of-the-social-media-stars-turning-to-unions

26 Zhu, Jane M., Arthur P. Pelullo, and Sayed Hassan. "Gender Differences in Twitter Use and Influence Among Health Policy and Health Services Researchers." *JAMA International Medicine* 179, no. 12 (October 14, 2019): 1726–1729. https://jamanetwork.com/journals/jamainternalmedicine/article-abstract/2753117

27 Woitowich, Nicole C., Vineet M. Arora, and Tricia Pendergrast. "Gender Differences in Physician Use of Social Media for Professional Advancement." *JAMA Network Open* 4, no. 5 (2021). https://jamanetwork.com/journals/jamanetworkopen/fullarticle/2779868

28 Demailly, Zoe, Geoffroy Brulard, Jean Selim, Vincent Compère, Emmanuel Besnier, and Thomas Clavier. "Gender Differences in Professional Social Media Use Among Anaesthesia Researchers." *British Journal of Anaesthesia* 124, no. 3 (2020): 178–184. https://www.sciencedirect.com/science/article/pii/S0007091219310207

29 "WikiProject Women in Red." Wikipedia, 2022. https://en.wikipedia.org/wiki/Wikipedia:WikiProject_Women_in_Red

30 Ha, Anthony. "Substack Faces Backlash over the Writers It Supports with Big Advances." *TechCrunch*, March 18, 2021. https://techcrunch.com/2021/03/18/substack-backlash/

31 Tait, Amelia. "'Influencers Are Being Taken Advantage Of': The Social Media Stars Turning to Unions." *The Guardian,* October 10, 2020. https://www.theguardian.com/media/2020/oct/10/influencers-are-being-taken-advantage-of-the-social-media-stars-turning-to-unions

32 Lorenz, Taylor. "The App with the Unprintable Name That Wants to Give Power to Creators." *The New York Times,* August 2, 2021. https://www.nytimes.com/2021/08/02/technology/fypm-creators-app-pay.html

Chapter 7: Misinformation for Mommies

1 Howorth, Claire. "Motherhood Is Hard to Get Wrong. So Why Do So Many Moms Feel So Bad About Themselves?" *TIME*, October 19, 2017. https://time.com/4989068/motherhood-is-hard-to-get-wrong/

2 Rapaport, Lisa. "More U.S. Mothers Diagnosed with Depression at Childbirth." *Reuters*, May 17, 2019. https://www.reuters.com/article/us-health-childbirth-depression/more-u-s-mothers-diagnosed-with-depression-at-childbirth-idUSKCN1SN21J

3 Druckerman, Pamela. *Bringing Up Bébé: One American Mother Discovers the Wisdom of French Parenting.* New York: Penguin, 2012, p. 30.

4 "Report from the U.S. Agency for International Development (USAID) to Congress on Female Morbidity and Mortality." USAID, May 13,

2019. https://2017-2020.usaid.gov/sites/default/files/documents/1869/USAID_Report_to_Congress_Female_Morbidity_and_Mortality_Web.pdf

5   Tuteur, Amy. *Push Back: Guilt in the Age of Natural Parenting.* New York: Dey Street Books, 2016, p. 70.

6   Haskell, Rob. "Serena Williams on Motherhood, Marriage, and Making Her Comeback." *Vogue*, January 10, 2018. https://www.vogue.com/article/serena-williams-vogue-cover-interview-february-2018

7   Anderson, Karen, Carmen R. Green, and Richard Payne. "Racial and Ethnic Disparities in Pain: Causes and Consequences of Unequal Care." *The Journal of Pain* 10, no. 12 (December 2009): 1187–1204. https://www.sciencedirect.com/science/article/abs/pii/S1526590009007755

8   Caryn Rabin, Roni. "Covid Worsened a Health Crisis Among Pregnant Women." *The New York Times*, March 16, 2023. https://www.nytimes.com/2023/03/16/health/covid-pregnancy-death.html

9   MacDorman, Marian F., Eugene Declercq, and Fay Menacker. "Trends and State Variations in Out-of-Hospital Births in the United States by Race and Ethnicity, 1990–2006." *Birth* 38, no. 1 (March 2011): 17–23. https://pubmed.ncbi.nlm.nih.gov/21332770/

10 Tuteur, Amy. *Push Back: Guilt in the Age of Natural Parenting.* New York: Dey Street Books, 2016, pp. 6, 236.

11 MacDorman, Marian F. and Eugene Declercq. "Trends and State Variations in Out-of-Hospital Births in the United States, 2004–2017." *National Library of Medicine*, December 10, 2018. https://pubmed.ncbi.nlm.nih.gov/30537156/

12 Filipovic, Jill. *The H-Spot: The Feminist Pursuit of Happiness.* New York: Nation Books, 2017, p. 253.

13 Druckerman, Pamela. *Bringing Up Bébé: One American Mother Discovers the Wisdom of French Parenting.* New York: Penguin, 2012, p. 30.

14 White, Tracie. "Epidurals Increase in Popularity, Stanford Study Finds." *Scope*, June 26, 2018. https://scopeblog.stanford.edu/2018/06/26/epidurals-increase-in-popularity-stanford-study-finds/

15   Pennell, Angela, Victoria Salo-Coombs, Amy Herring, Fred Spielman, and Karamarie Fecho. "Anesthesia and Analgesia–Related Preferences and Outcomes of Women Who Have Birth Plans." *Journal of Midwifery & Women's Health* 56, no. 4 (July 6, 2011): 376–381. https://onlinelibrary.wiley.com/doi/abs/10.1111/j.1542-2011.2011.00032.x

16   Tuteur, Amy. *Push Back: Guilt in the Age of Natural Parenting*. New York: Dey Street Books, 2016, p. 93.

17   Tuteur, Amy. *Push Back: Guilt in the Age of Natural Parenting*. New York: Dey Street Books, 2016, p. 238.

18   Vouloumanos, Victoria. "Women Are Sharing Medical Procedures They've Had Without Anesthetics or Pain Meds, and Why Is This So Normal." *BuzzFeed*, October 24, 2021. https://www.buzzfeed.com/victoriavouloumanos/gynecological-procedures-without-anesthetics-or-pain-meds

19   Klein, Jessi. "Get the Epidural." *The New York Times*, July 9, 2016. https://www.nytimes.com/2016/07/10/opinion/sunday/get-the-epidural.html

20   Hays, Sharon. *The Cultural Contradictions of Motherhood*. New Haven: Yale University Press, 1996, pp. 8, 97, 133.

21   Stern, Daniel N. and Nadia Bruschweiler-Stern. *The Birth of a Mother: How the Motherhood Experience Changes You Forever*. New York: Basic Books, 1998, p. 131.

22   Holcombe, Madeline. "Homemade Infant Formula Can Be Dangerous. Experts Share How to Feed Your Baby Through the Shortage." *CNN*, May 11, 2022. https://www.cnn.com/2022/05/11/health/infant-formula-shortage-misinformation-wellness/index.html

23   Moglia, Michelle L., Henry V. Nguyen, Kathy Chyjek, Katherine Chen, and Paula Castaño. "Evaluation of Smartphone Menstrual Cycle Tracking Applications Using an Adapted APPLICATIONS Scoring System." *Obstetrics & Gynecology* 127, no. 6 (June 2016): 1153–1160. https://doi.org/10.1097/AOG.0000000000001444

24   Keats Citron, Danielle. *The Fight for Privacy: Protecting Dignity, Identity and Love in the Digital Age*. New York: W. W. Norton & Company, 2022, p. 161.

25 Lomas, Natasha. "Clinic Reports Natural Cycles App for 37 Unwanted Pregnancies Since September." *TechCrunch*, January 17, 2018. https://techcrunch.com/2018/01/17/clinic-reports-natural-cycles-app-for-37-unwanted-pregnancies-since-september

26 U.S. Food and Drug Administration. "FDA Allows Marketing of First Direct-to-Consumer App for Contraceptive Use to Prevent Pregnancy." August 10, 2018. https://www.fda.gov/news-events/press-announcements/fda-allows-marketing-first-direct-consumer-app-contraceptive-use-prevent-pregnancy

27 Alaimo, Kara. "The Dangers of Abortion Misinformation." *CNN*, July 14, 2022. https://www.cnn.com/2022/07/14/opinions/abortion-misinformation-tech-platforms-alaimo/index.html

28 Pleasants, Elizabeth, Sylvia Guendelman, Karen Weidert, and Ndola Prata. "Quality of Top Webpages Providing Abortion Pill Information for Google Searches in the USA: An Evidence-Based Webpage Quality Assessment." *PLOS ONE*, January 21, 2021. https://journals.plos.org/plosone/article?id=10.1371/journal.pone.0240664

29 Umoja Noble, Safiya. *Algorithms of Oppression: How Search Engines Reinforce Racism*. New York: New York University Press, 2018, p. 38.

30 Rodriguez, Salvador. "Mark Zuckerberg Shifted Facebook's Focus to Groups After the 2016 Election, and It's Changed How People Use the Site." *CNBC*, February 16, 2020. https://www.cnbc.com/2020/02/16/zuckerbergs-focus-on-facebook-groups-increases-facebook-engagement.html

31 Chen, Brian X. "The Future of Social Media Is a Lot Less Social." *The New York Times*, April 19, 2023. https://www.nytimes.com/2023/04/19/technology/personaltech/tiktok-twitter-facebook-social.html

32 Hartley, Gemma. *FED UP: Emotional Labor, Women, and the Way Forward*. New York: HarperOne, 2018, p. 116.

33 Filipovic, Jill. *The H-Spot: The Feminist Pursuit of Happiness*. New York: Nation Books, 2017, p. 122.

34 Tuteur, Amy. *Push Back: Guilt in the Age of Natural Parenting.* New York: Dey Street Books, 2016, p. 5.

35 Tuteur, Amy. *Push Back: Guilt in the Age of Natural Parenting.* New York: Dey Street Books, 2016, p. 265.

36 Rizzo, Kathryn M., Holly H. Schiffrin, and Miriam Liss. "Insight into the Parenthood Paradox: Mental Health Outcomes of Intensive Mothering." *Journal of Child and Family Studies* 22 (June 30, 2012): 614–620. https://link.springer.com/content/pdf/10.1007/s10826-012-9615-z.pdf

37 Tuteur, Amy. "How Do Privileged Mothers Display Their Status If They Can't Breastfeed?" *The Skeptical OB*, January 9, 2020. https://www.skepticalob.com/2020/01/how-do-privileged-mothers-display-their-status-if-they-cant-breastfeed.html

38 Jankowicz, Nina. "The Internet Is Failing Moms-to-Be." *Wired*, January 21, 2022. https://www.wired.com/story/pregnancy-apps-disinformation/

Chapter 8: How Anti-Vaxxers Target Women

1 Mnookin, Seth. *The Panic Virus: A True Story of Medicine, Science, and Fear.* New York: Simon & Schuster, 2011, pp. 252–254.

2 Specter, Michael. *Denialism: How Irrational Thinking Harms the Planet and Threatens Our Lives.* New York: Penguin, 2009, pp. 7–8.

3 Smith, Naomi and Tim Graham. "Mapping the Anti-vaccination Movement on Facebook." *Information, Communication & Society* 22, no. 9 (January 5, 2017): 1310–1327. https://www.tandfonline.com/doi/abs/10.1080/1369118x.2017.1418406

4 Bloom, Mia and Sophia Moskalenko. *Pastels and Pedophiles: Inside the Mind of QAnon.* Stanford: Redwood Press, 2021, p. 71.

5 Bloom, Mia and Sophia Moskalenko. *Pastels and Pedophiles: Inside the Mind of QAnon.* Stanford: Redwood Press, 2021, pp. 4, 102.

6 Boseley, Sarah. "Half of New Parents Shown Anti-vaccine Misinformation on Social Media—Report." *The Guardian*, January 24, 2019.

https://www.theguardian.com/society/2019/jan/24/anti-vaxxers
-spread-misinformation-on-social-media-report

7   Jenco, Melissa. "CDC: Rate of Unvaccinated Toddlers Increasing." *American Academy of Pediatrics*, October 11, 2018. https://www
    .aappublications.org/news/2018/10/11/vaccinationrates101118

8   Specter, Michael. *Denialism: How Irrational Thinking Harms the Planet and Threatens Our Lives*. New York: Penguin, 2009, p. 59.

9   Moran, Megan Bridgid. "Anti-Vaxx Websites, We're Onto You." *TIME*, February 11, 2016. https://time.com/4213054/anti-vaxx-websites/

10 Mnookin, Seth. *The Panic Virus: A True Story of Medicine, Science, and Fear*. New York: Simon & Schuster, 2011, pp. 5, 236; Offit, Paul A. *Deadly Choices: How the Anti-Vaccine Movement Threatens Us All*. New York: Basic Books, 2011, p. 92.

11 Offit, Paul A. *Deadly Choices: How the Anti-Vaccine Movement Threatens Us All*. New York: Basic Books, 2011.

12 Mnookin, Seth. *The Panic Virus: A True Story of Medicine, Science, and Fear*. New York: Simon & Schuster, 2011, p. 304.

13 Mnookin, Seth. *The Panic Virus: A True Story of Medicine, Science, and Fear*. New York: Simon & Schuster, 2011, p. 302.

14 Hotez, Peter J. *Vaccines Did Not Cause Rachel's Autism*. Baltimore: Johns Hopkins University Press, 2018, pp. 60–63.

15 Mnookin, Seth. *The Panic Virus: A True Story of Medicine, Science, and Fear*. New York: Simon & Schuster, 2011, p. 266; Offit, Paul A. *Deadly Choices: How the Anti-Vaccine Movement Threatens Us All*. New York: Basic Books, 2011, pp. 172–174.

16 Offit, Paul A. *Deadly Choices: How the Anti-Vaccine Movement Threatens Us All*. New York: Basic Books, 2011, pp. 176.

17 Hotez, Peter J. *Vaccines Did Not Cause Rachel's Autism*. Baltimore: Johns Hopkins University Press, 2018, p. 155.

18 Hotez, Peter J. *Vaccines Did Not Cause Rachel's Autism*. Baltimore: Johns Hopkins University Press, 2018, pp. 126–130.

19 Hotez, Peter J. *Vaccines Did Not Cause Rachel's Autism*. Baltimore: Johns Hopkins University Press, 2018, p. 135.

20 Hotez, Peter J. *Vaccines Did Not Cause Rachel's Autism*. Baltimore: Johns Hopkins University Press, 2018, p. 125.

21 Hotez, Peter J. *Vaccines Did Not Cause Rachel's Autism*. Baltimore: Johns Hopkins University Press, 2018, p. 130.

22 "Measles, Mumps, and Rubella (MMR) Vaccination: What Everyone Should Know." CDC, January 26, 2021. https://www.cdc.gov/vaccines /vpd/mmr/public/index.html

23 Offit, Paul A. *Deadly Choices: How the Anti-Vaccine Movement Threatens Us All*. New York: Basic Books, 2011, p. x.

24 Mnookin, Seth. *The Panic Virus: A True Story of Medicine, Science, and Fear*. New York: Simon & Schuster, 2011, pp. 271–272.

25 Offit, Paul A. *Deadly Choices: How the Anti-Vaccine Movement Threatens Us All*. New York: Basic Books, 2011, p. 124.

26 Whyte, Liz Essley. "Spreading Vaccine Fears, and Cashing In." *HuffPost*, June 8, 2021. https://www.huffpost.com/entry/anti-vaccine -influencers_n_60be36b9e4b0ea8a1920d73f

27 "The Anti-vaxx Industry." *Center for Countering Digital Hate*, 2020. https://counterhate.com/research/the-anti-vaxx-industry/

28 Mnookin, Seth. *The Panic Virus: A True Story of Medicine, Science, and Fear*. New York: Simon & Schuster, 2011, p. 13.

29 Zadrozny, Brandy and Aliza Nadi. "How Anti-vaxxers Target Grieving Moms and Turn Them Into Crusaders Against Vaccines." *NBC News*, September 24, 2019. https://www.nbcnews.com/tech/social -media/how-anti-vaxxers-target-grieving-çmoms-turn-them -crusaders-n1057566

30 Bloom, Mia and Sophia Moskalenko. *Pastels and Pedophiles: Inside the Mind of QAnon*. Stanford: Redwood Press, 2021, p. 61.

31 Gregoire, Carolyn. "8 Things Your Brain Does Wrong Every Day." *HuffPost*, January 29, 2014. https://www.huffpost.com/entry/ you-make-these-mistakes-i_n_4675728

32 "Moving the Needle." *Royal Society for Public Health*, 2019. https://www.rsph.org.uk/static/uploaded/3b82db00-a7ef-494c -85451e78ce18a779.pdf

33 Crooks, Andrew T., Ross J. Schuchard, and Xiaoyi Yuan. "Examining Emergent Communities and Detecting Social Bots Within the Polarized Online Vaccination Debate in Twitter." *Social Media + Society* 5, no. 3 (2019): 1–12. https://journals.sagepub.com/doi/10.1177/2056305119865465

34 Sunstein, Cass R. *On Rumors: How Falsehoods Spread, Why We Believe Them, and What Can Be Done.* Princeton: Princeton University Press, 2014, pp. 15–16.

35 Whyte, Liz Essley. "Spreading Vaccine Fears, and Cashing In." *Huff-Post*, June 8, 2021. https://www.huffpost.com/entry/anti-vaccine -influencers_n_60be36b9e4b0ea8a1920d73f

36 Wong, Julia Carrie. "How Facebook and YouTube Help Spread Anti-vaxxer Propaganda." *The Guardian*, February 1, 2019. https://www .theguardian.com/media/2019/feb/01/facebook-youtube-anti -vaccination-misinformation-social-media

37 Alba, Davey. "Virus Misinformation Spikes as Delta Cases Surge." *The New York Times*, August 10, 2021. https://www.nytimes.com /2021/08/10/technology/covid-delta-misinformation-surge.html

38 "The Anti-vaxx Industry." *Center for Countering Digital Hate*, 2020. https://counterhate.com/research/the-anti-vaxx-industry/

39 "Facebook's Algorithm: A Major Threat to Public Health." *Avaaz*, August 19, 2020. https://secure.avaaz.org/campaign/en/facebook _threat_health/

40 "The Disinformation Dozen: Why Platforms Must Act on Twelve Leading Online Anti-vaxxers." *Center for Countering Digital Hate*, 2022. https://counterhate.com/wp-content/uploads/2022/05/210324-The -Disinformation-Dozen.pdf

41 Baker, Stephanie Alice, and Michael James Walsh. "'A Mother's Intuition: It's Real and We Have to Believe in It': How the Maternal Is Used to Promote Vaccine Refusal on Instagram." *Information, Communication & Society* (January 2022). https://doi.org/10.1080/13 69118X.2021.2021269

42 Aswell, Sarah. "Study Shows Anti-Vaxx Influencers Target Three Types of Moms." *Scary Mommy*, August 3, 2022. https://www.scarymommy

.com/parenting/anti-vaxx-influencers-target-these-three-types-of-moms

43 Schechner, Sam, Jeff Horwitz, and Emile Glazer. "How Facebook Hobbled Mark Zuckerberg's Bid to Get America Vaccinated." *The Wall Street Journal*, September 17, 2021. https://www.wsj.com/articles/facebook-mark-zuckerberg-vaccinated-11631880296

44 "The Anti-vaxx Industry." Center for Countering Digital Hate, 2020. https://counterhate.com/research/the-anti-vaxx-industry/

45 Altman, Drew. "Persistent Vaccine Myths." *KFF*, May 26, 2021. https://www.kff.org/coronavirus-covid-19/perspective/persistent-vaccine-myths/

46 "New Analysis Shows Vaccines Could Have Prevented 318,000 Deaths." *Global Epidemics*, May 13, 2022. https://globalepidemics.org/2022/05/13/new-analysis-shows-vaccines-could-have-prevented-318000-deaths/

47 Bloom, Mia and Sophia Moskalenko. *Pastels and Pedophiles: Inside the Mind of QAnon*. Stanford: Redwood Press, 2021, p. 58.

48 Kanno-Youngs, Zolan and Cecilia Kang. "'They're Killing People': Biden Denounces Social Media for Virus Disinformation." *The New York Times*, July 16, 2021. https://www.nytimes.com/2021/07/16/us/politics/biden-facebook-social-media-covid.html?referringSource=articleShare

49 Klein, Betsy, Maegan Vazquez, and Kaitlan Collins. "Biden Backs Away From His Claim That Facebook Is 'Killing People' by Allowing Covid Misinformation." *CNN*, July 19, 2021. https://www.cnn.com/2021/07/19/politics/joe-biden-facebook/index.html

50 Stolberg, Sheryl Gay and Davey Alba. "Surgeon General Assails Tech Companies Over Misinformation on Covid-19." *The New York Times*, July 15, 2021. https://www.nytimes.com/2021/07/15/us/politics/surgeon-general-vaccine-misinformation.html

51 Ball, Philip. "Anti-vaccine Movement Could Undermine Efforts to End Coronavirus Pandemic, Researchers Warn." *Nature*, May 13, 2020. https://www.nature.com/articles/d41586-020-01423-4

52 "Summary of Data Publicly Reported by the Centers for Disease Control and Prevention." *American Academy of Pediatrics*, November 30, 2022. https://www.aap.org/en/pages/2019-novel-coronavirus-covid-19-infections/children-and-covid-19-vaccination-trends/

53 Brumfiel, Geoff. "The Life Cycle of A COVID-19 Vaccine Lie." *NPR*, July 20, 2021. https://www.npr.org/sections/health-shots/2021/07/20/1016912079/the-life-cycle-of-a-covid-19-vaccine-lie

54 Sheikh, Knvul. "New Study Shows Covid Vaccines Can Temporarily Alter Menstrual Cycle." *The New York Times*, September 27, 2022. https://www.nytimes.com/2022/09/27/well/live/covid-vaccine-periods-delay.html?referringSource=articleShare

55 Brumfiel, Geoff. "The Life Cycle of A COVID-19 Vaccine Lie." *NPR*, July 20, 2021. https://www.npr.org/sections/health-shots/2021/07/20/1016912079/the-life-cycle-of-a-covid-19-vaccine-lie

56 Glaser, April and Brandy Zadrozny. "Distancing From the Vaccinated: Viral Anti-vaccine Infertility Misinfo Reaches New Extremes." *NBC News*, May 14, 2021. https://www.nbcnews.com/tech/internet/viral-vaccine-infertility-misinformation-finds-home-social-media-n1267310

57 North, Anna. "Why False Claims About Covid-19 Vaccines and Infertility Are So Powerful." *Vox*, August 30, 2021. https://www.vox.com/22639366/covid-19-vaccine-fertility-pregnancy-myths

58 Mandavilli, Apoorva. "The Covid Pandemic's Hidden Casualties: Pregnant Women." *The New York Times*, December 8, 2022. https://www.nytimes.com/2022/12/08/health/pregnant-women-covid-flu-vaccine.html

59 DiResta, Renee. "Anti-vaxxers Think This Is Their Moment." *The Atlantic*, December 20, 2020. https://www.theatlantic.com/ideas/archive/2020/12/campaign-against-vaccines-already-under-way/617443/

60 Diaz, Naomi. "1 in 5 Americans Consult TikTok for Health Advice Before Their Physicians." *Becker's Healthcare*, October 7, 2022. https://www.beckershospitalreview.com/digital-marketing/1-in-5-americans-consult-tiktok-for-health-advice-before-their-physicians.html

61   Seetharaman, Deepa, Jeff Horwitz, and Justin Scheck. "Facebook Says AI Will Clean Up the Platform. Its Own Engineers Have Doubts." *The Wall Street Journal*, October 17, 2021. https://www.wsj.com/articles/facebook-ai-enforce-rules-engineers-doubtful-artificial-intelligence-11634338184

62   McCabe, David, Kate Conger, and Daisuke Wakabayashi. "YouTube, Snap and Tiktok Executives Take Their Turn Answering to Washington." *The New York Times*, October 26, 2021. https://www.nytimes.com/2021/10/26/technology/youtube-snap-and-tiktok-executives-take-their-turn-answering-to-washington.html

63   Satariano, Adam and Mike Isaac. "The Silent Partner Cleaning Up Facebook for $500 Million a Year." *The New York Times*, August 31, 2021. https://www.nytimes.com/2021/08/31/technology/facebook-accenture-content-moderation.html

64   Alaimo, Kara. "One Way to Stop the Dangerous Spread of Vaccine Myths." *CNN*, July 20, 2021. https://www.cnn.com/2021/07/20/opinions/biden-facebook-white-house-section-230-alaimo/index.html

65   Bloom, Mia and Sophia Moskalenko. *Pastels and Pedophiles: Inside the Mind of QAnon*. Stanford: Redwood Press, 2021, pp. 125–126.

Chapter 9: The Flounce

1   Barry, Ellen. "How Russian Trolls Helped Keep the Women's March Out of Lock Step." *The New York Times*, September 18, 2022. https://www.nytimes.com/2022/09/18/us/womens-march-russia-trump.html

2   "Measuring the Prevalence of Online Violence Against Women." *Economist Intelligence Unit*, March 1, 2021. https://onlineviolence-women.eiu.com/

3   "Social Media Fails Women: Transforming Social Media Policies for a Feminist Future." *We Are Ultra Violet*, 2021. https://weareultraviolet.org/wp-content/uploads/2021/11/Social-media-fails-women.pdf

4   "Troll Patrol Findings." *Amnesty International*, April 4, 2018. https://
    decoders.amnesty.org/projects/troll-patrol/findings

5   Tumulty, Karen, Kate Woodsome, and Sergio Peçanha. "How Sexist,
    Racist Attacks on Kamala Harris Have Spread Online—A Case Study."
    The Washington Post, October 7, 2020. https://www.washingtonpost
    .com/opinions/2020/10/07/kamala-harris-sexist-racist-attacks-spread
    -online/?arc404=true

6   Selbie, Tamsin and Jonathan Peters. "'Fake Accounts Used My Pic-
    tures to Sell Sex'." *BBC News*, March 1, 2021. https://www.bbc.com
    /news/uk-scotland-56182060

7   Scheff, Sue. *Shame Nation: The Global Epidemic of Online Hate.*
    Naperville: Sourcebooks, 2017, p. 193.

8   Mack, David. "A Woman Is Facing Federal Charges Over an Alleged
    Bomb Hoax Against Boston Children's Hospital." *BuzzFeed News*, Sep-
    tember 16, 2022. https://www.buzzfeednews.com/article/davidmack
    /boston-childrens-bomb-threat-arrest

9   Powell, Laurel. "2021 Becomes Deadliest Year on Record for Trans-
    gender and Non-Binary People." *Human Rights Campaign*, November
    9, 2021. https://www.hrc.org/press-releases/2021-becomes-deadliest
    -year-on-record-for-transgender-and-non-binary-people

10 Quinn, Zoë. *Crash Override: How Gamergate (Nearly) Destroyed My
    Life, and How We Can Win the Fight Against Online Hate.* New York:
    PublicAffairs, 2017, p. 64.

11 Quinn, Zoë. *Crash Override: How Gamergate (Nearly) Destroyed My
    Life, and How We Can Win the Fight Against Online Hate.* New York:
    PublicAffairs, 2017, p. 62.

12 Wu, Brianna. "Doxxed: Impact of Online Threats on Women Includ-
    ing Private Details Being Exposed and 'Swatting.' Plus Greg Lukianoff
    on Balancing Offence and Free Speech." *SAGE Journals* 44, no. 3
    (Sepember 18, 2015): 46–49. https://journals.sagepub.com/doi
    /full/10.1177/0306422015605714

13 West, Lindy. "What Happened When I Confronted My Cruellest
    Troll." *The Guardian*, February 2, 2015. https://www.theguardian.

com/society/2015/feb/02/what-happened-confronted-cruellest-troll-lindy-west

14 Judd, Ashley. "Forget Your Team: Your Online Violence Toward Girls and Women Is What Can Kiss My Ass." *MIC*, March 19, 2015. https://www.mic.com/articles/113226/forget-your-team-your-online-violence-toward-girls-and-women-is-what-can-kiss-my-ass

15 Alaimo, Kara. "Trump: Cyber Bully-in-Chief." *The Hill*, December 12, 2016. https://thehill.com/blogs/pundits-blog/the-administration/309987-trump-cyber-bully-in-chief

16 Diaz, Daniella. "Trump Defends Tweet on Military Sexual Assault." *CNN*, September 8, 2016. https://www.cnn.com/2016/09/08/politics/donald-trump-military-sexual-assault/index.html

17 Syckle, Katie Van. "Five Years, Thousands of Insults: Tracking Trump's Invective." *The New York Times*, January 26, 2021. https://www.nytimes.com/2021/01/26/insider/Trump-twitter-insults-list.html

18 Thrush, Glenn and Haberman, Maggie. "Trump Mocks Mika Brzezinski; Says She Was 'Bleeding Badly from a Face-Lift'." *The New York Times*, June 29, 2017. https://www.nytimes.com/2017/06/29/business/media/trump-mika-brzezinski-facelift.html

19 Judd, Ashley. "Forget Your Team: Your Online Violence Toward Girls and Women Is What Can Kiss My Ass." *MIC*, March 19, 2015. https://www.mic.com/articles/113226/forget-your-team-your-online-violence-toward-girls-and-women-is-what-can-kiss-my-ass

20 Pagels, Jim. "Death Threats on Twitter Are Meaningless. You Should Ignore Them." *Slate*, October 13, 2013. https://slate.com/technology/2013/10/twitter-death-threats-are-meaningless-you-should-ignore-them.html

21 Hess, Amanda. "Why Women Aren't Welcome on the Internet." *Pacific Standard*, June 14, 2017. https://psmag.com/social-justice/women-arent-welcome-internet-72170

22 Hess, Amanda. "Why Women Aren't Welcome on the Internet." *Pacific Standard*, June 14, 2017. https://psmag.com/social-justice/women-arent-welcome-internet-72170

23 Elks, Sonia. "'I Will Rape You': Female Journalists Face 'Relentless' Abuse." *Reuters*, September 13, 2018. https://www.reuters .com/article/global-women-media-idUKL5N1VZ6FN

24 Foran, Clare. "'I Never Thought It Would Be Paul': Nancy Pelosi Reveals How She First Heard Her Husband Had Been Attacked." *CNN*, November 7, 2022. https://www.cnn.com/2022/11/07/politics /nancy-pelosi-interview-paul-pelosi-attack/index.html; Walsh, Deirdre and Susan Davis. "Speaker Pelosi Says She Will Step Down as Party Leader After Two Decades at the Top." *NPR*, November 17, 2022. https://www.npr.org/2022/11/17/1133397685/house-speaker-pelosi -step-down

25 Diaz, Daniella. "Alexandra Pelosi Reflects on Her Father's Attack: 'At Some Point, You're Just Done'." *CNN*, December 13, 2022. https://www .cnn.com/2022/12/13/politics/pelosi-documentary-cnntv/index.html

26 del Valle, Lauren. "Convicted Leader of Plot to Kidnap Michigan Governor Sentenced to 16 Years in Federal Prison." *CNN*, December 27, 2022. https://www.cnn.com/2022/12/27/politics/adam-fox-sentenced- whitmer-kidnapping-plot/index.html

27 Alaimo, Kara. "Opinion: The Attack on Paul Pelosi was Not an Isolated Incident." *CNN*, October 28, 2022. https://www.cnn. com/2022/10/28/opinions/paul-pelosi-attack-not-an-isolated-incident -alaimo/index.html

28 Sleigh, Sophia. "UK Lawmaker Says She Wears Stab-Proof Jacket to Meet Constituents." *HuffPost*, January 3, 2023. https://www.huffpost.com /entry/uk-lawmaker-stab-proof-vest_n_63b40673e4b0cbfd55e3c797

29 Franks, Mary Anne. "Unwilling Avatars: Idealism and Discrimination in Cyberspace." *Columbia Journal of Gender and Law* 20, no. 1 (2011): 224–261. https://doi.org/10.7916/cjgl.v20i2.2621

30 CareerBuilder. "Number of Employers Using Social Media to Screen Candidates at All-Time High, Finds Latest CareerBuilder Study." Cision, June 15, 2017. https://www.prnewswire.com/news-releases /number-of-employers-using-social-media-to-screen-candidates-at -all-time-high-finds-latest-careerbuilder-study-300474228.html

31   Keats Citron, Danielle. *Hate Crimes in Cyberspace*. Cambridge: Harvard University Press, 2014, pp. 182–185.

32   Kissell, Chris. "Home Insurance Cyber Protection Helps Defend Against Attacks, Cyberbullying." *Insurance*, August 9, 2021. https://www.insurance.com/home-and-renters-insurance/cyber-insurance

33   Keats Citron, Danielle. *Hate Crimes in Cyberspace*. Cambridge: Harvard University Press, 2014, pp. 10–11.

34   Frenkel, Sheera and Kellen Browning. "The Metaverse's Dark Side: Here Come Harassment and Assaults." *The New York Times*, December 30, 2021. https://www.nytimes.com/2021/12/30/technology/metaverse-harassment-assaults.html

35   Kang, Cecilia and Mike Isaac. "Defiant Zuckerberg Says Facebook Won't Police Political Speech." *The New York Times*, October 17, 2019. www.nytimes.com/2019/10/17/business/zuckerberg-facebook-free-speech.html

36   Alaimo, Kara. "Elon Musk Is Running Twitter Like Dictators Run Their States." *CNN*, December 16, 2022. https://www.cnn.com/2022/12/16/opinions/elon-musk-twitter-journalists-alaimo/index.html

37   Franks, Mary Anne. "Unwilling Avatars: Idealism and Discrimination in Cyberspace." *Columbia Journal of Gender and Law* 20, no. 1 (2011): 224–261. https://doi.org/10.7916/cjgl.v20i2.2621

38   Wu, Brianna. "Doxxed: Impact of Online Threats on Women Including Private Details Being Exposed and 'Swatting'. Plus Greg Lukianoff on Balancing Offence and Free Speech." *SAGE Journals* 44, no. 3 (September 18, 2015): 46–49. https://journals.sagepub.com/doi/full/10.1177/0306422015605714

39   Quinn, Zoë. *Crash Override: How Gamergate (Nearly) Destroyed My Life, and How We Can Win the Fight Against Online Hate*. New York: PublicAffairs, 2017, p. 47.

40   Quinn, Zoë. *Crash Override: How Gamergate (Nearly) Destroyed My Life, and How We Can Win the Fight Against Online Hate*. New York: PublicAffairs, 2017, p. 107.

41 Franks, Mary Anne. "Unwilling Avatars: Idealism and Discrimination in Cyberspace." *Columbia Journal of Gender and Law* 20, no. 1 (2011): 224–261. https://doi.org/10.7916/cjgl.v20i2.2621

42 McCamley, Frankie. "Robin Williams' Daughter Returns to Twitter After Abuse." *BBC News*, September 3, 2014. https://www.bbc.com /news/newsbeat-28773734

43 Bieber, Hailey. "Twitter Is Toxic." *The Purcell Register*, April 1, 2021. http://www.purcellregister.com/stories/hailey-bieber-twitter-is-toxic ,30556?

44 D'Aluisio, Alexandra. "Cardi B Deactivates Her Instagram Account After Grammys Rant: 'I F—king Worked My Ass Off'." *US Magazine*, February 12, 2019. https://www.usmagazine.com/celebrity -news/news/cardi-b-deactivates-instagram-after-grammys-2019 -rant/

45 Guglielmi, Jodi. "Lili Reinhart Says She's Taking a Break From 'Toxic' Twitter: 'There's Hate Everywhere'." *Yahoo*, December 18, 2018. https:// www.yahoo.com/entertainment/lili-reinhart-says-she-apos-193925146 .html?fr=sycsrp_catchall

46 Rothman, Michael. "Grieving Sarah Hyland Takes a Break From Twitter After 'Horrible, Negative, Ignorant Words'." *GMA*. https:// www.goodmorningamerica.com/culture/story/grieving-sarah -hyland-takes-break-twitter-horrible-negative-59622535

47 Coughlan, Maggie. "Why Aidy Bryant Quit Twitter." *The New York Post*, March 12, 2019. https://pagesix.com/2019/03/12/why-aidy -bryant-quit-twitter/amp/

48 Piner, Catherine. "Feminist Writer Jessica Valenti Takes a Break From Social Media After Threat Against Her Daughter." *Slate*, July 28, 2016. https://slate.com/human-interest/2016/07/feminist-writer-jessica-val enti-takes-a-break-from-social-media-after-threat-against-her- daughter.html; Goldberg, Michelle. "Feminist Writers Are So Besieged by Online Abuse That Some Have Begun to Retire." *The Washington Post*, February 20, 2015. https://www.washingtonpost.com/opinions /online-feminists-increasingly-ask-are-the-psychic-costs-too-much

-to-bear/2015/02/19/3dc4ca6c-b7dd-11e4-a200-c008a01a6692_story
.html

49   "USA: Twitter Scorecard: Tracking Twitter's Progress in Addressing
     Violence and Abuse Against Women Online in the United States."
     Amnesty International, December 7, 2021. https://www.amnestyusa.
     org/wp-content/uploads/2021/12/Twitter-Scorecard-Report-2021_
     FINAL.pdf

50   "Abuse and Harassment Driving Girls Off Facebook, Instagram and
     Twitter." *Plan International*, October 5, 2020. https://plan-interna-
     tional.org/news/2020/10/05/abuse-and-harassment-driving-girls-off
     -facebook-instagram-and-twitter; Batha, Emma. "Social Media Abuse
     Drives Girls Off Facebook, Instagram, Twitter—Poll." *Reuters*, Octo-
     ber 5, 2020. https://www.reuters.com/article/socialmedia-girls-abuse
     -idAFL8N2GP4RG

51   "Toxic Twitter—A Toxic Place for Women." *Amnesty International*,
     March 15, 2018. https://www.amnesty.org/en/latest/news/2018/03
     /online-violence-against-women-chapter-5-5/

52   "Toxic Twitter—A Toxic Place for Women." *Amnesty International*,
     March 15, 2018. https://www.amnesty.org/en/latest/research/2018/03
     /online-violence-against-women-chapter-1/

53   Scheff, Sue. *Shame Nation: The Global Epidemic of Online Hate.*
     Naperville: Sourcebooks, 2017, p. 167.

54   "Flounce." *Urban Dictionary*, September 29, 2013. https://www
     .urbandictionary.com/define.php?term=Flounce

55   "Social Media Fact Sheet." *Pew Research Center*, April 7, 2021. https://
     www.pewresearch.org/internet/fact-sheet/social-media/?menuItem
     =3814afe3-3f3c-4623-910b-8a6a37885ab8

56   Sumagaysay, Levi. "Christine Blasey Ford Got Doxed. Can Anyone
     Ever Really Scrub Their Online Presence?" *StarTribune*, September 25,
     2018. https://www.startribune.com/christine-blasey-ford-got-doxed
     -can-anyone-ever-really-scrub-their-online-presence/494166211/

57   West, Lindy. "What Happened When I Confronted My Cruellest
     Troll." *The Guardian*, February 2, 2015. https://www.theguardian.com

/society/2015/feb/02/what-happened-confronted-cruellest-troll
-lindy-west

58 Quinn, Zoë. *Crash Override: How Gamergate (Nearly) Destroyed My Life, and How We Can Win the Fight Against Online Hate*. New York: PublicAffairs, 2017, pp. 4–5.

59 Solnit, Rebecca. *Men Explain Things to Me*. Chicago: Haymarket Books, 2014, p. 134.

60 Bennett-Smith, Meredith. "Facebook Vows to Crack Down on Rape Joke Pages After Successful Protest, Boycott." *HuffPost*, May 29, 2013. https://www.huffpost.com/entry/facebook-rape-jokes-protest_n_3349319

61 "Hidden Hate: How Instagram Fails to Act on 9 in 10 Reports of Misogyny in DMs." Center for Countering Digital Hate, 2022. https://counterhate.com/wp-content/uploads/2022/05/Final-Hidden-Hate.pdf

62 Warzel, C. "'It Only Adds to the Humiliation'—How Twitter Responds to Harassers." *BuzzFeed News*, September 22, 2016. https://www.buzzfeednews.com/article/charliewarzel/after-reporting-abuse-many-twitter-users-hear-silence-or-wor

63 Jankowicz, Nina. *How to Be a Woman Online: Surviving Abuse and Harassment, and How to Fight Back*. New York: Bloomsbury Academic, 2022, p. 44.

64 Chang, Emily. *Brotopia: Breaking Up the Boys' Club of Silicon Valley*. New York: Portfolio/Penguin, 2019, pp. 236–237.

65 West, Lindy. "Twitter Doesn't Think These Rape and Death Threats Are Harassment." *The Daily Dot*, December 23, 2014. https://www.dailydot.com/unclick/twitter-harassment-rape-death-threat-report/

66 Warzel, Charlie. "Twitter Is Still Dismissing Harassment Reports and Frustrating Victims." *BuzzFeed News*, July 18, 2017. https://www.buzzfeednews.com/article/charliewarzel/twitter-is-still-dismissing-harassment-reports-and

67 "New Report Finds Twitter Continues to Fall Short on Protecting Women Online." *Amnesty International USA*, December 7, 2021.

https://www.amnestyusa.org/reports/new-report-finds-twitter
-continues-to-fall-short-on-protecting-women-online/

68 Quinn, Zoë. *Crash Override: How Gamergate (Nearly) Destroyed My Life, and How We Can Win the Fight Against Online Hate*. New York: PublicAffairs, 2017, p. 131.

69 *Hidden Hate: How Instagram Fails to Act on 9 in 10 Reports of Misogyny in DMs*. Center for Countering Digital Hate, 2022. https://counterhate.com/wp-content/uploads/2022/05/Final-Hidden-Hate.pdf

70 Hess, Amanda. "Why Women Aren't Welcome on the Internet." *Pacific Standard*, June 14, 2017. https://psmag.com/social-justice/women-arent-welcome-internet-72170

71 Chang, Emily. *Brotopia: Breaking Up the Boys' Club of Silicon Valley*. New York: Portfolio/Penguin, 2019, p. 247.

72 Kaplan, Katharine A. "Facemash Creator Survives Ad Board." *The Harvard Crimson*, November 19, 2003. https://www.thecrimson.com/article/2003/11/19/facemash-creator-survives-ad-board-the/; Brodsky, Sam. "Everything to Know About Facemash, the Site Zuckerberg Created in College to Rank 'Hot' Women." *Metro US*, April 12, 2018. https://www.metro.us/everything-to-know-about-facemash-the-site-zuckerberg-created-in-college-to-rank-hot-women/

73 Bhattacharya, Ananya. "In One Tweet, Elon Musk Captures the Everyday Sexism Faced by Women in STEM." *Quartz*, November 1, 2021. https://qz.com/work/2082746/elon-musks-tweet-captures-everyday-sexism-faced-by-women-in-stem

74 Isidore, Chris. "Elon Musk Calls Elizabeth Warren 'Senator Karen' in Fight Over Taxes." *CNN Business*, December 15, 2021. https://www.cnn.com/2021/12/15/investing/elon-musk-elizabeth-warren-taxes/index.html

75 Kendall, Mikki. *Hood Feminism: Notes from The Women That a Movement Forgot*. New York: Viking 2020, p. 58.

76 Quinn, Zoë. *Crash Override: How Gamergate (Nearly) Destroyed My Life, and How We Can Win the Fight Against Online Hate*. New York: PublicAffairs, 2017, p. 148.

77 Keats Citron, Danielle. *Hate Crimes in Cyberspace*. Cambridge: Harvard University Press, 2014, pp. 20, 84–85.

78 Quinn, Zoë. *Crash Override: How Gamergate (Nearly) Destroyed My Life, and How We Can Win the Fight Against Online Hate*. New York: PublicAffairs, 2017, p. 101.

79 Hattenstone, Simon. "Caroline Criado-Perez: 'Twitter Has Enabled People to Behave in a Way They Wouldn't Face to Face'." *The Guardian*, August 4, 2013. https://www.theguardian.com/lifeandstyle/2013/aug/04/caroline-criado-perez-twitter-rape-threats

80 Hess, Amanda. "Why Women Aren't Welcome on the Internet." *Pacific Standard*, June 14, 2017. https://psmag.com/social-justice/women-arent-welcome-internet-72170

81 Guardian News and Media. "Two Jailed for Twitter Abuse of Feminist Campaigner." *The Guardian*, January 24, 2014. https://www.theguardian.com/uk-news/2014/jan/24/two-jailed-twitter-abuse-feminist-campaigner

82 Merlan, Anna. "The Cops Don't Care About Violent Online Threats. What Do We Do Now?" *Jezebel*, January 29, 2015. https://jezebel.com/the-cops-dont-care-about-violent-online-threats-what-d-1682577343

83 Scheff, Sue. *Shame Nation: The Global Epidemic of Online Hate*. Naperville: Sourcebooks, 2017, p. 194.

84 Merlan, Anna. "The Cops Don't Care About Violent Online Threats. What Do We Do Now?" *Jezebel*, January 29, 2015. https://jezebel.com/the-cops-dont-care-about-violent-online-threats-what-d-1682577343

85 Bosman, Julie, Kate Taylor, and Tim Arango. "A Common Trait Among Mass Killers: Hatred Toward Women." *The New York Times*, August 10, 2019. https://www.nytimes.com/2019/08/10/us/mass-shootings-misogyny-dayton.html

86 "2018 Crime in the United States." FBI, October 7, 2019. https://ucr.fbi.gov/crime-in-the-u.s/2018/crime-in-the-u.s.-2018

87 Duffin, Erin. "Number of Federal Bureau of Investigation Employees in the United States in 2019, by Role and Gender." *Statista*,

October 2, 2020. https://www.statista.com/statistics/745497/number-of-fbi-employees-by-gender/

88 Alaimo, Kara. "Twitter's Removal of Nickelback Video Sends a Twisted Message." *CNN*, October 4, 2019. https://www.cnn.com/2019/10/04/opinions/trump-nickelback-tweet-is-a-limit-alaimo/index.html

89 Chang, Emily. *Brotopia: Breaking Up the Boys' Club of Silicon Valley.* New York: Portfolio/Penguin, 2019, pp. 247–249.

90 "Twitter Before and After Trump." *Edison Research*, February 17, 2021. https://www.edisonresearch.com/twitter-before-and-after-trump/

91 Quinn, Zoë. *Crash Override: How Gamergate (Nearly) Destroyed My Life, and How We Can Win the Fight Against Online Hate.* New York: PublicAffairs, 2017, p. 139.

92 "Upstander Pledge." Tyler Clementi Foundation. https://tylerclementi.org/pledge/

93 Quinn, Zoë. *Crash Override: How Gamergate (Nearly) Destroyed My Life, and How We Can Win the Fight Against Online Hate.* New York: PublicAffairs, 2017, p. 217.

94 Quinn, Zoë. *Crash Override: How Gamergate (Nearly) Destroyed My Life, and How We Can Win the Fight Against Online Hate.* New York: PublicAffairs, 2017, pp. 202, 207.

95 Quinn, Zoë. *Crash Override: How Gamergate (Nearly) Destroyed My Life, and How We Can Win the Fight Against Online Hate.* New York: PublicAffairs, 2017, p. 208.

Chapter 10: Meta Misogyny

1 Browning, Kellen. "Leader of Apple Activism Movement Says She Was Fired." *The New York Times*, October 15, 2021. https://www.nytimes.com/2021/10/15/technology/appletoo-apple-janneke-parrish.html

2 Chang, Emily. *Brotopia: Breaking Up the Boys' Club of Silicon Valley.* New York: Portfolio/Penguin, 2019, pp. 118–119.

3 Wakabayashi, Daisuke. "Alphabet Settles Shareholder Suits Over Sexual Harassment Claims." *The New York Times*, September 25, 2020. https://www.nytimes.com/2020/09/25/technology/google-sexual -harassment-lawsuit-settlement.html

4 Flitter, Emily and Goldstein, Matthew. "Long Before Divorce, Bill Gates Had Reputation for Questionable Behavior." *The New York Times*, May 16, 2021. https://www.nytimes.com/2021/05/16/business /bill-melinda-gates-divorce-epstein.html; Fernández Campbell, Alexia. "Women at Microsoft Say It's a Toxic Place to Work." *Vox*, April 11, 2019. https://www.vox.com/policy-and-politics/2019/4/11/ 18304536/microsoft-women-discrimination-harassment-complaints

5 Kelly, Heather. "Facebook Gets Sued for Gender Discrimination." *CNN Business*, March 19, 2015. https://money.cnn.com/2015/03/18 /technology/facebook-discrimination-suit/index.html

6 Greenway, Rebecca. "Gender Discrimination Lawsuits at Silicon Valley Tech Companies." *NBC Bay Area*, July 24, 2017. https://www .nbcbayarea.com/news/local/gender-discrimination-lawsuits-in -silicon-valley/27036/

7 Guynn, Jessica and Marco della Cava. "Silicon Valley's Dirty Little Secret: The Way It Treats Women." *USA Today*, March 3, 2017. https://www.usatoday.com/story/tech/news/2017/03/03/silicon -valleys-dirty-little-secret-sexual-harassment-discrimination-of -women/98646108/

8 Streitfeld, David. "Ellen Pao Loses Silicon Valley Bias Case Against Kleiner Perkins." *The New York Times*, March 27, 2015. https://www .nytimes.com/2015/03/28/technology/ellen-pao-kleiner-perkins-case -decision.html

9 Griffith, Erin. "Pinterest Settles Gender Discrimination Suit for $22.5 Million." *The New York Times*, December 14, 2020. https://www .nytimes.com/2020/12/14/technology/pinterest-gender-discrimination -lawsuit.html

10 National Center for Women & Information Technology. "By the Numbers." March 1, 2022. https://ncwit.org/resource/bythenumbers/

11   Bell, David A. and Dawn Belt. "Gender Diversity in the Silicon Valley." *Fenwick*, 2020. https://assets.fenwick.com/documents/Fenwick-Gender-Diversity-Survey-2020.pdf

12   Ma, Michelle. "Twitter Just Released Its Latest Diversity Numbers. Here's How It Stacks Up Against the Rest of Tech." *Protocol*, January 12, 2022. https://www.protocol.com/bulletins/twitter-2021-diversity-report

13   "Annual Diversity Report." *Facebook*, July 2021. https://about.fb.com/wp-content/uploads/2021/07/Facebook-Annual-Diversity-Report-July-2021.pdf

14   Chamberlain, Andrew, Daniel Zhao, and Amanda Stansell. "Progress on the Gender Pay Gap: 2019." *Glassdoor*, March 27, 2019. https://www.glassdoor.com/research/app/uploads/sites/2/2019/03/Gender-Pay-Gap-2019-Research-Report-1.pdf

15   Cech, Erin A. and Mary Blair-Loy. "The Changing Career Trajectories of New Parents in STEM." *PNAS* 116, no. 10 (March 5, 2019): 4182–4187. https://www.pnas.org/doi/10.1073/pnas.1810862116

16   Nayak, Malathi and Bloomberg. "Not 'Googly' Enough: Google Sued by Black Ex-employee Over 'Racially Biased' Culture." *Fortune*, March 20, 2022. https://fortune.com/2022/03/19/not-googly-enough-google-sued-by-black-ex-employee-over-racially-biased-culture-april-curley-san-diego-alaphabet-inc/

17   Wakabayashi, Daisuke. "Lawsuit Accuses Google of Bias Against Black Employees." *The New York Times*, March 18, 2022. https://www.nytimes.com/2022/03/18/technology/google-discrimination-suit-black-employees.html

18   Stylianou, Antonis C., Susan Winter, Yuan Niu, Robert A. Giacalone, and Matt Campbell. "Understanding the Behavioral Intention to Report Unethical Information Technology Practices: The Role of Machiavellianism, Gender, and Computer Expertise." *Journal of Business Ethics* 117 (2013): 333–343. https://link.springer.com/article/10.1007/s10551-012-1521-1

19 Martin, Asia. "Goodbye to the Good Life: The Cushy Perks of Tech Work Are Rapidly Disappearing." *Business Insider,* December 19, 2022. https://www.businessinsider.in/tech/news/goodbye-to-the-good -life-the-cushy-perks-of-tech-work-are-rapidly-disappearing- /articleshow/96343966.cms

20 Wagner, Kurt and Bloomberg. "Twitter Cuts Workers Address- ing Hate Speech and Trust and Safety as Elon Musk's Chaotic Revamp Continues." *Fortune,* January 8, 2023. https://fortune .com/2023/01/07/twitter-cuts-workers-hate-speech-trust-safety -elon-musk-revamp; Belanger, Ashley. "Twitter Sued for Target- ing Women and Staff on Family Leave in Layoffs." *ars Technica,* December 9, 2022. https://arstechnica.com/tech-policy/2022/12 /twitter-lawsuit-alleges-musk-layoffs-disproportionately-targeted -women/

21 Wakabayashi, Daisuke and Sheera Frenkel. "Parents Got More Time Off. Then the Backlash Started." *The New York Times,* September 5, 2020. https://www.nytimes.com/2020/09/05/technology/parents-time -off-backlash.html

22 Duffy, Brooke Erin and Becca Schwartz. "Digital 'Women's Work?': Job Recruitment Ads and the Feminization of Social Media Employ- ment." *New Media & Society* 20, no. 8 (2018): 2972–2989. https://doi .org/10.1177/1461444817738237

23 "Average Social Media Manager Salary." *PayScale,* 2021. https: //www.payscale.com/research/US/Job=Social_Media_Manager /Salary

24 Miller, Claire Cain. "As Women Take Over a Male-Dominated Field, the Pay Drops." *The New York Times,* March 18, 2016. https://www .nytimes.com/2016/03/20/upshot/as-women-take-over-a-male -dominated-field-the-pay-drops.html

25 McCarthy, Niall. "Where U.S. Tech Workers Get Paid the Most." *Statista,* June 17, 2020. https://www.statista.com/chart/22030/ average-tech-worker-salary-in-us-cities/

26 "Average Social Media Manager Salary." *PayScale*, 2021. https://www
.payscale.com/research/US/Job=Social_Media_Manager/Salary

27 Hempel, Jessi. "How Social Media Became a Pink-Collar Job." *Wired*,
May 26, 2018. https://www.wired.com/story/how-social-media
-became-a-pink-collar-job/

28 Levinson, Alana Hope. "The Pink Ghetto of Social Media." *Medium*,
July 16, 2015. https://medium.com/matter/the-pink-ghetto-of-social
-media-39bf7f2fdbe1

29 "Al Gore Hopes "Stalker Economy' Makes Us Gag." *NBC Los
Angeles*, March 10, 2013. https://www.nbclosangeles.com/news/
national-international/al-gore-says-we-live-in-stalker-economy
/2057337/

30 Zuboff, Shoshana. *The Age of Surveillance Capitalism: The Fight for a
Human Future at the New Frontier of Power*. New York: PublicAffairs,
2019, pp. 48–50, 521.

31 Valentino-DeVries, Jennifer. "Cellphone Carriers Face $200 Million
Fine for Not Protecting Location Data." *The New York Times*, February 28, 2020. https://www.nytimes.com/2020/02/28/technology
/fcc-cellphones-location-data-fines.html

32 Schneier, Bruce. *Data and Goliath: The Hidden Battles to Collect Your
Data and Control Your World*. New York: W. W. Norton & Company,
2015, pp. 51–53.

33 Alaimo, Kara. "Dating Apps Aren't Protecting You or Your Data."
Bloomberg, February 14, 2020. https://www.bloomberg.com/opinion
/articles/2020-02-14/online-dating-sites-can-and-should-protect
-users-and-their-data?leadSource=uverify%20wall

34 Singer, Natasha and Aaron Krolik. "Grindr and OkCupid Spread Personal Details, Study Says." *The New York Times*, January 13, 2020.
https://www.nytimes.com/2020/01/13/technology/grindr-apps
-dating-data-tracking.html

35 Schneier, Bruce. *Data and Goliath: The Hidden Battles to Collect Your
Data and Control Your World*. New York: W. W. Norton & Company,
2015, p. 26.

36 Schneier, Bruce. *Data and Goliath: The Hidden Battles to Collect Your Data and Control Your World*. New York: W. W. Norton & Company, 2015, p. 45.

37 Schneier, Bruce. *Data and Goliath: The Hidden Battles to Collect Your Data and Control Your World*. New York: W. W. Norton & Company, 2015, pp. 36–37.

38 Schneier, Bruce. *Data and Goliath: The Hidden Battles to Collect Your Data and Control Your World*. New York: W. W. Norton & Company, 2015, p. 57.

39 "Consumer Data Brokers Selling Lists of Rape Victims." *Jezebel*, April 2, 2014. https://jezebel.com/consumer-data-brokers-selling-lists-of-rape-victims-1557322995

40 Keats Citron, Danielle. *The Fight for Privacy: Protecting Dignity, Identity and Love in the Digital Age*. New York: W. W. Norton & Company, 2022, p. 13.

41 Cox, Joseph. "Data Broker Is Selling Location Data of People Who Visit Abortion Clinics." *Vice*, May 3, 2022. https://www.vice.com/en/article/m7vzjb/location-data-abortion-clinics-safegraph-planned-parenthood

42 Schneier, Bruce. *Data and Goliath: The Hidden Battles to Collect Your Data and Control Your World*. New York: W. W. Norton & Company, 2015, pp. 135–136.

43 Davis, Krystle M. "20 Facts and Figures to Know When Marketing to Women." *Forbes*, May 13, 2019. https://www.forbes.com/sites/forbescontentmarketing/2019/05/13/20-facts-and-figures-to-know-when-marketing-to-women/?sh=30b77f671297

44 Mc Mahon, Ciarán. *The Psychology of Social Media*. New York: Routledge, 2019, pp. 47–48.

45 Bensinger, Greg. "Americans Actually Want Privacy. Shocking." *The New York Times*, May 20, 2021. https://www.nytimes.com/2021/05/20/opinion/apple-facebook-ios-privacy.html

46 Lin, Johnny and Sean Halloran. "Study: Effectiveness of Apple's App Tracking Transparency." *Transparency Matters*, September 22, 2021.

https://blog.lockdownprivacy.com/2021/09/22/study-effectiveness
-of-apples-app-tracking-transparency.html

47 Kang, Cecilia. "Four Attorneys General Claim Google Secretly
Tracked People." *The New York Times,* January 24, 2022. https://www
.nytimes.com/2022/01/24/technology/google-location-services
-lawsuit.html

48 "Arizona Announces $85M Settlement With Google Over
User Data." *Associated Press,* October 4, 2022. https://apnews
.com/article/technology-business-lawsuits-arizona
-440a27f1e7c2c672d3ccc727439978b4

49 Nicas, Jack. "What Data About You Can the Government Get from
Big Tech?" *The New York Times,* June 14, 2021. https://www.nytimes.
com/2021/06/14/technology/personal-data-apple-google-facebook
.html

50 Chen, Brian X. and Daisuke Wakabayashi. "You're Still Being Tracked
on the Internet, Just in a Different Way." *The New York Times,*
April 6, 2022. https://www.nytimes.com/2022/04/06/technology
/online-tracking-privacy.html

51 Mc Mahon, Ciarán. *The Psychology of Social Media.* New York: Routledge, 2019, p. 41.

52 Mc Mahon, Ciarán. *The Psychology of Social Media.* New York: Routledge, 2019, p. 92.

53 Schneier, Bruce. *Data and Goliath: The Hidden Battles to Collect Your
Data and Control Your World.* New York: W. W. Norton & Company,
2015, pp. 229, 235.

54 Zuboff, Shoshana. *The Age of Surveillance Capitalism: The Fight for a
Human Future at the New Frontier of Power.* New York: PublicAffairs,
2019, p. 122.

55 Schneier, Bruce. *Data and Goliath: The Hidden Battles to Collect Your
Data and Control Your World.* New York: W. W. Norton & Company,
2015, p. 94.

56 O'Brien, Sara and Clare Duffy. "Nebraska Teen and Mother Facing
Charges in Abortion-Related Case That Involved Obtaining Their

Facebook Messages. *CNN*, August 10, 2022. https://www.cnn .com/2022/08/10/tech/teen-charged-abortion-facebook-messages /index.html

57	Keats Citron, Danielle. *The Fight for Privacy: Protecting Dignity, Identity and Love in the Digital Age*. New York: W. W. Norton & Company, 2022, p. 99.

58	Keats Citron, Danielle. *The Fight for Privacy: Protecting Dignity, Identity and Love in the Digital Age*. New York: W. W. Norton & Company, 2022, p. 163.

59	Browning, Kellen and Mike Isaac. "Activision, Facing Internal Turmoil, Grapples With #MeToo Reckoning." *The New York Times*, July 29, 2021. https://www.nytimes.com/2021/07/29/technology /activision-walkout-metoo-call-of-duty.html

60	Jankowicz, Nina. *How to Be a Woman Online: Surviving Abuse and Harassment, and How to Fight Back*. New York: Bloomsbury Academic, 2022, pp. 5, 7, 10–12.

61	Mele, Christopher and Daniel Victor. "'10 Concerts' Facebook Meme May Reveal More Than Musical Tastes." *The New York Times*, April 28, 2017. https://www.nytimes.com/2017/04/28/technology /facebook-concerts-attend.html?referringSource=articleShare

Chapter 11: The #Feminist Fallacy

1	Baggs, Michael. "Gillette Faces Backlash and Boycott Over '#MeToo Advert'." *BBC*, January 15, 2019. https://www.bbc.com/news /newsbeat-46874617

2	Smith, Tovia. "Backlash Erupts After Gillette Launches a New #McToo-Inspired Ad Campaign." *NPR*, January 17, 2019. https://www .npr.org/2019/01/17/685976624/backlash-erupts-after-gillette-launches -a-new-metoo-inspired-ad-campaign

3	Windels, Kasey, Sara Champlin, Summer Shelton, Yvetter Sterbenk, and Maddison Poteet. "Selling Feminism: How Female Empowerment Campaigns Employ Postfeminist Discourses." *Journal of*

Advertising 49, no. 1 (2019): 18–33. https://doi.org/10.1080/00913367 .2019.1681035

4   Etcoff, Nancy, Susie Orbach, Jennifer Scott, and Heidi D'Agostino. *The Real Truth About Beauty: A Global Report.* Dove, September 2004. https://www.clubofamsterdam.com/contentarticles/52%20Beauty /dove_white_paper_final.pdf

5   Bahadur, Nina. "Dove 'Real Beauty' Campaign Turns 10: How a Brand Tried to Change the Conversation About Female Beauty." *HuffPost*, January 21, 2014. https://www.huffpost.com/entry/dove-real-beauty -campaign-turns-10_n_4575940

6   Vega, Tanzina. "Ad About Women's Self-image Creates a Sensation." *The New York Times*, April 18, 2013. https://www.nytimes.com /2013/04/19/business/media/dove-ad-on-womens-self-image-creates -an-online-sensation.html

7   Murphy, Samantha. "Viral Dove Campaign Becomes Most Watched Ad Ever." *Mashable*, May 20, 2013. https://mashable.com/2013/05/20 /dove-ad-most-watche/

8   Silcoff, Mireille. "Dove's Latest Stand in the Virtue Wars." *The New York Times*, July 20, 2022. https://www.nytimes.com/2022/07/20 /magazine/dove-advertising-beauty.html

9   Zed, Olivia. "How Dove's Real Beauty Campaign Won, and Nearly Lost, Its Audience." *PR Week*, April 16, 2019. https://www.prweek .com/article/1582147/doves-real-beauty-campaign-won-nearly-lost-its -audience

10   Feloni, Richard. "Pantene Produces an Overtly Feminist Ad." *Business Insider*, December 10, 2013. https://www.businessinsider.com /pantene-philipines-whip-it-campaign-2013-12

11   Bahadur, Nina. "Pantene 'Not Sorry' Video Tells Women to Stop Apologizing So Much." *HuffPost*, June 18, 2014. https://www.huffpost .com/entry/pantene-not-sorry-shine-strong_n_5507461

12   "Our Epic Battle #LikeAGirl." *Always®*, June 26, 2014. https://always.com /en-us/about-us/our-epic-battle-like-a-girl; Goldberg, Hannah. "This

Ad Completely Redefines the Phrase 'Like a Girl'." *TIME*, June 26, 2014. https://time.com/2927761/likeagirl-always-female-empowerment/

13 Windels, Kasey, Sara Champlin, Summer Shelton, Yvetter Sterbenk, and Maddison Poteet. "Selling Feminism: How Female Empowerment Campaigns Employ Postfeminist Discourses." *Journal of Advertising* 49, no. 1 (2019): 18–33. https://doi.org/10.1080/00913367.2019.1681035

14 Banet-Weiser, Sarah. *Empowered: Popular Feminism and Popular Misogyny*. Durham: Duke University Press, 2018.

15 Ferguson, Majorie. "Images of Power and the Feminist Fallacy." *Critical Studies in Mass Communication* 7, no. 3 (2009): 215–230. https://www.tandfonline.com/doi/abs/10.1080/15295039009360175

16 Plank, Elizabeth. "10 Worst Ways Companies Have Used Feminism to Sell Women Products." *Mic*, June 26, 2014. https://www.mic.com/articles/91961/10-worst-ways-companies-have-used-feminism-to-sell-women-products

17 Traister, Rebecca. "'Real Beauty'—or Really Smart Marketing?" *Salon*, July 22, 2005. https://www.salon.com/2005/07/22/dove_2/

18 Sharma, Karuna. "Glow & Lovely Has Launched Its New Campaign, But Why Does It Look and Feel Exactly Like Fair & Lovely?" *Business Insider*, September 8, 2020. https://www.businessinsider.in/advertising/brands/article/glow-lovely-has-launched-its-new-campaign-but-why-does-it-look-and-feel-exactly-like-fair-lovely/articleshow/77986036.cms

19 "Unilever Sells Slim-Fast to Kainos Capital." *Unilever*, October 7, 2014. https://www.unilever.com/news/press-releases/2014/14-07-10-Unilever-sells-Slim-Fast-to-Kainos-Capital.html

20 Kendall, Mikki. *Hood Feminism: Notes from The Women That a Movement Forgot*. New York: Viking, 2020, p. 33.

21 Banet-Weiser, Sarah. *Empowered: Popular Feminism and Popular Misogyny*. Durham: Duke University Press, 2018, p. 47.

22 Kendall, Mikki. *Hood Feminism: Notes From the Women That a Movement Forgot*. New York: Viking, 2020, p. 253.

23 Gupta, A. H. "Crash Test Dummies Made Cars Safer (for Average-Size Men)." *The New York Times,* December 27, 2021. https://www.nytimes .com/2021/12/27/business/car-safety-women.html

24 Barroso, Amanda and Anna Brown. "Gender Pay Gap in U.S. Held Steady in 2020." *Pew Research Center,* May 25, 2021. https://www .pewresearch.org/fact-tank/2021/05/25/gender-pay-gap-facts; Kristof, Nicholas. "Are Vets and Pharmacists Showing How to Make Careers Work for Moms?" *The New York Times,* June 9, 2021. https://www .nytimes.com/2021/06/09/opinion/women-motherhood-jobs.html

25 Criado Perez, Caroline. *Invisible Women: Data Bias in a World Designed For Men.* New York: Abrams Press, 2019, pp. 48–49.

26 Povoledo, Elisabetta. "Pope Says High Number of Domestic Violence Cases Is 'Almost Satanic'." *The New York Times,* December 20, 2021. https://www.nytimes.com/2021/12/20/world/europe/pope-domestic -violence-almost-satanic.html

27 Wootson, Cleve. "A Dove Ad Showed a Black Woman Turning Herself White. The Backlash Is Growing." *The Washington Post,* October 9, 2017. https://www.washingtonpost.com/news/business/wp/2017/10/08 /dove-ad-that-shows-a-black-woman-turning-herself-white-sparks -consumer-backlash/

28 Alaimo, Kara. "A Little Predictability Could Go a Long Way for Working Moms." *Bloomberg,* May 10, 2020. https://www.bloomberg.com /opinion/articles/2020-05-10/mother-s-day-wishes-for-working -moms?leadSource=uverify%20wall

29 Fahrenthold, David. "Trump Recorded Having Extremely Lewd Conversation About Women in 2005." *The Washington Post,* October 8, 2016. https://www.washingtonpost.com/politics/trump-recorded-having -extremely-lewd-conversation-about-women-in-2005/2016/10/07 /3b9ce776-8cb4-11e6-bf8a-3d26847eeed4_story.html

30 Banet-Weiser, Sarah. *Empowered: Popular Feminism and Popular Misogyny.* Durham: Duke University Press, 2018, p. 177.

31 Brown, Emma. "California Professor, Writer of Confidential Brett Kavanaugh Letter, Speaks Out About Her Allegation of Sexual

Assault." *The Washington Post*, September 16, 2018. https://www
.washingtonpost.com/investigations/california-professor-writer-of
-confidential-brett-kavanaugh-letter-speaks-out-about-her-allegation
-of-sexual-assault/2018/09/16/46982194-b846-11e8-94eb-3bd52dfe917b
_story.html

32 Totenberg, Nina and Sarah McCammon. "Supreme Court Over-
turns Roe v. Wade, Ending Right to Abortion Upheld for Decades."
NPR, June 24, 2022. https://www.npr.org/2022/06/24/1102305878
/supreme-court-abortion-roe-v-wade-decision-overturn

33 Centers for Disease Control and Prevention. *Youth Risk Behavior Survey Data Summary & Trends Report: 2011–2021*. CDC, 2023. https://
www.cdc.gov/healthyyouth/data/yrbs/pdf/YRBS_Data-Summary
-Trends_Report2023_508.pdf

34 Griffith, Erin. "Silicon Valley Slides Back Into 'Bro' Culture." *The
New York Times*, September 24, 2022. https://www.nytimes.com/2022
/09/24/technology/silicon-valley-slides-back-into-bro-culture.html

35 Barnes, Brooks. "After #MeToo Reckoning, a Fear Hollywood Is
Regressing." *The New York Times*, October 24, 2022. https://www
.nytimes.com/2022/10/24/business/media/hollywood-metoo.html

36 Alaimo, Kara. "Opinion: This Verdict Is Much Bigger Than Depp or
Heard." *CNN*, June 1, 2022. https://www.cnn.com/2022/06/01
/opinions/verdict-bigger-than-depp-or-heard-opinion-alaimo/index
.html

37 Goldberg, Michelle. "The Future Isn't Female Anymore." *The New
York Times*, June 17, 2022. https://www.nytimes.com/2022/06/17
/opinion/roe-dobbs-abortion-feminism.html

38 Fischer, Mia. *Terrorizing Gender: Transgender Visibility and the Surveillance Practices of the US Security State*. University of Nebraska
Press, 2019, p. 5.

39 Tolentino, Jia. *Trick Mirror: Reflections on Self-Delusion*. New York:
Random House, 2019, p. 17.

40 Robertson, Katie. "After Roe v. Wade Reversal, Readers Flock to Publications Aimed at Women." *The New York Times*, August 14, 2022. https://

www.nytimes.com/2022/08/14/business/media/abortion-womens
-media.html

41 Crenshaw, Kimberlé. *On Intersectionality: Essential Writings*. New Press, 2023.

42 Clark-Parsons, Rosemary. *Networked Feminism: How Digital Media Makers Transformed Gender Justice Movements*. Oakland: University of California Press, 2022, pp. 3, 51.

43 History.com Editors. "Women's March." *History*, January 5, 2018. https://www.history.com/this-day-in-history/womens-march

44 Fadulu, Lola. "Why Lauren Smith-Fields's Friends Turned to Tik-Tok." *The New York Times*, February 15, 2022. https://www.nytimes
.com/2022/02/15/nyregion/lauren-smith-fields-tiktok.html; Fadulu, Lola. "Lauren Smith-Fields Was Found Dead. Her Family Had to Beg for Answers." *The New York Times*, January 27, 2022. https://
www.nytimes.com/2022/01/27/nyregion/lauren-smith-fields-bumble
-date-investigation.html

45 Jackson, Sarah, Moya Bailey, and Brooke Foucault-Welles. *#Hashtag Activism: Networks of Race and Gender Justice*. Cambridge: MIT Press, 2020, pp. xxix, 15, 26, 36, 71, 147.

46 Fremson, Ruth. "How Russian Trolls Helped Keep the Women's March Out of Lock Step." *The New York Times*, September 18, 2022. https://www.nytimes.com/2022/09/18/us/womens-march-russia
-trump.html

47 Tolentino, Jia. *Trick Mirror: Reflections on Self-Delusion*. New York: Random House, 2019, p. 29.

48 Manjoom Farhad. "We Might Never Know How Much the Internet Is Hiding From Us." *The New York Times*, August 25, 2022. https://www
.nytimes.com/2022/08/25/opinion/social-media-algorithms.html

49 Keats Citron, Danielle. *The Fight for Privacy: Protecting Dignity, Identity and Love in the Digital Age*. New York: W. W. Norton & Company, 2022, pp. 70–71; Umoja Noble, Safiya. *Algorithms of Oppression: How Search Engines Reinforce Racism*. New York: New York University Press, 2018.

50 Metz, Cade and Mike Isaac. "Meta, Long an A.I. Leader, Tries Not to Be Left Out of the Boom." *The New York Times*, February 7, 2023. https://www.nytimes.com/2023/02/07/technology/meta-artificial -intelligence-chatgpt.html; Grant, Nico. "Google Calls In Help From Larry Page and Sergey Brin for A.I. Fight." *The New York Times*, January 20, 2023. https://www.nytimes.com/2023/01/20/technology /google-chatgpt-artificial-intelligence.html

ACKNOWLEDGMENTS

For anyone who doesn't believe in paid maternity leave, I hatched the idea for this book while on maternity leave with my second daughter. I'm grateful to my husband, parents, Wendy Deja, and my children's many saintly childcare providers for giving me the space to write this book.

I'm fortunate to have worked with an incredible team of brilliant, supportive women on this book designed to empower women. Thank you to Robin Straus for connecting me with Gail Winston, and thanks to Gail for connecting me with my incomparable agent, Gráinne Fox at United Talent Agency. I'm unthinkably fortunate to be represented by her. Thanks as well to Madison Hernick, Kelly Karczewski, and Veronica Goldstein at UTA.

Thanks to my amazing editor Laura Apperson at Alcove for believing in this project and for improving it tremendously.

Thank you to all the people who granted me interviews for this book, including the women who spoke to me anonymously to help me understand perspectives on homebirths that are different from my own.

Thank you as well to Elizabeth Lanphier for valuable input and to my research assistants, Kimberley Casey and Aaliyah Solis-Castillo.

This book was born out of my writing for CNN Opinion over the past eight years about the social impact of social media and issues women are up against. I'm grateful to my editors Rich Galant and Jane Carr for championing my work—as well as to my past CNN

Opinion editor Pat Wiedenkeller, my Bloomberg Opinion editor Jhodie-Ann Williams, and my previous Bloomberg Opinion editor Tracy Walsh.

I finished this project at Fairleigh Dickinson University, where it's been life-changing for me to have colleagues who unbegrudgingly accommodate my need for a work schedule that allows me to balance my caregiving responsibilities. It's an essential part of what makes my work possible. I owe special thanks to our visionary interim provost, Ben Rifkin, and to my exceptional interim dean, Janet Boyd, and outstanding chair, Gary Radford.

Most of all, thank you to my husband and daughters for their bottomless love and support. My views on these issues have been deeply informed by my experiences as a mother—and my hope to leave the world a better place for my girls, and for yours.

INDEX